WHY CAN'T I FALL IN LOVE?

by the same author

Kosher Sex
Dating Secrets of the Ten Commandments

WHY CAN'T
I FALL IN
L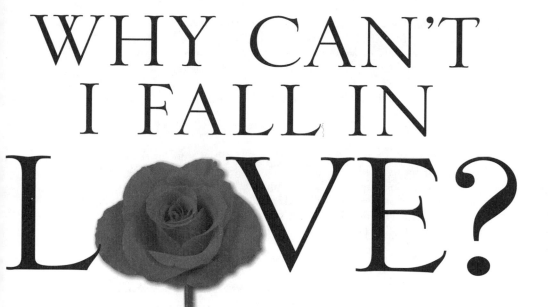VE?

A 12-STEP
PROGRAM

SHMULEY BOTEACH

ReganBooks
An Imprint of HarperCollinsPublishers

HarperCollins books may be purchased for educational, business, or sales promotional use. For information please write: Special Markets Department, HarperCollins Publishers Inc., 10 East 53rd Street, New York, NY 10022.

FIRST EDITION

Designed by Nancy Singer Olaguera

Printed on acid-free paper

Library of Congress Cataloging-in-Publication Data

Boteach, Shmuley.
    Why can't I fall in love? : a 12-step program / Shmuley Boteach.—
    1st ed.
      p. cm.
    ISBN 0-06-039346-7
    1. Love. 2. Intimacy (Psychology) 3. Man-woman relationships.
      I. Title.
BF575.L8 B65 2001
306.73—dc21   2001019404

01 02 03 04 05 ❖/RRD 10 9 8 7 6 5 4 3 2 1

What kind of fool am I?
Who never fell in love
It seems that I'm the only one
that I have been thinking of
What kind of man is this?
An empty shell, a lonely cell
in which an empty heart must dwell
What kind of lips are these
That lied with ev'ry kiss
That whispered empty words of love
that left me alone like this
Why can't I fall in love
like any other man
And maybe then I'll know
what kind of fool I am.

What kind of fool am I?
Who never fell in love
It seems that I'm the only one
that I have been thinking of
What kind of man is this?
An empty shell, a lonely cell
in which an empty heart must dwell
What kind of clown am I?
What do I know of life?
Why can't I cast away
the mask of play
and live my life
Why can't I fall in love
'til I don't give a damn
And maybe then I'll know
what kind of fool I am.

—"What Kind of Fool Am I?"

Contents

In Gratitude

A brief word about the people you'll meet on the following pages.

But first a word *to* them: I offer my sincere and heartfelt thanks to everyone who has shared openly and freely of their lives with me. The experiences and insights you've volunteered through your E-mails, phone calls, in-person meetings, and letters have not only informed me and so much of this book, they have also inspired me. I hope they do the same for readers.

Because of the intimate nature of people's revelations, I have altered many details about their lives to protect their privacy; in a few cases I have combined elements of two or three people's stories into one. But the incidents and anecdotes are truthfully represented; the emotions recounted are very real. If you think you recognize any of these people, it is because by now the common themes of so many single men's and women's lives have been woven from a common thread into a fabric called the human love condition.

Blessings and shalom.

Acknowledgments

First, I wish to thank my publisher, Judith Regan, who is responsible for this book. When an author makes a statement like this, two things are meant. One, that the publisher is responsible for the publication of the book. And two, that the author is desperately trying to grovel to the person who decides whether or not he will be published again and how many advertising dollars will be involved.

In my case, I can truthfully say that it's only because of Judith that this book was conceived at all. I had originally intended to write a book solely about the mystical nature of gender difference. Judith, however, warned me that if I wanted to compete in the big leagues I needed to write a broader book about relationships, rightly pointing out that "John Gray" is infinitely easier to remember than "Shmuley Boteach." I was convinced, and I uncharacteristically bowed my head in silent submission. Judith has become a close friend and confidante; she believed in me from the moment of my first appearance on her TV show, even though the ratings immediately plummeted, and I am honored to be part of her impressive stable of authors (even if my presence brings down the average a bit).

Of course I also want to thank my long-suffering editor Cal Morgan, known in many circles as the very best editor in publishing (in this case I am groveling but not exaggerating). I still remember a conversation I had with him recently. "I once heard," he told me, "of a new, environmentally friendly method of taking old rags and refuse and recycling them into paper in order to save the trees. But I never heard of this new technique of yours, Shmuley, which reverses the process." Well, Cal, if you're listening, I just want to say how much I appreciate all the professional encouragement you gave me—like the time you asked me, "Ever consider giving up writing and joining the WWF?"

I especially want to thank my good friend Perry Garfinkel for the Herculean effort he brought to this manuscript. Not only did Perry sift through, organize, and edit the vast amount of material I produced on this subject, but he also offered invaluable insights, ideas, and tips that were instrumental in enhancing the presentation and content of the manuscript. (Who said you can't improve on perfection?) Aside from being highly intelligent and well-read, Perry is an extremely good-natured man who cares deeply about others. I still remember how, toward the end of the book, when my nerves were completely frayed and I threatened to throw myself from the window, Perry looked at me ever so lovingly and, with tears in his eyes, asked me, "Can I keep your laptop?" If the book is a huge success, then it's entirely due to the brilliance of my insights and the profundity of my thoughts. If it's a colossal failure, it's entirely due to Perry's choosing all the worst material and having deleted all the best bits.

I wish to thank my seven children, who are the inspiration behind my writing—which is another way of saying I will do anything to escape the responsibilities of parenthood, including sitting in front of a mind-numbing computer screen for eight hours a day. When Debbie and I married, I told her that in the aftermath of the Holocaust I felt it was every Jew's responsibility to try to replenish lost Jewish numbers. What I did not tell her was that I intended for us to undertake the project entirely on our own. But my children are a great blessing to me, and the joy they bring is matched only by the expense. So thank you for buying this book and sharing in my parental project.

Now for the serious part. I want to thank my wife, Debbie, to whom I've dedicated this book. After all, I have, thank God, been one of those really lucky ones who have fallen in love. And this year is especially important to our marriage. My parents divorced in the thirteenth year of their marriage. Their breakup scarred me in a way that will probably never completely heal. It also led directly to my writing books on relationships. March 2001 marks the thirteenth year that Debbie and I will be married. So this is the big one, and I've been thinking a lot about it. I decided that as a husband I would have to undertake new precautions to ensure that our marriage gets through the traumatic thirteenth year without a glitch.

The first thing I decided to do was keep my fingers crossed for the entire year. But three things ruined my plan. One, it became impossible to hold a fork, and I started to wither from malnutrition. Two, I remembered that I was Jewish (and just try keeping your fingers in the shape of a Star of David for a year). Three, my hand turned a dark shade of blue from lack of blood circulation. Clearly, I had to find a more profound way of getting through this year. While I was fortunate enough to fall in love, I'd now have to work on a way of *staying* in love. So I decided that a far better plan was to go the extra mile in undertaking loving acts that would make my wife feel special. Whereas before I would buy Debbie flowers every year on our anniversary, I now buy them on our anniversary and the day of the Super Bowl. Whereas before I would shower for her once a month, I now shower once a week, whether I need it or not. And whereas before I would buy her gold necklaces and pearl earrings, I now buy her poster-size portraits of myself and copies of my published books. Who said I wasn't a romantic at heart?

Last, but certainly never least, I would like to thank God Almighty, Creator of love, Progenitor of affection, Matchmaker-in-Chief, who created Adam from the clay of the earth but dignified his being by giving him a helpmate to brush off the dust. It was in Eve's love that Adam found redemption; it was in Adam's devotion that Eve found paradise. And it is in the Almighty's constant and unconditional blessings toward me and my family that I find purpose and happiness. May I always prove myself worthy of His love and deserving of His protection, and be the beneficiary of His omnipotence—especially when it comes to book sales.

Wishing you the joy of falling into, and the happiness of remaining in, the eternal grasp of love,

Rabbi Shmuley Boteach
February 2001
Englewood, New Jersey

1

The Problem

The story of a love is not important—what is important is that
one is capable of love. It is perhaps the only glimpse we are
permitted of eternity.

—Helen Hayes

My friend Henry has a problem. At the ripe old age of forty, this real
estate mogul is already so wealthy he doesn't have to work another
day in his life, and neither will his children—that is, if he ever has
any. Handsome and charming, he has a penthouse overlooking Central Park in Manhattan, an enormous retreat in Westchester
County, and perhaps another vacation home in Vail, Colorado
(frankly, I've lost track). He owns a personal jet and a couple of lim-
ousines, collects Picassos, and has just installed a bowling alley at his
weekend getaway. He dates so many beautiful women they practically have to take a number to get a night out with him.

We should all have such problems, right? So what could be bothering this fortunate soul?

Every week Henry and I get together and talk about the predicament that has cast a shadow over his otherwise enviable life. A life,
he laments, that is missing one little thing: love.

"Why can't I fall in love?" he wondered aloud to me one day
after recounting his previous week's experiences with women he'd

met. Our visits had taken on a kind of pattern. Each week he would weigh the pros and cons of the women he'd been seeing (and there were usually several a week), going into elaborate detail about their strong points and weaknesses. Henry's a thoroughly good man, but sometimes I get the feeling he reviews the properties he buys and sells with more passion. None of the women in his life, he invariably concludes, is a keeper. And though the parade of women through his life seems endless, he claims he has never once fallen in love. When I first expressed incredulity at this and giggled nervously, he looked me square in the eye. "Why don't you believe me, Shmuley? I'm completely serious. I have never once been in love."

Laura is another friend of mine with a problem. Though not as wealthy as Henry, this bright and ambitious attorney in her early thirties works long, hard hours to maintain her lifestyle: dinners at hot new restaurants with colleagues, getaways with girlfriends at a Napa Valley spa, membership in a popular health club, ownership, with the bank, of a condo in one of L.A.'s trendier districts. Laura gives every appearance of savoring the West Coast good life she has created for herself. But whenever I see her on my frequent trips to California, her usually bright face turns sour when she talks about her love life.

"What love life?" she exclaims, enumerating the false starts and dead-end relationships she's had. "Some of them are really great guys," she admits. "But no matter how many times I go out, I just can't seem to fall in love." This man is too short; that one doesn't make as much money as she does; another is perfect, except for one problem: He's married.

For all their success in the world, Henry and Laura are failing at what I believe is life's most important mission: finding someone with whom they can share a rich and lifelong love affair, someone who will cherish and worship them. Instead, like millions of their counterparts, they have thrown themselves into their careers, hoping that professional success will plug all the leaky holes in their hearts. But for all the many ways they find to fill their days—from seemingly benign pastimes such as overworking or spending time with friends and family; to the distracting entertainment of TV,

movies, and the Internet; to the endless pursuit of material possessions—they pass every moment with a great empty cavity in the
middle of their chests where their hearts are, or should be.

Henry and Laura are not alone. Theirs is an affliction I have witnessed countless times since 1988, when I first started a program for
young singles at Oxford University in England. In the intervening
years I have served as an adviser for Internet matchmaking websites
and a matchmaker on singles cruises; I have met, listened to, and
counseled tens of thousands of single people of all ages, religious
backgrounds, and nationalities; and I have received and responded
to hundreds of sad, sometimes desperate, letters and E-mails from
lonely, love-starved people. After fielding countless questions on
the lecture circuit, I have come to see that millions of single people
share this problem.

These days the question seems to echo everywhere: "Why can't I
fall in love?" Even among those who have been married for some
time, I hear its variation: "Why can't I *stay* in love?"

At first I merely felt bad for Henry and Laura. I listened, offered
what encouragement I could, tried to understand their individual
personalities well enough to advise them wisely. But before long I
realized that single men and women like these two—those aware
enough of their problem to express it in the form of that six-word
question—are the lucky ones. They have a problem, and they know
it. They admit that the lack of a loving, intimate relationship is causing them pain, pain that ebbs and flows but at times grows unbearable. This pain preoccupies them so persistently that they have
taken two crucial steps toward solving their problem: first admitting
that they *have* a problem and then doing something about it.

The unlucky ones, the ones I'm really concerned about, are those
who can't see that they have a problem. Along with thoughtful singles
like Henry and Laura, I have met countless young men and women in
the last several years who appear emotionally anesthetized, who seem
almost willfully to have numbed themselves to that emptiness in their
hearts. These unfortunate souls, so many of them charming, attractive, and successful in every other aspect of their lives, have become
unable even to think about the obstacles standing between them and

a joyous love affair. So accustomed are they to living without love, so adept are they at treating the symptoms with everything but the one sure cure, that they assume this is the human condition, this is the way their lives were meant to be. "Love? Who, me?" they say. "That's for Hallmark cards and country-and-western songs and corny Hollywood movies and romance novels. Love? That's for needy people. I don't need love. I'm fine. Really." It's a sentiment sadly reflected in a *Time*/CNN poll in 2000 that showed a diminishing number of American women, fewer than 50 percent, looking toward marriage as the source of their happiness. "Marriage is not what it used to be," Barbara Dafoe, co-director of the Rutgers University National Marriage Project concluded bluntly.

To me, the saddest part of this worldwide phenomenon is that so many people have become numb to the pain of their loneliness, desensitized by the wide range of cultural influences that tell us it's okay to live without love. With no one to welcome their love and no one to love them in return, they live with the sense that something is missing, but they never quite understand what it is. And they accept their woe as if this were the human condition.

Make no mistake about it—this is not natural. It's not the way things were meant, or ought, to be. The human condition, as I will contend in this book, is meant to be enriched and rewarded, made deeper and fuller, by love. And when we human beings are without love, we are meant to dream and aspire, to yearn and strive, to prepare for, to pray for, and ultimately to rise up to this vital emotion. To love, to be intimately in love with another person, is the defining expression of our existence. It fulfills the most basic human need: to feel special. Loving and being loved satisfy that need. Love is a fundamental part of the universe, the cohesive factor that propels and promotes humankind. It is both a learned behavior and an instinctive human trait. And, too, it is a tradition that we pass down from generation to generation, through our genes and through our belief and through our reenactment of it at home—in our living rooms, around our kitchen tables, in our beds. We first learn about love when it comes to us, unconditionally, from our parents, and we pass that same unconditional love down to our children. Detach from love, and you detach from the life force.

But many of us have grown used to living without love. Often, usually with the help of our contemporary culture, we fashion an almost (almost!) impenetrable fortress of intellectual argument around our lives, reassuring ourselves that frivolous love has no place in our lives. Yet this is a defensive fortress, and its only effect can be to isolate us, to cut us off from the most potent and nourishing of human experiences, until we are left desolate and alone.

These people, living alone in their well-guarded shells, are the ones who move me to write this book. If you recognize yourself among them, perhaps you've taken the first step. You may be ready to confess that your heart's deepest desire is to step across the line from cynic to believer, from doubting love to believing in love, and more: to believing in your own ability to experience love.

The world was not always overrun with such cynicism. In truth, for centuries before our time, men and women have understood that love is the pivotal event in the human drama. The search for love was matched only by the search for God as a central theme of art, music, and philosophy. It was a noble cause, an almost spiritual aspiration. In the days of courtly love, men won women's affections by vanquishing their enemies or rivals in battle. They courted their fair ladies, sought the approval of their parents, earned their respect. In Victorian America—and until, perhaps, the early 1960s—the dating game was similarly genteel. Men and women would meet, and if they liked each other they'd meet again. And again. Walks, talks, drives, picnics, movies, dances, meeting each other's friends and family—this was the stuff of dating, and there was an innocence about it that would be difficult to find today. People looked forward to dating; it was seen as a journey of exploration, as a way to find and win one's lover for life. Indeed, for many, life itself was a journey toward love.

There was, it must be admitted, a certain amount of evaluation involved in the process, at least at first. No partners have ever successfully grown together without watching and listening to each other closely, without learning what there was to know about each other. But as young men and women of previous generations spent ever more time together, slowly their relationship would change, from objective analysis to subjective attraction. As these couples spent more and more time together, they developed an affection for each other that transcended any early judgments. Why? In part, because each of them was growing as a person through the time they spent together, in part because the finer qualities one found in a mate eventually came to seem more important than his or her inevitable human weaknesses. As the two grew together, they would spend less time comparing the other to others they had dated. They began, instead, to create a world unto themselves. Before too long, they'd begin missing each other when they were apart; that's when they'd realize they needed to be around each other to experience a deeper, more contented sense of personal fulfillment. Through steps like these—an almost intuitive process, devoid of today's facile psychotherapies—they fell in love. Exclusivity and commitment usually followed, to the excitement and pleasure of all involved. Engagement and marriage were the logical outcomes. Prenuptial agreements were unheard of; divorce was a rarity.

In our grandparents' day, men and women seemed to be made of Velcro, destined to hold fast to each other. The single men and women of our time, on the other hand, seem increasingly to be made of Teflon; men and women just can't seem to stick together. We go out on dates conscientiously, relentlessly, almost obsessively. We have become Olympic gold medalists of the event called "dating." And yet many of us find ourselves curiously unaffected by the experience. In fact, I've come to realize, the more we date, the less able we are to fall in love.

Ironically, even as we invent ever more amazing means of communication—phone, FedEx, fax, cell phone, E-mail, wireless—those three most intimate words seem to be harder to communicate than ever before. "I love you" still gets caught in men's and women's throats like dry Shredded Wheat. (Not the word *love* itself, mind you. That we use so often it's lost its meaning for us: I love my Toyota, I love this game, I ❤ New York.)

Why? How did so many people get to this state? And more important, how can we find our way out of it and back into a state of grace? Where is the path back to the Garden, as it were, where Adam and Eve invented the love affair?

My answers may jolt you. You may find them disturbing, for they will challenge existing ideas many hold dear. In many respects, they contradict conventional wisdom. And yet what have you—what has any of us—got to lose? If you, like so many others, are living each day without love, I think you'll find that my ideas merit your attention. If nothing else has worked, maybe it's time to take a radical approach to falling in love.

But why, you may ask, should you take advice from me, an Orthodox rabbi who married the first woman he ever dated; who has remained married to the same beloved woman since 1988, with whom, thank the Lord, he has brought seven blessed children (and counting) into the world? What do I know about modern dating? Plenty. Over the years I have made the complexities of relationships my ongoing field of study, perhaps because I myself was the child of a difficult marriage that ended in divorce, perhaps because my time at Oxford showed me just how tormented the men and women of my generation have been by their inability to find lasting love. It is a part of my role as a rabbi to listen to people, to evaluate their problems and offer advice, and after years of doing so I am flattered that I've become known as a sympathetic counselor to people of all ages. If I seem immodest—if I cannot refrain from mentioning that some of my friends have in recent years begun referring to me only somewhat humorously as the Love Prophet—I trust you'll accept it as (ahem) one of my very few weaknesses.

Hard, Cold Truths

Why is it so hard to fall in love? How have the last several generations—baby boomers, Generation Xers, and now Generation Nexters—lost that universal understanding of love? By way of an answer, let me offer a little tough love. Consider:

❤ *As a culture, we have become shallow.* We have lost our respect for depth, for truth and beauty. Our criteria for allowing ourselves to fall in love are based on superficial values that don't strike to our core. And in our shallowness we have become boring. We're bored with each other, bored even by ourselves, certainly bored with the whole dating ritual.

❤ *Each of the two sexes has lost its sense of wonder about the other.* We have lost respect for the differences between men and women; at the same time, we have lost respect for the harmony that men and women are capable of achieving together. By becoming oh-so-familiar with each other, ironically, we have become oh-so-distant from each other. We have become brothers and sisters, not lovers.

❤ *We have declared our independence from each other.* We shun the notion of need. Needing someone else—for love and support, for physical affection and emotional attention—has been reclassified as a bad thing, a sign of weakness. And in our society, showing signs of weakness, exposing our vulnerabilities, is a *very* bad thing.

❤ *Our unwillingness to show weakness has robbed us of our innocence.* Another irony: Though as a culture we're more willing and eager every day to bare all in every forum imaginable, from Calvin Klein ads and MTV videos to Jerry Springer romps, as individuals we've grown deathly afraid to go *emotionally* naked before each other. (Where's that fig leaf when you need it?) The innocence required to bare one's soul before another, one of our most valuable qualities, is now dismissed as naïveté.

❤ *We have become fiends of premature judgment, the sitting justices on the Supreme Court of Relationships.* We approach each encounter with the opposite sex with a list of nonnegotiable requirements. Fail to meet one item on the list? *Next!* And how did we grow so unforgiving? Because judgment, of course, is hard to resist as a short-term defense; it is the quickest and cheapest way to avoid the humiliation of being judged first ourselves.

❤ *We have deluded ourselves into thinking we deserve the best relationship we can find.* You may be happy at work, satisfied with the station you've reached in life. And yet, ask yourself: Do you have the best job you could possibly have? Do you live in the best neighborhood in America? For that matter, are you the best person you know? We have forgotten that *good*—not better, not best—can be wonderful.

❤ *We have come to view love as a luxury rather than a necessity.* Nice work if you can get it, but not worth any real sacrifice. Our parents understood the importance of marrying the right person even at the wrong time or even in the wrong place; today, on the other hand, we put the timing of our careers and education, and the place we want to live, well before romance and love.

♥ *We love with our head rather than our heart.* We have become so "smart" about love and romance—thanks to magazine articles, books, tapes, lectures, and the collected street wisdom of the armies of singles who have gone before us—that intellect now rules over gut instinct. Our minds talk us out of relationships, with reason and logic, before a spark of passion can get ignited in our hearts.

♥ *We have lost faith in the institution of marriage.* I am certainly not the first to make this observation. The divorce rate now exceeds 60 percent. And the latest findings confirm our worst fears: The children of divorce approach marriage with all the enthusiasm of a visit to the dentist. Can you imagine living in a world where more than half the nations on the globe are at war with each other? Civil wars are raging in more than half our households, and we have no United Nations of Relations to declare a state of emergency. Rather, the citizens of those households, the children of divorce, have fled the scene as soon as they reached the age of majority, and they have become refugees from marriage.

♥ *We have become a disposable society.* It's now easier to throw away most household items and buy new ones than to fix the old ones, and our view of relationships is much the same. Problems with a marriage? Splitsville! Issues that can't be resolved? Who has time? Time for a trade-in! Spouse putting on a little weight? Trade up! We have lost the willingness to accept flaws, to take responsibility for regular care and maintenance of each other.

♥ *We have also become a distractible society.* Blame it on information overload, the quick-cut imagery of MTV, too many choices, too little time. We have lost the appetite for concentration; with so many stimuli floating around us, it can feel impossible to pay attention to one other person, much less to our own minds. It's no wonder attention deficit disorder (ADD) has become the disorder du jour. Men, especially, suffer from a form of the disease that might be called chronic wandering eye, which leads to severe

commitment phobia. As my friend Dennis Prager says, the average guy on a date these days resembles a radar tower, constantly
homing in on every pair of legs that passes by.

♥ *We have pigeonholed the pursuit of love, made it a mere pastime.*
We've penciled it in on our Day Planner: *Next week I'll turn
thirty; next year I'll be ready to fall in love.* On alternate Tuesdays,
between kick-boxing class and group therapy, we schedule blind
dates. Rather than approaching love as an all-encompassing
state of mind and heart, learning to build it from the inside out,
extending one's love from oneself to family and friends and
then to a lover, we treat it like a hobby, fitting it in where convenience allows.

In short, we have lost touch with the essential qualities Adam
and Eve learned in the Garden: comfort with our own nakedness, a
respect for innocence, an appreciation of the pain that comes from
loneliness, a sense of wonder, compatibility, selflessness, respect for
the differences between the sexes, and an understanding that closeness comes from shared experience.

That's the bad news, a splash of cold water, perhaps. But a nice,
bracing splash in the morning can be invigorating, and who doesn't
need a little help waking up?

There's good news, too. Notice that I say we have *lost* all these
qualities. That is because I believe we once had them, that we have
misplaced them, and that we can bring them back into our lives.
That won't be easy, you may protest, and I'd agree. It will involve flying in the face of some of our strongest cultural currents. Yet those
are the very currents that all too easily pull us into the sea of unhappiness. I am recommending that you abandon the deeply ingrained
patterns that have deprived you of lasting love. It will mean changing attitudes not only about love but about yourself, your life, and
the priorities within it. But the rewards will be worthy indeed.

It may provide solace to hear that you're not the only one going
through all this. Singlehood is on the rise, and as its legions grow,
"Sgt. Pepper's Lonely Hearts Club Band" may be our theme song for
a long time to come. According to the U.S. Census Bureau, the

number of never-married adults almost doubled between 1970 and 1994, from 21.4 million to 44.2 million. An estimated 43 million American women are either unmarried or divorced, more than 40 percent of all adult females. The ranks of single men have grown at roughly the same rate. And the marriage rate among women fell by one-third since 1970, according to a report by the National Marriage Project at Rutgers University in 1999.

Even more interesting: A recent poll for *Time*/CNN indicates that nearly 80 percent of men and women say they think they'll find a "perfect mate" but that only 34 percent of women and 41 percent of men say they'd marry someone they didn't consider a perfect match. And the desire to start a family seems to be outpacing the desire to have a mate to help start it: According to an astonishing report in the *New York Times*, the proportion of out-of-wedlock births has gone from one in sixty in 1960 to one in three in 1995.

It may come as no surprise that those who do marry are putting marriage off longer and longer. The median age at first marriage in 1994 was 26.7 for men and 24.5 for women, the oldest since the Census Bureau began counting in 1890.

But isn't it possible that these are all *good* signs, you ask? Evidence that, in this era of increasing education and career opportunity, we're all being more careful about choosing our partners? Well, that may be so. But to me it also confirms a growing sense that we as a culture are finding it easier to fall in love with fantasy than with reality. Instead of taking the leap of faith required to nurture a relationship from potential to reality, we are clinging to the notion that perfection will fall into our laps—no work, no worry—if only we have the patience to wait for it.

That may sound right to you. *After all, don't I deserve the best? Shouldn't I hold out for quality?* Yet while you wait, and each new day slips by, your own quality of life may be slipping as well. A growing body of research is demonstrating that single men and women may be running a gamut of risks. Consider these statistics:

❤ Twenty percent of single and divorced women suffer from a chronic health condition, compared with about 14 percent of married women, according to the National Center for Health Statistics.

❤ Unmarried men between the ages of forty-five and sixty-four, whether they live alone or with someone, are twice as likely to die within ten years as married men in the same age range, according to the journal *Longevity*.

❤ Compared with married women, divorced women have five times the risk of requiring psychiatric care. (*Physician* magazine)

❤ Automobile fatalities among divorced men and women alike are triple the rates for married men and women. (*Physician* magazine)

❤ Divorced adults, particularly men, suffer a much higher rate of physical and emotional illness than married adults and are more prone to risky behaviors that could shorten their lives. (*Colorado Chiropractic Journal*)

❤ Divorced people suffer higher rates of psychological problems, are more likely to develop cancer, and are more likely to develop alcohol problems than married people. (National Institute for Healthcare Research)

❤

Henry knows few of these statistics and would probably recoil at the idea of being considered just another number. Yet, despite his successful career, that's exactly what he is, another admirable yet impoverished single person struggling to understand why he can't fall in love. In large part, meeting Henry (and so many others like him) is what inspired me to write this book. In our weekly meetings, as I listened to him, I heard echoes of conversations I've had with singles of all ages, of all economic, ethnic, and religious backgrounds, for more than a decade. Some have been as open and honest about their problem as Henry was, but almost every unhappy single I have encountered had crafted a garrison of defensive excuses, perfected, no doubt, after years of warding off the kindly inquisition of family and friends. Men and women alike have learned to blame everyone and everything except themselves when love eludes them. The opposite sex, they plead, is too insensitive, too commitment-phobic, too passive, too aggressive, too confused, too immature. Or the timing is off: "She's on the rebound." "I just started a new job." Or the local soil is barren: "It's hard to meet people in this town." Or the dating gods just weren't in sync: "I just haven't met the right person" (in other words, "I'm not giving my love to someone I don't think deserves it"). One evening, as I was arriving at a banquet hall in Washington, D.C., to address a group of four thousand singles, I encountered a young friend from Florida. "Have you met anyone nice here yet?" I asked. "Are you kidding?" she said, waving her hand dismissively. "I've already checked out the scene; there's nobody here." Two thousand eligible men all in one hotel, and she'd rejected the lot in five minutes.

We have become a defensive culture. Our obsessive need to build walls around ourselves—walls designed to protect ourselves from exposure, risk, rejection, heartbreak—has dwarfed our eagerness to forge connections with others. Walls may be effective in keeping other people from getting too close, but they also keep us from extending ourselves. We've taken the wrong lessons from the business world: Toughness, strength, self-sufficiency, and control may be assets to a burgeoning career, but they make a sorry strategy for finding love.

Sometimes, too, the walls we form around ourselves are made of other people. Many singles I've met—and poor, successful Henry is no exception—surround themselves with friends and colleagues, filling their every nonworking hour with social banter and activity. Yet too many of us value our friends as buffers against our own loneliness, as time-fillers to fall back on when there's no romance on the radar screen.

Henry was like that. Whenever we got together in purely social circumstances, I took time out to watch him discreetly as he worked the room. On the surface he seemed to be doing everything right with women. He knew what to say, when to offer a compliment, when to open the door and appear chivalrous. But after I watched him for a while, it dawned on me that something was wrong. His every gesture seemed practiced, pro forma; he seemed to be performing by rote, without passion or intention. I knew Henry well enough to know he was a good person, charming and in most ways confident. Yet somehow, when it came to meeting women, his spontaneity slipped away. Something inside was holding him back, working overtime to prevent him from appearing unsure of himself or vulnerable.

Eventually, I realized that if I was successful in helping Henry overcome the obstacles keeping him from happiness, I might be able to help others as well. And so each week, after our conversations, I would suggest a new issue for Henry to focus on, along with a new project or exercise—homework assignments, we called them—that I thought might help him, slowly but surely, to change his outlook and his behavior. It wasn't easy at first, but one day I hit upon something I thought might get at the heart of the problem. I asked him a simple question: "What is your greatest fear?"

"I have none," he said abruptly. *Aha*. I'd hit a nerve.

"I mean, what's the last thing you worry about before you go to sleep, the first thing on your mind when you wake up?" I pressed him. "What is it that could topple your whole world?"

That got him. I knew he was reluctant to open up, but I can be as persistent as an Olympic-class Jewish grandmother. So he finally admitted that two private fears had been haunting him. The first had to do with his business. The success of his company depended in large part on the other agents he hired, on whether they put in the kind of effort he did, whether they fared well or poorly, and whether they remained loyal to his firm or defected to another company; these were all matters, he complained, that he could influence but not control. The other problem had to do with his older brother, Henry's partner in building the business and a man Henry greatly admired and relied on for business guidance and emotional support. His brother was recovering from a terrible car accident, and Henry found that if he dwelled too long on the possibility of his death, his own heart rate would skyrocket. "My brother is the only person I really trust," he told me.

At the time Henry was dating a woman he said he liked but did not love. Why not love? "I just think we don't have enough in common," he explained. "She doesn't understand my work, and she doesn't understand me. We don't really have anything to talk about, either, other than the usual platitudes. To be honest, she's starting to bore me."

"So give her something to work with," I suggested. "Tell her about these two fears."

And now Henry revealed a third fear: opening himself up to someone else, especially a woman. "No way!" he objected. "It's not going to happen. I don't trust her. Who knows? Later, she could use it against me."

"You haven't entrusted anything to her yet," I responded. "How do you know she's not trustworthy?" In truth, after weeks of dating, I could tell he still knew relatively little about the woman. "How will you ever get to know her if you don't give her a chance?" He agreed that on their next date he would give it a try.

Part of Henry's problem was a kind of insecure arrogance, a presumption that no woman could deserve his trust. This isn't meant to condemn him; it's hard to find successful people who don't have a little extra ego propelling them forward. But falling in love with someone is the ultimate act of equalization. It's about finding a lover you can recognize as your counterpart, with glorious qualities and equally glorious faults that stack up as impressively as your own. That's why love can never coexist with condescension. If you think you're in a league of your own, sooner or later you're going to run out of people to play ball with.

Laura's problem was quite the opposite. Besides the lack of self-confidence so many women—deemed the second sex for so many years—struggle with, Laura had also been raised by a mother who viewed her as the not-good-enough daughter—not smart enough, not pretty enough, not thin enough, not devoted enough. Though she had plenty going for her, Laura insisted on setting her sights on men who met the ideals her mother held over her own head: effortlessly brilliant, catalog-gorgeous, ostentatiously successful. Not surprisingly, often they were also emotionally distant, self-involved, workaholic, and in some cases married or otherwise involved. And Laura's approach rarely varied. Though she dated quite a series of these magnificent mannequins, including a few who were actually promising, invariably she would reject them prematurely, out of fear that if she stuck it out they would reject her first. She always had to "beat them to the punch," as she put it several times. Unable to figure out how to build a powerful relationship with a potential mate, she settled instead for a strategy that gave her the upper hand but left her alone.

"Why don't you try dating someone more like you?" I suggested. "Perhaps you should look for more substantive qualities than looks and money." I encouraged her to seek out a *nice* guy for a change, the kind of guy, in other words, she might never have looked at twice before, the kind who cares about more than his bank account and his bathroom mirror. More on how she fared later on.

Both Henry and Laura needed to be reminded that what they really deserved, and wanted, was *depth*—not just an affectionate business partner or a facile dinnertime conversationalist, but someone with whom they could share their deepest selves without fear of rejection. What they needed to do was to reexamine their own goals, to reach beyond their preconceptions about what love is and what makes a successful relationship. They needed help in recognizing people who might be worthy of their love—and in making themselves worthy as well.

If I can accomplish one thing in this book, it will be to encourage you to do the same. Today you may believe that only a few of the men or women in the city where you live—maybe one in twenty?—might be potential mates. No doubt you've got plenty of criteria you use to narrow the field. (Don't worry, everyone does.) Perhaps you categorically reject men who are your height or shorter. But really, what's a foot or two between lovers? Maybe you refuse to date women who would rather take a drive through the country than watch men in shoulder pads chase a pigskin up and down a muddy field. So what if you miss Super Bowl XXXXXX? Take the plunge. Resist the urge to run or reject. Date the short guy at least a few times; he may turn out to be the best man you've ever met. Spend time with the sports-challenged woman; she might provide comforts you didn't know you were missing. Open yourself up, and you'll find that others around you do, too. Listen to others, and they will be both grateful and interesting. Look around and be thoughtful, and you'll find that the potential for romance and lasting love is everywhere.

If you're reading this book, chances are you bought it for a reason. (Unless you're Jewish, in which case your mother bought it for you and inscribed it with a directive that you have one year to produce a grandchild or you're out of the will.) If you're reading with an open mind; if you're willing to abandon your old, discouraged perspective on dating; if you have enough faith to imagine yourself happily married to a man or woman who loves you, then I believe you can fall in love.

For I believe that a successful relationship is like a religion, a religion involving mutual worship. Our universal desire for romance springs from our spiritual core. We all long to be noticed, understood, and cherished; we all feel special and yearn to enjoy mutual admiration with another as special as ourselves. We want someone to choose us and place us, like God Himself, at the center of his or her universe. We want romance to make us feel alive, necessary, irreplaceable. It is no accident that marriage, a domestic arrangement, is also a sacred vow, for it is a conviction of faith.

All I ask is that you engage with the challenge of falling in love. There's no use pretending it's an easy or predictable process. Love, the simplest, most natural process known to man and woman, is also our most enduring mystery. Yet every one of us can conjure up that mystery in our own life. It will take commitment; it will require you to confront yourself with hard questions; it will demand that you second-guess your most self-protective instincts. Throughout this book, I offer many of the "homework assignments" I used with Henry, Laura, and others. I invite you to try them in your own life and use them to confront the obstacles that are holding you back.

But falling in love isn't all work, either. Relax with it. Enjoy it. Have fun with it. Dance with it. Appreciate the contradictions of love. Accept that someone out there besides yourself may hold the key to your eager heart, that you are both in control and not in control of the outcome.

Trust me on this. After all, I'm not just another short, unshaven Jew. I'm the Love Prophet.

2

What's Wrong with Love?

This is what is the matter with us, we are bleeding at the roots, because we are cut off from the earth and sun and stars, and love is a grinning mockery, because, poor blossom, we plucked it from its stem on the Tree of Life, and expected it to keep on blooming in our civilized vase on the table.

—D. H. Lawrence, "A Propos of *Lady Chatterley's Lover*"

For one human being to love another; that is perhaps the most difficult of all our tasks, the ultimate, the last test and proof, the work for which all other work is but preparation.

—Rainer Maria Rilke

Mom, romance is dead. It was acquired in a hostile takeover by Hallmark and Disney, homogenized, and sold off piece by piece.

—Lisa Simpson, *The Simpsons*

Dear Rabbi Shmuley:

When I hear you lamenting the increasing tendency of single people to remain single, I feel you must be talking specifically to me. I have dated a number of wonderful, successful, and charming men, and yet none of them made my heart flutter in that way that I know it is supposed to. What's more, I don't feel my life is severely lacking without the presence of a relationship. Rather, I feel quite content. And yet I wonder if it is this atti-tude that keeps me alone. Or perhaps I have simply forgotten how to love. I feel like I knew when I was sixteen; then, somewhere along the way—per-haps as a result of failed relationships or heartbreak—I have forgotten. What am I to do? What if I never remember?

—Lonely Lucy

Before we can look forward optimistically, we need to look back-ward honestly. To learn how to fall in love, or fall back in love, we must retrace the steps that led us off the path to the loveless condition in which Lucy and so many like her find themselves. After all, who would have thought that an entire generation of men and women would have such difficulty falling in love? Can you imagine waking up one morning starving, but making no effort to find food? What, then, can be said about the silent army of men and women like Lucy, who stave off their loneliness and whose search for love is, at best, half-hearted? Once we identify how the average Jane and John are drafted into that army, we can march our way back to the other side.

There was a time when it could truly be said: Whatever the ques-tion, love is the answer. Love was the pièce de résistance of human achievement. It was praised in music, art, and philosophy. It was, and still is, the heart and soul of every religion. And there was no debate about its status as life's most important goal. Love was what little girls dreamed of, what poets wrote of, what philosophers spec-ulated on, and what men and women worked at. Love and marriage were understood to be critical pieces in life's jigsaw puzzle. All young boys and girls hoped someday to meet the man or woman of their dreams, fall in love, and spend the rest of their lives together. Sure, we knew there would be good days and bad; it was right there in the wedding vows: "for better or for worse." But we knew love was what gave our lives meaning. And we knew it was worth every ounce of our energy to find it, nurture it, feed and water it, and watch it grow.

The rules of love also seemed simpler back then, better defined. A man and a woman met, dated, got engaged, and got married in relatively short order. It all happened organically, with little effort. Most often they were from the same town. Their families knew each other. They may even have been childhood friends or sweethearts. Couples married at a younger age, but rather than feeling trapped by marriage, they felt liberated by it. It was what they most looked forward to: a universal pinnacle nearly everyone wanted and was able to achieve.

I remember what it was like for me, growing up in a rabbinical seminary. We studied hard, kept our eyes fixed on our desks; just about the only recreation we had came when we attended the weddings of our older friends. At any given time, it seemed, another fleet of couples was lining up to get married. I remember standing there, sometimes in the bitter cold (Jewish tradition encourages us to get married outdoors, beneath the stars), just a little envious, as I watched my older friends bring wonderful young women into their lives. And what I wanted most of all was to do the same. We all did. People often think that religious people aren't romantic, but my fellow seminarians were the most romantic-minded specimens I've ever spent time with. Half of me loved going to those weddings and dancing my heart out, but the other half hated the feeling of emptiness as I watched yet another couple bring love into their lives, while I was still too young to do so.

The idea of young men and women flocking into marriages with their childhood neighbors or friends, their nascent relationships nurtured along by their families, may strike terror or revulsion into the hearts of single men and women today. For some it will even recall the specter of arranged marriages, a concept that may, gentle reader, put you in mind of dusty period dramas or, for that matter, the little scheme your Aunt Ruth cooked up for you when you were in eleventh grade and Mrs. Sofransky's awkward son Jason needed a date for the high school prom.

But the concept of matchmaking—involving arranged *introductions*, not mandated marriages—is making a comeback, and I'd suggest that there's a simple reason: We're growing frustrated with the "independence" we've clung to proudly for so long. We're starting to realize that it's no crime to seek out help, especially from those who know us best. And we're remembering that the intimate connection of a human relationship isn't merely a luxury; it's something we need.

Nature's Plan

Humankind (well, all right, life as we know it) is dependent on the natural gravitation between the sexes, a pull toward each other that both parties welcome. That's the way the sexes were built. That's what nature intended. Unlike business or football or music, it's not an acquired skill; it's instinctive, intuitive. A woman walks by, and the guy's head turns, and he wonders, "What if?" Girls look at boys they like and ask themselves, "Could he be the man of my dreams?" We love with our hearts and souls, not our heads and our checkbooks.

But, Shmuley, you may say, it's never been *easy*. And you're right. Dynamic tension—push and pull, give and take—has always been part of the deal. We call that compromise. A woman brings certain things to a relationship, a man others, but when they blend together, the result belongs to both of them. Love has always meant giving oneself over to another completely, merging with another into a new being. Falling in love was about finding pleasure in giving, rather than taking, about turning the focus of our lives away from ourselves and onto another. That's what made love so liberating; it actually freed us from the burdensome occupation of self-preoccupation. That fact is embedded in the etymological roots of the word: *Love* comes from the Latin *libere*, "to please." If you give up something of yourself—some indulgence, some freedom—to please your lover, what you gain by the union far outweighs the sacrifice.

In recent years, thinking this way has fallen out of favor. *Protect yourself*, single men and, especially, women have heard for years. Look out for number one. Work the opposite sex to your advantage. Don't reveal your vulnerabilities; he can't be trusted with them. Don't lose your freedom. Build your career; love yourself; find a mate later, if you have time. Constantly on guard against the sacrifices love entails, we've thrown the benefits out with the bathwater. The words associated with love run against the grain of every self-help message of the last quarter-century: *compromise, sacrifice, dependency, need*. Like the woman who signed herself Lonely Lucy, we've grown so fearful of all these ideas that we wonder whether we're capable of love at all.

We live in the age of the individual: the overnight entrepreneur, the eighteen-hour management consultant, the twenty-four-hour webhead. We race through the airline terminal, twenty-four/seven road warriors, PalmPilot in one hand, cell phone in the other. We define ourselves in purely professional terms, not through who we are but by what we do. We wear the blue bags under our eyes with pride, the honor badge of our workaholic ways. And so we cruise along, convinced that success in life can come only through self-interest and self-sufficiency. To *need* is no longer fashionable, no longer even acceptable. We don't want anyone owning our heart.

In the movie *Wall Street*, in 1987, the voracious trader, Gordon Gekko, intoned the memorable line, "Greed is good." With apologies to Gekko, in this book I will suggest a different perspective: *Need is* good.

Just as no flower can grow without sunshine and no blade of grass can rise without water, our hearts cannot live without love. None of us can lead healthy or productive lives without it. The Beatles may have overstated the case; love isn't *all* you need, not as long as there's food to chill and bills to pay and an Internet to surf. But it is the first thing you need, because without it all the rest is hollow and uninspiring.

Control Isn't Everything

Not long ago, I received a bracing E-mail message from a hardworking forty-five-year-old woman who owns a successful advertising agency in Los Angeles.

"People just don't want to believe that I don't want a husband," she wrote. "I really and truly don't. In fact, I never did. I had my first love child almost twenty years ago, before it was the fashion, and I knew then and now that it was nonsense to give your man an ownership position. Never again . . . and I mean, truly, never. And as for sex and great companions, I feel passionate about both . . . but I am not marriage material."

There are people who see "falling" in love as a weakness. Falling, they argue, means losing control, having the ground give way under you. Who wants to lose control? Fall and you'll break something—your heart, naturally.

Yet losing control may be exactly what many of us need. In fact, isn't passion itself a matter of being carried away by something greater than yourself? Isn't the essence of pleasure being overtaken by a feeling so strong that it lifts you to a higher place? And don't we regard people who can't let go as hopelessly lost? Aren't rigid and anal-retentive people the least appealing in society—not to mention the worst lovers? "Give me liberty or give me death," Patrick Henry cried, yet we all voluntarily sacrifice elements of our freedom daily in order to have the kind of life we want. We give up the first four years of our adult lives to go to college in return for an education. We then give up forty to sixty hours or more of our week, every week, in order to put food on the table. Many of us volunteer—sacrifice—even more time and effort in order to give something back to society. We give up our *freedom* to do this. But we never regret a minute of it.

The same is, or should be, true of love. If love is a kind of religion, what is most important is the faith that's at its center, a faith that allows the lover to surrender a part of himself or herself to the greater good of the relationship, without ever doubting that the sacrifice will be worthwhile.

Faith is necessary to the very act of committing to a relationship, precisely because the future is unknowable. I'm reminded of the story of my friends Jon and Lisa, one of the happy romantic outcomes I've had the pleasure of watching firsthand.

Jon and Lisa were doing just fine as a couple. In fact, after three months they were already getting serious about making plans to marry. It looked like a happy beginning, especially for Jon, who as an only child had been burdened with the difficult responsibility of taking care of his mentally challenged mother. Then one day Lisa, who was a nurse, told Jon that she'd done a little research into Jon's mother's condition and discovered it was hereditary. Because of this, she told him, she felt she had no choice but to break off their relationship. She just didn't want to gamble with her own child's life.

Jon was devastated. So was I. Not only had I introduced them to each other, but everything else in their relationship bode so well for a lifetime of commitment. So I asked if I could meet with Lisa alone. Now I should note that, as loving as she is, Lisa is nothing if not logical. As a health-care worker, she'd been trained to deal with empirical knowledge, and as a person she was naturally inclined to this kind of thinking. So I knew I had to speak to her on her terms.

I started with one simple question: "Do you love Jon?"

"Very deeply," she answered without hesitation.

That was all I needed to hear.

"Look," I said, "it's fear that's holding you back. And if you choose fear, you won't be able to walk out on the street. There are fears ad infinitum." (I thought using Latin with her might add intellectual heft to my argument.) "You want facts, you want proof, you want confirmation that your marriage will last forever, that your children will be healthy, that everything is going to work out just the way you want it to. In short, you want certainty. But, Lisa, as a nurse, you more than anyone know that there are no guarantees. Sick people live long lives. Healthy people die unexpectedly. God's plan is incomprehensible.

"If you try to consider everything that could go wrong in a marriage, in life, before you commit, you'll never make it out of the starting gate."

I paused to let that sink in, then took a different tack. "But marriage is the quintessential statement of hope, and hope negates fear. In your case, your fear is robbing you of the possibility of hope. The fears of your mind are overruling the joys of your heart. Hope and love emanate from the same organ, Lisa: the heart. Stay in your heart. Get out of your head. Your heart will take care of everything."

And against almost every fiber in her body, against all her medical training, she took the leap of faith and decided to trust her heart. Today, Jon and Lisa are the proud parents of three gorgeous children—three mentally and physically healthy, gorgeous children. To this day Lisa says they beat the odds. To this day I say it wasn't even a contest.

Which Is More Important—Lookin' for Love or Just Chillin' Out?

When it comes to finding a mate, many singles have bamboozled themselves with their own rhetoric. They insist that they'll never settle for anything less than the best. And in an odd twist, very often "the best" represents a version of themselves. The term *soul mate* has become a fixture in the lexicon of love, but its meaning has become twisted. Instead of searching for someone to *become* our soul mate, we go through life just waiting to stumble upon someone who already is. We aren't satisfied until we find our mirror image, our duplicate. If you're a guy, so the thinking goes, just take yourself, redo the plumbing, and presto—you have the perfect woman!

Ultimately, searching for your superficial "match" will lead only to dissatisfaction. For what makes a relationship work isn't necessarily whether two people have a common taste in movies, or hate the opera, or dream about traveling the globe. Soul mates are made, not born. They grow together, learning from one another, thriving on each other's energy and spirit, and reveling in the differences that make each one irresistible.

Recently, on the TV show *Men Are from Mars, Women Are from Venus*, I found myself in a debate with an advocate of premarital sex. "Rabbi," this woman taunted me, "the problem with you is that you make such a big deal out of sex. It really *ain't* no big thing. So chill out. Take a cold shower."

But if sex is no big deal, I wondered, then what is? What is left for men and women to experience that is intense and passionate? If lovemaking *ain't* gonna do it, as she contends, what is there to sew two strangers together as one flesh? Talking about their IRAs? Demonstrating against genetically modified food?

It's a popular sentiment: Take it easy. Be cool. Love is great if you have it, but we can all live without it. Money? That has the power to move us. But divorce? Happens every day. Philosophers and research scientists have been trying to convince us of the same thing for over a century. Love, they insist, is no great mystical force; it's nothing more than an illusion, evolved craftily to ensure that we remain devoted to the act of procreation. As two members of the Center for Evolutionary Psychology at the University of California, Santa Barbara, recently wrote in a paper that appeared on the center's website: "Our natural competencies—our abilities to see, to speak, to find someone beautiful, to reciprocate a favor, to fear disease, to fall in love, to initiate an attack, to experience moral

outrage, to navigate a landscape, and myriad others—are possible
only because there is a vast and heterogeneous array of complex
computational machinery supporting and regulating these activities." How's that for pillow talk?

The attempt to pacify passion, to desexualize sex, to reduce love
to evolutionary terms—to *chill*, as it were—goes against human
nature. Its only real accomplishment is to explain away the allure of
the opposite sex. Countless studies have been performed to demonstrate that there is no significant difference between men and
women. But the academics who follow this path are ignoring a more
obvious and fundamental natural law, which is that differences are
what keeps the world in balance. Attempts at homogeneity nearly
always fail. Hitler's attempt to create One Race, fortunately, was
resoundingly rejected by society. Communism, the experiment that
tried to obliterate socioeconomic differences, also proved hopeless.
In political and economic terms, the truth is universally acknowledged every day: The world is composed of opposing yet complementary component parts. The same perspective should be brought
to bear on our struggle to understand the delicate play between the
sexes: *Vive la différence!*

How to Recognize Mr. or Ms. Right

With so much confusion about what we're even supposed to be
looking for in a partner, how are any of us supposed to recognize a potential soul mate? Here are a few exercises to help you
start answering that question.

   While you're looking . . .

What Are You Looking For?

Give this question some thought: What are your primary needs
in life? More specifically, what qualities do you need to make
you feel more complete, more whole and well-rounded? Do
you need, for example, to be more extroverted? Less judgmental? Perhaps you need to be more open to new ideas.

   Then think about what might be your greatest gift. What is it
you have that makes you special? You're a good listener, for

instance. Or you're empathic. Or you know how to make people feel good about themselves. Now imagine a person who has qualities that complement yours: perhaps a gregarious, easygoing type, who's looking for understanding. What you come up with just may form a kind of pencil sketch of your soul mate.

This can also be a good, honest way to learn a little something about your own weaknesses and begin thinking about working on them. If you can admit that you tend to be a little too preoccupied with material things, then look for somebody with a more spiritual bent. It'll help you be drawn toward the right people, but it also may help you become a more soulful and attractive person.

Go Talk to That Wallflower in the Corner

Finding a soul mate can feel like looking for the proverbial needle in a haystack And sometimes that needle does all it can to hide from you. It's possible that your soul mate is not the flashy man or woman everyone else is drawn to but that more reserved and unassuming person off in the corner. Here are some physical and psychological cues that will tip you off that someone has the makings of a soul mate. Look for a person who

💜 Has a quiet confidence, whose facial muscles are not all tensed up.

💜 Maintains strong and steady eye contact.

💜 Doesn't fidget.

💜 Doesn't mumble.

💜 Leans forward when talking or listening, without folded arms.

💜 Doesn't start every sentence with *I, me,* or *my.*

💜 Asks you questions about your life.

💜 Is a sincere listener.

💜 Compliments you without sounding like a used car salesperson.

💜 Raises the conversation easily to a serious level.

Once you've found a potential soul mate. . . .

Listen to the Sounds of Silence

When two people can simply hold each other, saying and doing absolutely nothing but being together, and the pain of loneliness, the stress of the day, the pressure to impress each other all fall away, then it's very likely they're soul mates. Try this silent hug exercise with your partner, and listen to your heart (and your partner's) as you do so.

Take Each Other to Meet the Folks

That's right. Bring your partner home to meet the parents. For some couples, this is the most stressful prospect in the early stages of dating. Many save it until just before they marry, sometimes with disastrous results. So why not get it over with as soon as possible, before it takes on profound implications? Like that moment in Woody Allen's *Annie Hall,* when Allen stops Diane Keaton on the street and suggests that he kiss her now to avoid the embarrassing attempt later in the evening.

Make it a casual visit, perhaps just dropping in one Sunday afternoon. Or invite your parents to join you two for a theater outing. This will diffuse the intensity of the "interview" across the dinner table. If your partner fits in with your family, it's a good sign that he or she might make it as your life mate. And the truth is, whether we can admit it or not, we all want our parents' approval. Because they know you pretty well, your parents might have some useful feedback on whether the two of you are compatible.

Not that you'd take their advice, of course. When was the last time you did?

We Don't Need No Stinkin' Lovers— We've Got Lives

Our culture's obsessive emphasis on independence has led too many singles to back-burner their search for love and turn instead to their like-minded, sympathetic friends for solace. Now I don't want to go on record saying we should cut off all our friends if we're going to find romance. But I will take a stand that may prove controversial: For too many of us, our attachment to friends threatens to dull our longing for a long-term romantic relationship. The wildly popular HBO series *Sex and the City* offers a fascinating window into this problem, though I hardly think its writers intended it this way. The series presents its four central characters as avid manipulators of men; ultimately, they always seem happier complaining to each other about the flawed opposite sex than pursuing the men they bemoan. To be sure, they make brief forays into the world of dating, but it's when Samantha, Charlotte, Carrie, and Miranda return and regale each other with the stories of their encounters that each episode reaches its stride. In fact, I believe the secret of *Sex and the City*'s success isn't just that it's funny and sexy, but that it captures the camaraderie many women today have come to think of as more important and more lasting than the romantic relationships they claim to crave. For these women, men are a means to the end of their own friendships, rather than vice versa; they derive greater stimulation from each other than they could ever derive from a man.

Of course, some of us never even have time for a night out with the girls (or boys, as the case may be). Dana, a British acquaintance of mine, is a case in point. A highly successful investment banker, at forty-seven she is attractive and vivacious. She would like to have a man in her life, she tells me, but she unashamedly, almost proudly, lets on that she works every night until midnight and simply has no time to date. When I tried to set her up with a friend of mine on a weekend, she told me she spends even Saturday nights in the office. She takes pride in being the group leader for an office of three hundred fifty employees, nearly all of them men. When once I asked her if she was missing anything in her life, she responded, "Sure, three things. First, the promotion I've been awaiting for two years. Second, my parents' health has not been too great; I wish they were well. Third, a good man, as if I could ever find one."

"It's funny," I said to Dana. "I've spent my whole life trying to cure myself of raw, masculine ambition, the kind that pulls you away from your wife and kids and tells you that money and hobnobbing with the rich and the powerful are everything. I feel this way because I've always believed in the natural superiority of women.

And so has Judaism. It has long advocated that those who beat their swords into ploughshares, who spend their time nurturing and caring for each other rather than killing each other, are superior to those testosterone-driven maniacs whose only purpose in life is to outdo their colleagues in war, in the marketplace, and on the golf course. But you? You haven't even mentioned wanting to bring children into the world. I don't mean to sound insulting, but you're so proud of yourself and your work, you're starting to sound like a man."

She seemed offended by the comment. "Motherhood isn't for everyone," she said defensively. "I don't want kids. I love my work."

That may be so, I told her. And indeed, maybe motherhood isn't for everyone. But the nurturing instinct of motherhood is a totally different thing. We all need to be needed by someone or something. "But tell me," I said to Dana, "who is it that needs *you*? And don't say 'my bank.' The moment one of your underlings learns how to do what you do, and surely some of them are catching up, your bank will need you no longer. What about *unconditional* love? As someone's wife, or mom, you are irreplaceable. You're not an institution, you're an individual. Work is something you do; being a lover is who you are."

I don't know yet what will happen with Dana. As she adds millions to her net worth, her bank account increases in size, but her heart will never keep pace with it unless she learns to fall in love. If we approach the search for love the way we do our search for riches, building our careers craftily and defensively, guarding our positions and creating self-serving alliances, we will be the poorer for it.

3

Games Daters Play

Every time I date a man, I think: Is this the man I want my children to spend their weekends with?

—Rita Rudner

When we talk about dating today, the language we use offers a window into just how ambivalent we are about the whole exercise. Before World War I, we described the early romantic stage between men and women as "courting." With its reminder of ancient rituals, it was one of the first terms to fall by the wayside of political correctness. But the idea of courting was intriguing. It suggested a spatial context to the experience that has almost entirely disappeared. It conveyed the fact that this man and woman were meeting in the same "court," that they were trying to establish a home. It was about creating their own private space, one that would be theirs to share exclusively. It also put women in the driver's seat, by allowing them to choose whom to allow into their court. Today, of course, they more often wait to be asked out.

What has replaced *courting* is a far more nebulous term: *dating*. Now the playing field has switched from the spatial to the temporal. Dating is limited; it's time-specific and time-limited. Two people are scheduled to meet on a certain date, at a predetermined time, at a convenient place. Their appointment, once avidly remembered, now booked coldly into a Day Planner, will have a beginning, a middle, and an end. Call someone "my date," and you are essentially labeling him or her as a time commitment, a responsibility, a burden. The emphasis shifts from being with someone, as it always was in the days of courting, to *doing something* with the person, ranging from seeing a movie to, well, getting your groove on. Subconsciously, the date has become an end in itself, not a means to further growth in your relationship. And if you're not "dating" someone, perhaps the two of you are just "going out," again, with all the emphasis on what you're doing, and none on whom you're doing it with.

People who are dating often say they are "seeing" each other. But among all the five senses, seeing involves the greatest potential for distance. You can see people from much farther away than you can hear them, smell them, touch them, or taste them. Claire never says, "I *smelled* Tom last night," but rather that she "saw" him, as if she merely happened to encounter him on a street corner. And Tom never says, "I *touched* Claire last night," even though that may have been just what he was doing (or wanted to be doing).

One of the reasons we've developed this elaborate vocabulary is that, from adolescence on, the fears that color our every thought about the opposite sex—fears of rejection, of embarrassment, even of revealing our true feelings to our friends—have made us experts at defensive strategy. As teenagers, people of my generation talked about "hanging out with" our pals; now, singles of all ages have co-opted this wonderfully commitment-phobic phrase, as void of intimacy as you can get, to describe their romantic involvements. Recently, a friend told me he was attending the tenth-anniversary celebration of a couple who lived in Woodstock, New York. "Oh, they've been married ten years?" I asked. "Who said anything about being married?" came the reply. "They're celebrating hanging out together for ten years." And in the past few years, teenagers have hit upon the phrase "hooking up" to describe their increasingly casual sexual relationships, as if they were describing the connection between a pickup truck and a U-Haul trailer. Cultural observers, among them Tom Wolfe, who called his most recent book *Hooking Up*, have expressed great angst over the growth in popularity of "hooking up." But it shouldn't have come as a surprise. As a society, we've been backing away from intimacy for almost a century.

The Unbearable Process of Dating

We may be shying away from intimacy, but many of us sure aren't shy about filling up our evenings with one date after another. "Shmuley," I hear often, "I date constantly. My life is nothing but a series of setups, a barrage of blind dates." But the mere fact of dating isn't enough, as many singles know all too well. And part of what's wrong may be the way we approach the process; in fact, the notion that it's a *process* may itself be a problem. We are so practical-minded today, so analytical, so critical. In our maze of self-protective phobias, we undertake the search for a romantic mate oh, so gingerly, as if it were roughly equivalent to picking a new stock or reviewing the stereo system ratings in *Consumer Reports*. By the time we reach adulthood, many of us think of dating as a purely evaluative experience. Through sheer repetition it becomes an exercise, in which "applicants" are paraded past us one by one, and we judge them with the cold practicality of a wizened judge.

What's wrong with that? you ask. *Don't we have the right to make an informed choice?* Well, yes, but . . .

The trouble is that this kind of smart-shopper dating can make us so self-conscious, so coldly calculating, that it robs us of the spontaneity that makes for romance. When all we can think of is trying to ferret out our potential partners' flaws—to avoid making a mistake, God forbid—we are only sabotaging our ability to grow together in mutual trust and thus to fall in love.

As Erich Fromm wrote in *Love, Sexuality, and Matriarchy*:

We all know the person who can never be spontaneous, who can never feel free, because he insists on controlling his feelings, thoughts, and actions. He can never act unless he knows precisely what the result will be. He cannot stand any doubt. He frantically seeks certainty, often to be tormented by more doubt when this certainty cannot be found. Such people who are obsessed with the need to control may be kind or cruel, but one condition must be fulfilled: The subject of their interest must be controllable.

And it's exactly this appetite for control that can stand in the way of love.

Denise, an intelligent thirty-nine-year-old unmarried writer, dates an average of six different men per month. She considers herself an "expert dater." "I disagree with you, Shmuley, that dating a lot just leads to confusion," she told me one afternoon. "I've come light-years since my college days, when I didn't even know what I wanted. How can you know what type of guy you're looking for unless you've gone out with a whole bunch of different men and gradually eliminated the possibilities?"

"But what if it takes until you're eighty before you find what you're looking for?" I asked.

"Well, I hope it doesn't take that long," she replied. "But it's better to remain single all that time than to make a mistake and marry the wrong person."

Like so many of us, Denise is convinced that variety leads to greater discernment in dating. But nothing could be further from the truth. Statistics have shown that people who date more frequently before marriage are at a much greater risk of divorce. Why? Because once you've hardwired your brain to rate your potential spouse's behavior on a kind of point system, it can be almost impossible to change when you enter married life. Dating too much sows confusion; it leads men and women alike to think of potential mates as nothing more than a collection of attributes, to be scored and tallied in the endless search for a perfect formula. Worse, the very profusion of faces and dates can itself become a burden. When opportunities for bonding start to feel like no more than wearying exercises, rather than inspiring and exciting moments when anything can happen, only cynicism can result.

One Day at a Time

The Two-Date Minimum Policy

No matter how inappropriate the date, go out on a second date anyway, with obvious exceptions. Granted, there are cases when you'll know in the first five minutes, or sooner, that this isn't the person you want to marry, or even a person you want to spend much time with. But once you know that, it might take the edge off and help you be more thoughtful about getting to know the person. It may take two dates to find something you have in common, or something this person knows about that you've always been intrigued by, or even something you *like* about the person. Spend time looking for the person's good qualities, instead of simply toting up the reasons to reject him or her. Look for agreement, not disagreement. In the meantime, you're getting practice in withholding judgment.

Now, here's a left-field rule: Gourmet coffee-shop dates don't count. Dates should last a minimum of two hours, even if you're gritting your teeth all the way. Without that, how can you ever sink into one another? You're going to get only a cursory look, and depth of personality will never be revealed. Short dates only encourage you to fixate on the obvious, the kinds of features you're bound to get bored with quickly.

And who knows, a lousy first date could lead to a better second, and even a third.

No Double Booking

If you schedule a date at 9:30 when you've already got another one at 7:00, in effect you've already decided the first date is going nowhere. Dating isn't like lining up ducks to be shot down one at a time, or like being a salesman who knows that the more calls he makes the better are his odds of meeting a quota. Take dates one at a time. Invest 100 percent of your attention on each date when you're on it. If it doesn't work out, *then* move forward. Double-booking sabotages your intention, unless your intention is merely to date and not to meet Mr. or Ms. Right.

This rule also means never booking dates with more than one person per week. What should you do with the other six days if your Monday blind date doesn't work out? First, you've already agreed—haven't you?—to a second date, even if the first was a disaster. Second, you can always watch *Temptation Island* or *Survivor* on TV, which should eat up some time and leave you feeling lucky. Then, when you're still left with time on your hands, read this book over and over again, until you have memorized it, and analyze it for hidden codes.

Would You Cheat on Your Children?

In my seminars, I often ask audiences to suggest one-word synonyms for love. Many offer *devotion* or *affection*. Some throw in *trust* or even *communication*. For a variety of reasons, none of these words quite captures the essence of love. The word I then suggest as an alternative is surprising. It sounds technical, scientific; it's hardly likely to show up in anyone's love poetry. But as a synonym for love, there is no better word than *subjectivity*. To love is to be subjective, to favor beyond the constraints of reason.

That's why, although there are a billion parents on this planet, every single one believes that his or her children are the smartest, the cutest, the best-looking, and the best-behaved of all. They can't all be right. But their love for their children renders more rational evaluation impossible—and irrelevant. Consider: Although husbands and wives sometimes cheat on each other, no parents ever cheat on their children. We never hear stories of Mr. Jones secretly going next door in the middle of the night to see eight-year-old Mikey and telling him, "Mikey, you're the boy I really love. My own son doesn't understand me. For now we'll have to keep our love for each other a secret and go to Yankee games together in disguise. But the time will come when I will get rid of my own kid and adopt you instead. In the meantime, here is a secret baseball mitt as a token of my affection. Make sure not to show it to anyone, especially my son."

Why is this scenario preposterous? Because parents never objectively compare their kids with other kids. They are entirely *subjective* in their appraisal of their children, so why would they ever cheat on them? To be sure, they may compare their children's performance in school or on the Little League field, but they never compare the love they have for their children with love for other kids. It's that simple. Even the children God gives us to punish us for our sins—who come into our lives looking all innocent and cute, but whose only precocious childhood ability is in the field of shattering Ming vases, whose only goal in high school is to wreck our car, and whose fifteen minutes of adult fame will be spent on *Jerry Springer* complaining about how their parents ruined their lives—even these children we love, *because they are ours*.

I learned this firsthand on a recent airplane flight. As I took my seat, I happened to notice a small child sitting with his mother behind me. Sometime after we took off, the airline served pasta for lunch. Slowly, I began to feel my yarmulke move in a circular motion around my head, as if of its own volition. A moment later a wet trickle—marinara sauce—started down my temple. This kid was mushing his spaghetti into my hair. "Damian, stop that right now," I heard his mother say. And yet, when I turned around later to lecture the child on the spiritual virtues of obedience—or lock him in an overhead compartment—his mother smiled back at me obliviously. "Oh, you want to play with him! Isn't he a darling?" Now, how can two people have such radically different views of the same person? Answer: She loved him; I felt otherwise. And love, whether familial or romantic, can succeed only if it's entirely subjective.

Just as we want our partners to love us subjectively, we also want them to love us unconditionally, freely and unreservedly, the way a parent loves even a child like my little airborne buddy. We want to be adored and accepted by our partners, regardless of how old and wrinkled we get or how our fortunes in life vary. As we've seen, that's what's so beautiful about parental love. It is offered freely and without regard for deservedness, like a gift, and it never wavers.

On the other hand, there's a difference between parental love and romantic love that bears noting. (Yes, I know, there's more than *one* difference.) While our parents can make us feel loved, they cannot make us feel special in quite the same way a lover can, because they do not choose us. In a sense, then, we're also in search of *conditional* love: We long to be appreciated for our qualities, for the "conditions" we as unique individuals bring to a relationship. In the recent Nicolas Cage movie *The Family Man*, a wildly successful yet emotionally unfulfilled man believes he has everything he could want, until he is given a glimpse of how happy he could have been had he opted for a simpler, less extravagant life with a wife and kids. "I choose us," he says to the woman he could have married, who had said the same thing to him years before, in vain. It's something we all long to hear. We seek corroboration of our own sense of worth.

Shopping for Love

When it comes to romance, most of us take enormous pains to preserve a sense of objectivity, even if it's only an illusion. We compare constantly. Whereas once you asked a woman out and felt thrilled that she said yes, and were drawn by her attractiveness and confidence, now, after dating forty women, you notice at once that your newest date's front teeth are a bit crooked and her breasts are rather more pear-shaped than you prefer. Whereas once you went out with a guy and were pleased to have a date and go to a nice restaurant, now you spend most of the evening counting the number of hairs left on his head and trying to figure out if his Rolex was bought at a bazaar in Bangkok.

Simply put, overdating leads to boredom. "Every night I take out a different girl," my friend Ron confided. "I go through the same routine. I know which stories to share about myself to soften her up. I know which lines are going to make her laugh. I know which confessions are going to win her sympathy. And my objective throughout is to win her over so that she comes home with me and sleeps with me. And you know what? It rarely fails to work. But how can I be impressed with people whose buttons are so easy to push?"

Here's another letter I got from a woman who was clearly fed up with dating:

Dear Rabbi Shmuley,

I am dangerously close to swearing off dating altogether. I hate everything about it: waiting for phone calls, desperately seeking eye contact at the bars and art museums, and, worst of all, the torturous event we commonly refer to as a first date. Invariably, the following ensues: Fifteen minutes' talk about the weather and the latest political news. Then I tell him what I do; he feigns interest in my fun and foibles as a marketing director; then he

*tells me about his latest trial, or patient, or web venture, or consulting proj-
ect. Blah, blah, blah. Worse yet, four dates later and we're usually on the
same exact page—the only difference being level of physical contact. Does
it get any better than this? I am beginning to wonder.*

What can I do to dig out of this rut?

—Bored in Boston

With so much serial dating by both men and women, the process
has turned into a game in which they match their own finely honed
techniques with those of each new victim.

"I took this girl out for dinner and I would have liked her," one
guy told me after a lecture I gave. "She was pretty; smart, too. Good
sense of humor. Good values, or so I thought. But then she started
to slurp her spaghetti. She was so unsophisticated." So he dumped
her. Because she slurped her spaghetti!

A woman friend of mine similarly ended a seven-month relationship because the man she dated talked too much about his
accounting job, which she found boring. She honestly told me that
she had no other complaint against him; she actually found him an
attractive gentleman in every way. "So why don't you just work on
the relationship?" I asked. "You know, put some effort into it? Steer
the conversation to something you find a bit more engaging?" She
sighed. "I work the whole day on my job. I don't want to come
home and have to work on a relationship as well. Relationships
should just work out naturally. If you have to work on a relationship, it's a sign that something's just not right." You wonder what's
going to happen to this woman once she has a kid who doesn't
jump when she tells him it's time for a bath.

We are so quick to embrace such ill-advised judgments. *He's not
tall enough. She's not smart enough. He wears the most ridiculous ties.
She wears too much makeup. He is too close to his sister. She doesn't get
along with her mother. He doesn't kiss right. She's a Republican.*

At base, there's a kind of arrogance involved in this judgmental
attitude that's antithetical to the very idea of romance. Humility—
the belief that you are capable of being infinitely enriched by being
exposed to another person—is a prerequisite to falling in love, and

those who grow too full of themselves often leave no room for someone else. When single people explain that they just haven't met "the
right person," what they usually mean is that they haven't met the
best person. Whenever I hear someone pining away, wondering who,
or where, that best person is, I suggest that a bit of humility might be
helpful. "Are *you* the best person you know?" I ask. "Do you have the
best car? The best job? The best home? If you were starving for something to eat, would you hold off until you found the best food?" The
answer, of course, is always no, and so it should be with relationships.
For the best relationships are not ones in which everything is perfect; those exist only in fantasy. The best relationships—and they're
more common than you think—are those in which each partner's
idiosyncrasies (the judgmental would call them "flaws") are understood and embraced by the other, becoming the mortar that holds
together the foundation of the union.

Good Enough Is Good Enough

> Infatuation is when you think that he's as sexy as Robert Redford,
> as smart as Henry Kissinger, as noble as Ralph Nader, as funny as
> Woody Allen, and as athletic as Jimmy Connors. Love is when
> you realize that he's as sexy as Woody Allen, as smart as Jimmy
> Connors, as funny as Ralph Nader, as athletic as Henry Kissinger,
> and nothing like Robert Redford—but you'll take him anyway.
>
> —Judith Viorst

Here's a radical concept that flies in the face of common inclina-
tion but that may open up boundless possibilities: Sometimes good
enough is good enough! If we learn to consider love a necessity
rather than a luxury, then we find that good enough can mean
something quite different from settling for second best. In fact, the
very act of accepting a lover's difficult qualities, along with the
beautiful ones that drew us in at first, can serve to enhance our own
capacity for love.

Once, on an airplane, I was seated near a woman who spent the
first few minutes of the flight with her head in her hands, her eyes

red with tears. She started telling me about a guy she had been see-ing for a year. Thirty-five, unmarried, she said that she really wanted this to work. She was looking forward to buying a house, having kids, the whole nine yards. The man, she said, was loving and attentive, but there was one problem: He earned less money than she did. Not much, but enough that it mattered to her. (Each of them alone, it should be noted, made more than enough to sup-port a family.) She told him that she came from a wealthy back-ground and that she was used to the good things in life. And she questioned whether he would be able to sustain her in the lifestyle to which she'd grown accustomed. She pestered him about the problem for months, never letting up, making him feel inadequate and unwanted. After six months, he decided to break off the rela-tionship. "You don't love me for the right reasons," he told her. He said he felt like a failure around her, even though by any normal measure he was doing very well indeed. "When I'm around the woman I love I want to feel like a winner, not a loser," he said. And he terminated the relationship. I didn't blame him.

Then, naturally, she went into a tailspin. She called him every day, apologizing profusely, begging him to take her back, telling him how sorry she was and how miserable she was without him, but he wouldn't take her calls. She started seeing a therapist—and told the ex-boyfriend about it, hoping he'd recognize her commitment to change. Still, he refused to have her back.

And why was she crying now? Because she'd just bumped into him at a conference. "I was just getting over him," she bawled. "And now I'm devastated again. He looked so good; he seemed so happy. I had something so good, and I gave it up for luxuries."

But she wasn't that superficial, I told her; it wasn't a thirst for an even higher quality of life that had caused her to scuttle the relation-ship—not exactly. "No," I said, "you just chose to value yourself on the basis of how much money he was making. What made you give him up was your own inflated self-worth. You judged yourself to be too valuable to throw your life away on him. What you couldn't do was change your own self-image. And if you want to save yourself from having the same thing happen again, that might be a good place to begin."

Love Is Neither a Merger nor an Acquisition

Is it any wonder that people are losing the knack for falling in love? The philosopher Immanuel Kant defined immorality as treating people as means rather than ends. Too many single people see love and marriage in calculating terms, as a *merger,* and not of their lives but of their lifestyles, so to speak. Instead of looking forward to blending their two personalities into a family unit, they dwell on the trappings of their lifestyles, making sure their partner's tastes in food, or favorite movies, or golf handicap, or income is the same as their own. As in the merger of two corporations, parties who approach marriage with this cynical attitude are often looking to ensure that each is contributing proper value—and it's all too often monetary value we're talking about—to the relationship. "Oh, she has a gorgeous weekend getaway; that will be *ours* now!" "He's good friends with a bunch of wealthy people I can sell my line of jewelry to." Women, especially, want to feel they're merging their firm with a bigger company that can leverage their lives to higher plateaus.

I have nothing against profiting from a union or even from marrying up. But when bettering one's station in life becomes more than the happy accident of marriage, when it becomes the reason for marriage, then the partnership is founded on shaky ground.

I once conducted a *Love Boat*–style singles cruise to the Bahamas. My group, fifty in all, consisted of singles in their twenties and thirties. There was one woman the guys acknowledged was the best-looking of the bunch. Not surprisingly, she got the most attention, and not surprisingly, she was also the most difficult for any of the guys to pin down (both literally and figuratively). I watched from afar for a few days as she played different guys off each other, dancing with one this night, taking a midnight stroll with another the next. We then had a session in which each person confessed his or her inability to love. When it came to her turn, I spoke up. "Let me guess. A lot of guys ask you out, and you date them once, sometimes twice, each. A lot of them are nice, but you can't commit to any because you're afraid that the moment you do, some much better catch is going to come along, and you'll regret your impetuousness." She looked at me, mouth ajar. "How did you know that? Are you some kind of prophet?"

"Well, yes," I said. "I am the *Love* Prophet." But anyone could have perceived her problem. She was treating potential boyfriends as job offers, and anyone with any sense holds out for the best possible package.

Make Love, Not Lust

> God gave men both a penis and a brain, but unfortunately not enough blood supply to run both at the same time.
>
> —Robin Williams, on the Lewinsky affair

> The true feeling of sex is that of a deep intimacy, but above all of a deep complicity.
>
> —James Dickey

There's another troublesome aspect of dating that clouds our understanding of what we want and how to get it: the matter of lust. By this point in our "enlightened" age, everyone professes to recognize that love and lust are two different animals. Yet night after night, date after date, we persist in confusing the two. Perhaps a moment spent parsing out the differences would be an instructive way to get at just what love is all about.

Love, I would suggest, is about giving. We want to give our love to another, and when we do (and the stars are in alignment), we receive love in return. Lust, on the other hand, is about taking, about having our own needs or appetites fulfilled. When a man loves a woman, he wants to make her happy; when he lusts after her, he merely wants to make himself happy—*at her expense*. Love is the supreme expression of selflessness; lust is the basest manifestation of selfishness. Love is the highest acknowledgment of another's individuality; lust is the supreme denial of it. Love is about recognizing the humanity of the one we love; lust is about turning him or her into an object. Love animates; lust renders the animate inanimate. Love is specific; lust is indiscriminate. Love affirms; lust denies.

The perfect act of love is the embrace, the joining together of two as one. Hugging, as Rabbi David Israel points out, involves creating a circle with our arms; it bespeaks our desire to create space within our own lives for the person we love. The person need not morph into us in order to be accepted. We recognize that he is his own person and we must accommodate him. We symbolically tell our beloved that we are happy to love her on her terms. Lust is a different matter altogether. When we lust, we do not hug but rather grope, stealing a selfish touch rather than opening a space to let another in. We seek to objectify the other, to appropriate him or her into our own identity.

All of which, of course, isn't to say there's anything wrong with sex itself. What's important is the difference between the two kinds of sexual desire: hormonal and erotic. Lust is a matter of hormonal desire; it's all about releasing an inner need. A person engages in hormonal sex not because he or she has been aroused by someone else, but rather because there is a hormonal buildup within the body that needs to be released. Hormonal sex usually ends up brief, boring, and uninspired, because it engages only the outer, animalistic layers of being. Hormonal sex is all about the release of an inner buildup of sexual steam, what I call "sexual ventilation." It pulls us into ourselves, rendering sex a form of masturbation with another.

Erotic desire, on the other hand, is all about satisfying a need that comes from something greater than ourselves, that comes from an awareness of the power of our union with another. When we feel erotic desire, we are not guided by our hormones. Whether we've been out for a romantic dinner together or engaged in a challenging tennis match, we're suddenly compelled to make love because we find our *lover* irresistible, not our bodily urges. Love, like all the finer emotions, draws us outside of ourselves, teaching us that real fulfillment can be achieved only in tandem with our fellow human beings.

Sex, as I've said elsewhere, is kosher. It's a part of life and love, to be enjoyed and celebrated as one of the blessings unique to our species. We are the only organisms who make love face-to-face, who kiss while we make love, and who engage in sex as an act of emotional bonding rather than as a purely reproductive exercise. But when two human beings meet and fall in love, the connection between their bodies can far transcend what happens in the bedroom. One of my favorite stories concerns one of the great rabbis of this century, who once accompanied his wife on a visit to the doctor. When the doctor asked what was the matter, the rabbi answered, "Our leg hurts, Doctor, and we won't be able to continue walking for much longer."

"Now wait a second; whose leg is injured?" the doctor said.

"*Ours*," the rabbi replied.

It's an unforgettable image. For these two, so long in love, the border between self and other had dissolved entirely. He and his wife had achieved the biblical promise: They had become one flesh.

Is It Love or Lust?

Especially at the start of a new relationship, it can be hard to distinguish between the two "L" words when your hormones are raging in every direction. Lust is a fine thing when it's directed toward a person you love and to whom you're committed. The problem comes when you're using someone as a means to an end, when the only direction you have in mind is the bed or a way to bolster your bruised ego. Remember: Some people feign love so they can have sex; others feign sex so they can have love. Both come up empty. Women, particularly, often go to bed with guys not because they're interested in the sex but because they're interested in the guy. And they mistakenly think that sex will create instant intimacy. They assume, wrongly, that it will make the man feel closer to them and more appreciative. Here are some ways to tell the difference between lust and love.

♥ You know it's love when you fall for the face. You know it's lust when you fall for the figure. If it's love you want, look at a person's face, especially the eyes, which are the direct route to the soul. If it's lust you want, go and buy a rubber doll, which has plenty of air but no spirit.

♥ It's lust when someone is talking, but you don't hear a word, because your eyes keep stealing glances at cleavage and bulges, distracting your ears from listening. It's also lust when you *are* listening but only so that you can convince the person of how caring and kind you are, so he or she will let you at that cleavage or those bulges.

💜 It's lust when you're not in the moment, thinking not about the date itself but about what you can say or do to take the next step (into the bedroom). This prevents the relationship from developing and unfolding organically, rendering it only a means to an end.

💜 If you wouldn't go out with a person again if you knew the encounter wasn't going to end in sex, it's lust. If you consider it a darn shame but well worth the wait if you don't have sex for six months—or, better yet, until you're married—then it's love.

💜 If you'd still make love to this person if he or she had a completely different mind and personality, it's lust. If you'd make love if he or she had a completely different body but the same attractive mind and personality, it's love.

💜 If you forget to play all the manipulative games you've mastered on the dating circuit, it's love.

Breaking *The Rules*

When it comes to advice on relationships, singles today are confronted with a surfeit of opinion but a dearth of meaningful, helpful counsel. Newsstand shelves are filled with glossy women's magazines, offering cynically crafted, ready-made recipes for disaster. *Cosmopolitan* tempts readers with "Six Fantasies That Could Wreck Your Relationship" and offers "Nine Super Sneaky Ways to Snag Him." Even mom's old familiar *Redbook* is ready to let you in on "Eight Sizzling Sex Secrets (Only Lovers in the Tropics Know)." And the new breed of men's magazines is even more shameless: *Maxim* promises: "Tonight's the Night!—40 totally unfair pickup tricks," while *Stuff* cuts to the heart of one male fantasy: "Twice the Sex! Half the Foreplay!"

But for sheer mercenary zeal, it was the publication of *The Rules*, Ellen Fein and Sherrie Schneider's recent guide to luring unsuspecting men into marriage, that took home all the awards. What concerns me isn't just that *The Rules* sold about a million copies more than my own *Kosher Sex*. (Oh, all right, it doesn't make me *happy*.) I'm not even mad because *The Rules* encourages women to play hard to get. Rather, what bothers me is that Fein and Schneider, two otherwise lovely young women I've had the pleasure of debating, encourage women to think of dating as "playing." *The Rules* was designed to show women how to take their time-honored feminine mystique and twist it into manipulation, how to transform feminine modesty into a masquerade. As part of the bargain, it trains women to overlook organic love in the search for superficial commitment. *The Rules* mistakenly equates curiosity, the lifeblood of a relationship, with unavailability. If love is a natural grass football field, then *The Rules* is AstroTurf. It may seem to work better, but it isn't real, and when you take a fall it leaves a nasty burn.

Women who took *The Rules* to heart soon found themselves stripped of one of their sexiest qualities: their innocence. It also took away what I believe is the greatest benefit of a truly strong, loving relationship: the opportunity, at long last, to be yourself, to be natural, to love someone openly, without guile or artifice. It might be easier to rope a man in using these bait-and-switch methods, but it's a lot harder to keep a relationship growing and thriving once he realizes he's been played.

Fein and Schneider's pitch played well, in part because it was carefully larded with feel-good messages and appeals to its readers' feelings of loneliness and lack of control. "When things slow down," they advised, "take care of yourself; take a bubble bath, and build up your soul with positive slogans like 'I am a beautiful woman. I am enough.'" But in my debate with the authors, I recommended a different approach. When you're feeling lonely, feed your soul by forgetting about yourself and giving to others. They recommended having a nose job; I suggested forming an opinion. They suggested preparing for a date by putting on makeup for an hour; I advised reading a book for four or five hours and then putting twenty minutes into makeup. They recommended that women play hard to get, and I urged women to indulge their natural mystery and become unknowable. If he calls on Friday, they warned, you're not available on Saturday. I took a different approach: If he calls on Friday, I said, tell him you *are* available—to go with him to synagogue or church, or to volunteer at a soup kitchen. Stay one step ahead of him—not with Machiavellian guile, but with pious virtue. Inspire him to be a better man when he's around you, and he'll never get bored.

Ultimately, the *Rules* phenomenon isn't really the authors' fault. They simply put into words a dating style that was one kind of predictable response to a superficial dating scene. But the truth is, after all the fads have faded, what most of us really want isn't to trap a mate. Women don't want to wake up one day and realize they've blindfolded a man and led him to the altar. For love is about not cynicism but trust, not craftiness but innocence.

4

Roadblocks to Falling in Love

To fear love is to fear life, and those who fear life are already three parts dead.

—Bertrand Russell

True love is the absence of fear.

—Anonymous

The only thing we have to fear is fear itself.

—Franklin D. Roosevelt

If it's all as simple as that—innocence, trust, honesty—then what gets in the way? I've mentioned it before, but it's time to return to the one overwhelming obstacle that keeps most of us from falling in love: fear. Fear of what? Don't we live in an age when many of the basic fears that beset previous generations have been more or less assuaged? Well, yes, but not in the hearts of singles. Relationship-related fears still hold many of us back, perhaps more than ever.

Well, then, let us count the fears; there are at least as many ways to fear as to love. Among those who have immediate romantic prospects, there's the old favorite, fear of commitment, once the sole province of men who wanted to play the field, now a unisex proposition. A subset of this is the fear that there might be someone better out there, a perfect man or woman scheduled to pop into your life right after your honeymoon and taunt you with the specter of lost opportunity. Some people even suffer from fear of breaking someone's heart by dumping him or her; the prospect of carrying around a yoke of guilt has been enough to prevent many from pursuing a relationship and even to push a surprising number of mismatched lovers into ill-advised marriage.

Perhaps more potent is the fear of being rejected, the paralyzing insecurity that we first experience during puberty and that visits all but the most confident among us at some point during our adult lives. When we're without a regular boyfriend or girlfriend, we fear we'll never be good enough to attract potential suitors. We're not attractive enough, not smart enough, not rich enough, not funny enough. When we prove ourselves wrong and succeed in sparking an attraction with someone, we live in fear of blowing it: of saying the wrong thing, of revealing too much, of letting our lover down. We become afraid that our partner has fallen in love with a good front, with the performance we've pressed ourselves into giving, and that after the wedding he or she will bolt on discovering the truth. Even well into marriage, we persist in fearing that we'll become boring or lose our physical appeal. Women and men alike increasingly consider plastic surgery a viable alternative to aging, a phenomenon that even extends (if you'll pardon the pun) to the previously arcane practice of penile elongation surgery, which has emerged from the shadows as an expensive ego boost for some among the 86 percent of men who feel their penis isn't large enough. (And who said men weren't shallow?)

Fear can even force people to stay in relationships they should leave. One friend of mine is currently engaged to marry a woman he has been with for five years. Twice he and his fiancée have broken off their engagement; twice they have gotten back together. I believe, in all honesty and with a great deal of sadness, that it's a relationship both would be better off without. Both of them are unsatisfied; both have separately confessed to me that they secretly have dated, and even cheated with, other people on the side, although both deny that the things on the side are serious. Yet when I ask my friend why he doesn't simply put this relationship out of its misery and end it, he says, "Because I'm afraid I'll regret it as soon as we break up." These two are hanging on to a moribund relationship out of fear, and they are wasting their lives, while hurting each other.

Then there's the fear that risks becoming self-fulfilling: the fear of never falling in love. I sense this fear among nearly all the young singles I meet. It's an unsettled feeling, a distressed uncertainty that begins in one's mid-twenties and grows with every passing day. If you reach your mid-thirties without getting married, the fear can grow so strong that it's incapacitating. Numb with fear, you resign yourself to living alone. Love, for you, is relegated to the status of myth, of fairy tale; you refuse ever again to be misled by its charms. Your heart, you resolutely announce to anyone who will listen, will belong to no one but yourself.

This is a fear to be taken seriously, for left unchecked it can have the power to enshroud your heart with a sadness that, in turn, blocks your very ability to love. Feeding off the fear of rejection, it can make you nervous and uptight in the company of a suitor, depriving you of your natural confidence and hurting your ability to be completely open and share your heart with the one you love.

The Mother of All Fears

All these fears are superficial in the face of the greatest fear we all face, not death or public speaking, contrary to conventional wisdom, but the living equivalent of death: We fear anonymity. We fear not being recognized, whether for our heart and soul or our personality, for our contribution to society or for making a difference in another person's life. Fear of anonymity underlies our reaction to many difficult events, such as being fired from a job or discovering that our partner has been unfaithful. Events such as these tell us that we are not special, that we are less than unique. Being told one is redundant, as the English so politely put it, and being cuckolded both send a painful message. They suggest that someone else out there has a value that surpasses ours, that we have been weighed in the balance and found wanting.

The feeling of being insignificant, or invisible, can have positive effects. It drives some men and women to succeed at their life's calling or to do meaningful volunteer work in their community. But for many of us, whether we know it or not, the fear of anonymity is a heavy burden.

I suggest that the role of love in the world is to give each human being the chance to face down that fear. Finding someone who loves you, whom you love in return, is an urgent mission. It is the search for recognition, for affirmation. The poet Emily Dickinson wrote eloquently of this feeling in these childlike, yet profound, lines:

> *I'm nobody! Who are you?*
> *Are you nobody, too?*
> *Then there's a pair of us—don't tell!*
> *They'd banish us, you know.*

Dickinson captured that moment of recognition that comes for anyone who finds his or her great love: that sense of gentle conspiracy, that precious knowledge that you are making a difference in someone's life. We all yearn to share our secret selves, our "nobodies," with another.

Love and Fear

In the end, fear and love are incompatible, antithetical emotions. They cannot coexist; one negates the other. Knowing this, and understanding the power of love, is the secret to conquering fear.

This isn't just a philosophical issue. The effects of fear can be traced right down to the basest physical level. Fear shuts us down. When we're afraid, we pull our shoulders down, bend our necks, lower our eyes. Fear also triggers what is known as the fight-or-flight response, which sends one message to the nervous system directing the body to contract, and simultaneously instigates a hormonal chain reaction that can send the heart rate and blood pressure soaring. Throat muscles and nostril passages open wider. Our throat goes dry, we sweat, our pupils dilate, we blush or get goose pimples. Imagine how such a transformation can affect our chances on a date, as we turn from a charming Jekyll to a hideous Hyde. Can we blame our dinner date for picking up the nearest steak knife in self-defense?

Love, on the other hand, is all about expansiveness. It breaks down walls; it's inclusive, accepting. Love is emotional yoga. It flexes our heart muscles, makes us more elastic. When we're in love, we feel hope; we find ourselves able to believe with confidence in another person's goodness. Fear hardens, but love softens; it softens the eyes and softens the heart. Fear is about shrinkage; love is about enlarging. Love enables us to look less judgmentally at others, because we know there is one person who can look at us without judgment.

Of these two powerful motives, love and fear, most of us are too often moved by the latter. And yet we all have it within our hearts to overcome fear, to trust in love. The actress Drew Barrymore recently told *Rolling Stone* magazine about writing her millennium resolution and burying it in the sand. "I will not fear anymore," she wrote. "I will not have the fear that is stopping me from living." It is no surprise that she reached this milestone just as she was finding a new love. By literally burying her fears, she made herself capable of love.

Two Ways to Start Overcoming Your Fears

Get Comfortable with Decision Making

It may seem like a roundabout approach, but in my experience most relationship fears come down to the fear of making a wrong decision, which can paralyze people into refusing to make any decision at all. So start small. When planning a dinner-and-movie date, don't spend half an hour on the phone debating restaurant and film choices. Go with the first suggestion, and live with it. Let this approach expand to other decisions, like what to wear on a date and what people you want to date. Once you get accustomed to quicker decision making, you'll realize that all the angst was for naught. And you'll be able to live with your decisions—good, bad, and ugly—much more easily.

Face Down Heartbreak

Now you're ready for a major fear face-off. Another fear that I see keeping people from opening up to new mates is the fear of rejection. This often springs directly from a traumatic experience in the past, an unexpected or particularly harsh breakup, for example. So marshal all your courage, call the one who broke your heart, and invite him or her to meet for a quick hello. The point of this isn't to rake either one of you across the coals or, for that matter, to stir up any old flames. (In fact, this is advice you should follow only if you're sure there's no chance of falling for him or her all over again.) Tell the person it's simply to touch base, catch up, perhaps bury the hatchet. For you, though, this is an opportunity to measure the distance you've come, to discover that this was just another person in your life, not some all-powerful Icon of Rejection. It may hurt for a moment, but later, after you discover you're still breathing, you'll realize that it's about time life went on.

Fears, Lies, and Consequences

How can we learn to conquer our fears? First, we have to understand the effects they have in our lives.

Many men and women try to short-circuit their fear of inadequacy by flat-out lying, making themselves out to be healthier, wealthier, or wiser than they truly are. Not surprisingly, it's a strategy that almost always backfires. Case in point: my friend George.

An extraordinarily handsome, charming man with a good job, George dated a woman named Charlene for two years. Throughout his twenties he'd dated models, but he'd never settled into a long-term involvement. "I didn't want a serious relationship," he told me. "Who needed commitment? I was having too much fun."

He was surprised, therefore, to discover just how quickly he fell for Charlene, whom he met at his own twenty-ninth birthday party. "It was incredible," he recalled. "I had never been in love before. It was so passionate. We spent every waking minute together. I idolized her."

But then, for predictable reasons, George started doing something he himself calls "really stupid." He began lying to Charlene about almost every aspect of his life. "The more I fell in love with her," he says, "the more scared I was that she would think that I wasn't good enough for her. I mean, this woman had everything; she was beautiful, smart, and sexy. I was terrified that she would see right through me."

First George started lying about his financial worth, telling Charlene he had millions of dollars invested in securities, when in truth his total net worth wasn't more than about $250,000, which for many of us, of course, wouldn't be bad at all. Then he lied about his education, saying he'd graduated from the University of Pennsylvania, an Ivy League school, when he'd actually gone to Penn State. He fed that lie to her parents as well. He even told Charlene that his own parents had divorced; in fact, they were separated, and his mother had been living with another man for ten years, but he was afraid that such an arrangement made him sound as though he came from what he termed a "trailer-trash family."

George managed his deceptions so well that it took Charlene a year and a half to discover the truth. When she did, she hit the roof. She was especially angry because he had embarrassed and humiliated her before her parents, the rest of her family, and her friends. Not only did she break off the relationship, but when George started calling her at work, begging for a reconciliation, she took out a restraining order against him. "I will have nothing to do with a man who lies to me," she screamed at him over the phone.

"But why does she hate me so much?" he asked me. "I know what I did was wrong, but I've apologized, and I'm trying to make it right."

But George was missing the point. The most important thing a woman wants in a relationship, I told him, is to feel respected, valued, and secure. She wants to know that she can get naked with a man, literally and metaphorically, and always feel safe. By lying to her, George had persuaded Charlene not only that he didn't value or respect her but that he was essentially untrustworthy. "You've become like a stranger to her," I told him. "And nobody trusts a stranger."

But there's a bigger lesson in George's story. Besides feeling betrayed, Charlene realized something that had never even dawned on George: that he didn't value himself. His compulsion to fabricate a glamorous life story grew out of his own fear that what he had to offer Charlene was not enough. He began to worry that what she was attracted to was what she saw on the surface: good looks, a charming personality, big bucks. But then the house of cards fell down, and Charlene was just as embarrassed by her own misjudgment as she was by George's behavior. She found she'd fallen in love with an apparition, a ghost with no substance.

George misunderstood—undervalued—what made him special. He grew afraid that his inadequacies would overshadow his positive qualities. He may never reunite with Charlene, but he has learned a valuable lesson: that choosing fear over love can lead only to trouble.

Stop Lying!

As a *USA Today* survey suggests, almost two-thirds (64 percent) of adults have told a spouse or significant other a lie to avoid an argument. More than a third (38 percent) have lied about what something costs. And 47 percent of couples admit that their marriages might benefit from more honesty.

Stop Lying—and Stop Stretching the Truth

We tell lies in relationships out of fear and insecurity, the insecurity that the truth of who we are isn't enough. We also lie when we want to get something, something we don't think we can get with the truth or something we're embarrassed to want in the first place. We lie to manipulate people, when we fear our own truth won't win their respect. Here are some popular lies people tell to cover their insecurity:

- 💜 They earn more money.
- 💜 They've traveled more extensively.
- 💜 Their family has greater financial means.
- 💜 They've had more sexual experience.
- 💜 They've had less sexual experience.
- 💜 Their future plans are loftier.

♥ They're more driven or motivated.

♥ They're better-educated.

♥ Their bodies are more natural.

♥ They know important people.

♥ They're more interested in the relationship with you.

♥ They're less interested in the relationship with you.

Have you ever told one of these lies? This exercise is in the spirit of radical honesty; if you've been telling such lies, stop. Then go to the person you're currently lying to, and 'fess up.

If you're just starting a relationship, show good faith by telling a truth about yourself that you've lied about to others. Again, start small; that one about abducting Patty Hearst in the 1970s might have to wait until the engagement party. But after you've confessed, when the roof doesn't cave in and your partner hasn't left you, you'll have learned that the truth can set your heart free. When it becomes second nature, you'll be much freer and happier as a result.

Don't Fib to Yourself

Self-deception, almost by definition, is the hardest kind of lie to detect; only you will know how truthfully you answer the following questions. But there's nothing more self-defeating than trying to fool yourself. If you've been telling yourself any of the following lies, you're obstructing your own path to love.

♥ I can change him.

♥ He *will* leave his wife.

♥ She's ignoring me because she's under a lot of pressure at work.

♥ He hasn't called because he lost my number.

♥ He says he doesn't love me because he has a problem with intimacy.

♥ He *will* propose this year.

> ❤ He's not abusive; he just has a bad temper.
>
> ❤ He would fall back in love with me if I lost fifteen pounds.
>
> ❤ He doesn't have to tell me he loves me; I know he does.
>
> ❤ It's okay that she spends more time with her friends than she spends with me.
>
> ❤ I know she demanded complete financials before dating me, but it's *me* she loves.
>
> ❤ I know he trusts me completely. This prenup he wants is just standard procedure.

Fear Destroys True Intimacy

A woman sent me an E-mail message not long ago confiding an incident I've since found to be increasingly common. "I have been dating Brad for three months," she began. "We started having sex on the fourth date. And I can't explain why this happens, but every time he tries to stimulate me sexually to the point where I am about to lose control, where I'm really just going to submit entirely to him and my body is going to become his, I stop him. He finds this a real turn-off. Is there something wrong with me?"

Her hesitation, I wrote back, was entirely understandable; it's all a matter of trust. "Simply stated," I told her, "you don't want Brad having that degree of control over you. Or, to put it somewhat differently, you always want to remain in control when you're around Brad." After all, I asked her, what was Brad to her? A boyfriend? How serious was her commitment? Was she hoping to marry him? How special was he to her, and vice versa? "The reason you stop him," I said, "is that you're afraid of lighting a fire that you won't want to, or be able to, douse. What if you fall in love with him and he doesn't reciprocate? What if he doesn't call you in the morning? What if he lifts you up to the clouds and then lets you drop with no parachute? Or, on the other hand, what if he falls for you and you don't reciprocate his feelings? Then you'll feel guilty for hurting him." This woman wasn't suffering from sexual dysfunction or frigidity. She was afraid. At the end of the day, her lover was still a stranger; she hadn't allowed him into her world.

This isn't an isolated problem. It's this kind of fear that explains why so many people these days complain that the thrill is gone from their sex lives. The essence of sex is being able to let go. What makes sex so pleasurable is that it's the only thing we do that involves submitting entirely to instinct. We awaken the beast within, and that makes it intense and passionate. Sex is the most natural of all experiences, because during the sexual act we give up thinking about what we're doing; we simply try to *be*. And a generation that finds it hard just to *be,* to let go, to lose control, isn't going to have an easy time with sex. (Which explains why, when husbands today ask their wives, "Honey, how about a quickie tonight?" their wives respond, "As opposed to *what?*")

Fear Douses the Fire of Love

Ultimately love, like sex, is about throwing caution to the wind. It's about taking flight, being carefree. It's about spreading one's wings and soaring, opening all the doors—emotional, sexual, spiritual—as wide as we can. Fear weighs us down, prevents us from proceeding. When people ask me, "Why can't I fall in love?" very often what they're really asking is, "Why can't I soar? How did my wings get clipped? Why can't I forget these regrets about my past, these worries about my future, forget all my concerns and anxieties, and just commit to someone? What is it that's holding me back?"

The answer is fear. And the solution is love.

Love and fear do have one thing in common. They are two of life's most powerful motivating forces. They can make us run our fastest: either into the arms of the one we love or away from the things that terrify us. We've all heard stories of the average-size mother who, seeing her child pinned under a car wheel, unbelievably lifts a small car by herself. Or of the man who, less dramatically but no less remarkably, gives up a self-defeating, bad habit for the love of a good woman. In one of the most memorable lines in recent screen history, Jack Nicholson, in the film *As Good as It Gets*, tells Helen Hunt's character that he has changed his life because she makes him "want to be a better person." This from the same actor who, thirty years earlier in the film *Carnal Knowledge*, played a character whose inability to commit to a woman was irreparable, making him a revolting male chauvinist and two-timer to the end. For those of us who grew up with Nicholson on the screen, it was a memorable transformation.

Loneliness: You're Not Alone

> The most terrible poverty is loneliness and the feeling
> of being unloved.
>
> —Mother Teresa
>
> All the lonely people—
> where do they all belong?
>
> —John Lennon and Paul McCartney, "Eleanor Rigby"

Loneliness is the great incubator of fear. It is also a condition that's central to human experience. Indeed, the first lonely person was the first man: Adam. Of all the things God could have observed about His first human creation, it was Adam's loneliness He noted first. Even Paradise was not perfect without love; for all the beauty there was in the world He had made, there was no light of love to illuminate those things for Adam. Loneliness is also the very first "bad" thing mentioned in the Bible: "It is not good for man to be alone," God says. "I will make a compatible helper for him." Some theologians have even suggested that God created Adam, and then Eve, because He too was lonely.

What is loneliness? It is what we feel when we begin to suspect that we are ordinary, or lacking any special quality that sets us apart from others. We feel lonely when there is no one around who listens to our opinions, no one who takes our views seriously, no one who admires us or respects our individuality. No one, in short, to choose us, from among all the others and make us feel we stand out.

Some have suggested that we live in a kind of paradise today, a time of prosperity and plenty—at least in the Western world. Yet just as Adam felt alone without a mate, so we as a culture are lonelier than ever. The feeling of loneliness has never left us, from the beginning of human history, but we have never become accustomed to it. Our lives and everything we do can be seen as one long, end-less flight from loneliness. We build businesses, we build towering structures, we create great works of art to fill the void, but what we all hope for is to find that one other person with whom we can share the love that is the ultimate antidote to loneliness.

The first step is to admit that we are lonely. In a strange yet nec-essary way, loneliness is the engine that drives us to love. It propels us to overcome all the sacrifices and risks that love entails.

"Who here is lonely?" I frequently ask large audiences of single people. In a crowd of a thousand, six hands or so might go up. It's hard to find people who are confident enough to admit such a thing in public. Some simply don't recognize its symptoms. But admitting that you feel lonely is nothing more than admitting that you're a human being. You're a healthy person; you feel pain, which is an essential part of the human condition. God help those who cannot recognize their own loneliness.

Today, rather than doing something positive about our loneli-ness, many of us simply pursue distractions. We watch more TV, go to more movies, call more friends, have more casual sex, or simply immerse ourselves more deeply in our work.

When I was twenty-one years old, I was so lonely that at times I felt a physical pain. I was in a seminary, studying to be a rabbi. Although my fellow rabbinical students were the closest friends I could imagine, I hungered for a nurturing feminine presence who would love me and whom I could love. And I have to tell you that it was that internal feeling of loneliness that allowed me to be drawn so surely to the woman I married. For me, love wasn't a luxury; I almost literally couldn't live without it. I wasn't desperate—desper-ation can be counterproductive, even debilitating, when one is look-ing for love—but my parents' divorce and the subsequent breakup of our family had bred in me a very idealistic understanding of love. So when I met a woman who was very warm and loving to me, that was all I needed. I didn't have to date twenty women to compare her with. I didn't need to see her face in *Cosmopolitan* or *Vogue* (though my beautiful wife would stand out even there). All I needed was a caring, affectionate woman who shared my values, who appreciated me for who I was and was grateful for the love I offered her. Like

Dickinson's "nobodies," we looked at each other and saw "a pair of us," and our loneliness, thank heavens, was conquered.

Loneliness: Spotting It and Stopping It

Are you a lonely person? It's a confession few are eager to make. But if you answer yes to any of the following questions, you may well be suffering from loneliness.

- 💜 Do you leave the television on all day when you're at home alone?

- 💜 Do you call a lot of people on the telephone just to talk, even though you don't have a lot to say, and some of them aren't even your favorite people in the world?

- 💜 Would you rather spend New Year's Eve alone than be the one person in the room who isn't passionately kissing someone when the clock strikes midnight?

- 💜 Do you avoid going to movies alone because everyone else goes as a couple or a family?

- 💜 Do you call your cat "Sweetheart"? Have you given your golden retriever an engagement ring?

- 💜 Have you stopped taking your favorite walk because you hate doing it alone?

- 💜 Do you hate looking in the mirror because the face staring back at you looks forlorn?

- 💜 Do you suffer bouts of depression that you don't tell anyone about?

- 💜 Do you get bitter whenever you hear that your friends have fallen in love?

- 💜 Do you find yourself sobbing without being able to identify why?

- 💜 Do you find yourself shopping compulsively whenever you begin to feel a bit down?

If you answered yes to any of these, that's okay, and it's a good first step. Because recognizing loneliness, and accepting it as a normal stage in life, is critical in helping to conquer it. Remember: Loneliness is the problem; love is the cure.

Embrace Loneliness

Here's an exercise designed to help you face the demon of loneliness up close and personal, but at the same time with a steely objectivity that will jolt you out of your cozy little solitude.

Go to the local singles bar. Alone. Even if you never go there and hate singles bars, go. Find a stool or table where you can observe the whole room and all the goings on: the cat-and-mouse games men and women play, the slick guy eyeing the woman at the end of the bar, the women giggling over some "loser," the ordinary quiet man whom no one will approach and who won't approach the shy woman sitting near him. Pretend you're invisible. If someone asks to join you, for once I give you permission to say, "Actually, I'm waiting for someone." Your job is to remain aloof, a fly on the wall, objectively watching the scene.

It's not a pretty picture. The dating scene can be awkward and embarrassing—for *everyone*. See it for what it is: a strange and unsettling social endeavor no one should have to be put through. Now imagine that *this* is your life, that every night you're condemned to sit there and watch this travesty, this single person's purgatory.

This is the belly of the beast called loneliness, the desolate corner of the earth known as the singles scene. If this is what it takes to move you out of your acceptance of being single, so be it. Now can I introduce you to that ordinary man or that shy woman? I thought so.

Loneliness in Its Many Forms

The simplest form of loneliness is, literally, the state of being alone, being physically separated from everyone else. Sometimes, solitude is welcome. When the world is too much with us, we seek out solitude

by going off on our own to reflect on our lives, to regroup, to revital-
ize. In the eighteenth century, Daniel Defoe's Robinson Crusoe left
the bustle of London to discover peace of mind at sea, and he found it
after being shipwrecked on a deserted island. The transcendentalist
writer Henry David Thoreau did the same in the nineteenth century,
when he withdrew to the woods at Walden Pond and wrote about the
importance of self-reliance. Today, many of us seek solitude on
retreats, on vacations, at spas, even on long walks in the country. Others find peace of mind through various traditions of meditation.

Like all things, when taken to the extreme, solitude can be
unhealthy. Those who isolate and insulate themselves for long periods of time, guarding their hearts against emotional interaction, are
going against a basic human principle. As Aristotle noted, we are
by nature social creatures.

Most of us, at most points in our life, avoid being alone like a
house afire. When we do find ourselves alone, we distract ourselves
with other voices, through television or music or talk radio. Some
people leave the TV or radio on all day while they're at home, to
break the silence and perhaps to distract them from the thing that
scares them the most: their own thoughts. Introspection makes us
confront aspects of ourselves we dislike. We fear aloneness because
we do not enjoy our own company or are bored with ourselves.

For those who abhor aloneness, there is the quick and simple
remedy of being in the company of others. When the TV or the
radio talk shows finally won't suffice, people trot off to the local pub
or join thousands of like-minded comrades in giant sports arenas or
concert halls. Even Thoreau eventually rejoined civilization when
it got too lonely out there in the woods.

Modern technology, among its many benefits, has enabled us—
some might say condemned us—to experience aloneness more easily. Today, we can sit in front of a computer monitor, alone, and
simulate being surrounded by others in chat rooms, through E-mail,
or by viewing live streaming video. Of course, like the medium
itself, the solution is only virtual. A recent study at Carnegie Mel-
lon University showed that those who spend more than five hours a
week surfing the Internet are ten times more prone to depression.
Only true human company can combat aloneness.

But there is another, deeper level of loneliness—existential lone-liness, the feeling of being lonely even while in the company of oth-ers. As we all know, you can be at Yankee Stadium, surrounded by eighty thousand people, and still feel lost. Even as a man or woman is surrounded by friends, he or she may, paradoxically, feel the cold-ness of seclusion. Standing in a room full of couples at midnight on New Year's Eve, those without a loving mate to share a kiss know exactly what I mean. And you don't have to be unmarried to be lonely. Simply being in a relationship is no cure for the condition.

Existential loneliness occurs when a person no longer feels spe-cial, because nobody recognizes her or his distinctiveness. As the great Jewish thinker Abraham Joshua Heschel once said, "The great-est human need is to become a need." We all need to be needed. To alleviate existential loneliness, we seek the company of people who recognize and appreciate what makes us unique, who lessen our sense of ordinariness. It's a sense that can be found in a close-knit community, or within one's immediate family, the people who know us and love us for what makes us different from all other people. Above all else, this is a feeling that comes in the context of marriage. When we commit to the exclusivity of marriage, we bestow on each other a great blessing, the recognition that we are special. *Only you make me feel this way*, husband says to wife; *only you open my heart this way, make me laugh this way, make me love this way.*

By the same token, when someone who had recognized that gift rejects or replaces us, our loneliness returns with a vengeance, because our greatest fear seems to be on the verge of confirmation: We feel not just betrayed, but also ordinary, mundane, redundant. Anyone who has ever been cheated on by a spouse understands this. It's impossible to avoid the feeling that you've been replaced, that you're expendable. Whatever it is that you gave to the person you love, he or she has chosen to get it from someone else. Wives who discover that their husbands have been unfaithful often describe the emotion as feeling as if they were present at their own funeral.

Each of us deals with loneliness in a different way. Some people wallow in it; they let the loneliness bring them down, like a heavy weight. Others actually revel in their loneliness; their identity seems predicated on it, in the mode of great cinematic loners like

James Dean. Some deny their loneliness altogether, numbing themselves by surrounding themselves with distractions.

There are ways to use loneliness as a positive force, as a spur to searching out romance. We can use the power of loneliness, in other words, to defeat itself. But there's one big, bad habit that keeps too many of us locked in a vicious circle of loneliness, and that's commitment phobia, as we're about to see in the next chapter.

Ten Signs That You're in Love

What, or who, will break you from the grip of a loneliness that has been with you since ice was first invented? How will you recognize that person with whom you will want to move through the stages of a relationship? Here are some clues:

1. When you have a piece of good news, is this the first person you run to tell? (If it's still your mother, you're probably not in love.)
2. When you experience something beautiful—a gorgeous piece of music, a magnificent vista, a sublime work of art—is this the person you wish were there sharing it with you? And is the experience incomplete without him or her at your side?
3. When you see this person in pain, do you wish to drop everything and take away the pain? Or is popping an Altoid the first thing that comes to mind?
4. Do you find yourself thinking about this person in the middle of staff meetings and while you're stuck in traffic? Is he or she the first person you think of when you wake up and the last you think of when you go to bed?
5. Do you defend him whenever someone criticizes him? Do you find yourself taking pride in her achievements?
6. Do you get jealous when you see this person show affection to someone else?
7. Do you love talking about this person to other people? Do you bring him or her up gratuitously in conversations?

8. Do you fantasize about sharing a life with this person?
9. Do you find yourself dressing better in this person's presence? Wanting to do better at work? Clean up your room? Shower more than once a week?
10. Do you feel slightly self-conscious around the person?

If you answered yes to more than five of these questions, chances are good that this person has broken through the hard tissue that surrounds your heart. And my advice is that you let down your guard and let him or her in.

5

Addressing the "C" Word—Are You a Commitment-Phobe?

Of all the reasons we can't seem to fall in love, commitment phobia is by far the most common.

Fear of commitment is something that for many years we ascribed only to men. For decades, the scenario went as follows: Man and woman start dating. Man enjoys the casual connection, a regular Friday date, and a warm body to hold. Woman enjoys the emotional connection, a regular Friday date, and a warm body to hold her. Three months pass; the man still enjoys the casual connection and the warm body, but the woman is hankering for more. She'd like Friday, Tuesday, and Sunday dates and wants him to meet her parents. Man runs for cover. Relationship ends; game over.

But now—and many of you readers will know this if you'll just look into your hearts—the monopoly has been crushed. Women have caught up to men in the can't-catch-me marathon of commitment phobia.

A Brief History of Commitment

So what happened? Why is it that today no one wants to commit? Why is our civilization being dominated, for the first time in history, by a "singles" culture? Who are all these people who claim to be happy being single, who just date for fun, and for whom the idea of "settling down" is no more than a vague goal for the future, when everything else starts getting stale?

Up until the sixties, men and women dated to get married. They had no pretensions that they had to be passionately and madly in love in order to do so. What they needed was to be "in like." As long as they were strongly attracted to each other and shared common goals and values, they could make a go of it. Men would come a-courting, and women would act their naturally coy and mysterious selves; they would go out on dates but only until the man was so captivated that he had to ask this woman to marry him. People went dancing in clubs and restaurants, not as a prelude to a one-night stand but because they wanted to dance. They enjoyed simple male-female interactions that didn't involve bumping and grinding. It was simply expected of couples to get married and without waiting around too long. The idea of "keeping your options open" was unheard of.

And sex? Well, sure, some people had it before marriage. But they were the exception, not the rule. Indeed, one heck of a lot of people married just to have sex. The rule was "no chupa, no shtupa"—no wedding, no bedding. And this caused more than a few suitors to pop the question as soon as their desire began to consume them. In those days, after all, sex was still looked upon as something glorious and transcendent.

But then the sixties roared across America and changed everything. A revolution swept our culture, and protest became de rigeur. Young people rebelled not only against government but against the boring conservatism of their parents' way of life. They rejected the nine-to-five job at the bank and the wife and two kids and split-level in the suburbs. What they wanted was freedom, and that meant sexual freedom.

The sexual revolution sprang from many causes. The birth control pill was one; no longer did unmarried women need to worry about getting pregnant, and no longer did randy men have to worry about shotgun weddings. Feminism was another. Women rightly revolted against the strict confines of housewifery and clamored for careers. But some overzealous feminists took a more extreme position, trying to prove, in the words of Gloria Steinem, that "a

woman without a man is like a fish without a bicycle." They
shunned patriarchy because it was oppressive and sought freedom
from what they saw as a life of drudgery.

But all of these changes removed the idea of "need" from the
context of relationships. People saw their parents' commitment as
something stifling, so free love and multiple partners were
embraced. Women no longer needed men to support them, so they
no longer felt obliged to accept men's marriage proposals. Suddenly,
commitment became passé.

Today, the aftershocks of the sixties are still with us. America
and the rest of the Western world are no longer in a state of
protest—if anything, we're in a state of ennui—but we've yet to
recapture the innocence of the first part of the century. We may
have lost the need for commitment, but it has yet to be replaced
with anything better. And what is left in its wake is our "singles culture," a culture dedicated to putting off commitment.

As a relationships writer and counselor, I hear constant complaints about just how awful the singles culture has become. But it's
hard to look back in nostalgia at a kinder, gentler singles culture
from the past, because there's never *been* a singles scene before, at
least not the way we understand it. People never devoted an entire
decade of their lives to dating for recreation. We're flying blind.

But commitment phobia is not incurable. It's an issue that can be
confronted and dealt with in a forthright, direct manner. The first step
is to admit that one has a problem and wants to change and to recognize the problem as an addiction. The addiction in question may be to
a number of things: to stalwart independence, to ambivalence, to
autonomy, or simply to affairs of the heart that are fated to fail.

If you're one of those brave souls who don't mind being called
"old-fashioned," and you're ready to break through the commitment barrier, then gird your loins and follow me. First we'll look at
the defining characteristics of the modern singles culture.

1. Dating Just to Date

People today reserve their twenties to date and have fun, in the
belief that they can settle down when they reach their thirties. If

you're a man or woman in your twenties, you probably expect to go to college and even graduate school, find a good job, become financially successful, all the while having girlfriends or boyfriends around to fulfill your emotional and sexual needs. Yet these relationships never get too serious, because to you it doesn't seem like the right time. Some people date each other for *years* and then break up because "it doesn't feel right." It's not that people don't want to be in relationships. It's that they don't want to be in a relationship that maps a path for the future. What they're interested in is what's happening *right now*.

2. One-Night Stands

It used to be that people who wanted sex without commitment had to pay for it. Prostitution was the only way a man could relieve his unbearable urges without having to worry about making a phone call the next day, or marrying the woman, or at least taking her out to dinner. Today people enter nightclubs like tigers on the prowl, seeking out partners they can chat up with some lame pickup lines that will help pave their way into the sack. People want sex free— without paying for it, but also without courting—and because our society has no need for commitment, they get it. Men and women alike go hunting for partners in what is essentially mutual masturbation. Sex has become a casual activity, divorced from true meaning—and devoid of true pleasure. We don't even know what we're missing.

3. Cohabitation

Today, couples gladly agree to live with each other without officially tying the knot. This is no longer a shameful proposition. If a couple have been dating for a number of years and still aren't sure about things, they might move in together "to see how it goes," the same way you might test-drive a car. For that matter, they figure they can save money by cutting their rent in half. Cohabitation ensures that men and women can have all the benefits of marriage, leaving many to wonder what difference the official status could make. Yet the idea of cohabitation is a little like a bank offering a mortgage with no collateral. With no obligation, nothing at stake, who wouldn't just say "Great, see ya!" and walk out the door with the money?

4. Delayed Commitment

People might argue that there's really no such thing as a "singles culture," that eventually everyone gets married. Today, though, people are doing that later and later. The average age for a man to be married is now thirty-one. Fifty years ago it was twenty-four. The average age for a woman to get married is now twenty-eight. Fifty years ago it was twenty-two. Today people talk about not committing to the "wrong" person, and they want to keep their options open. For men, commitment to the institution of marriage sounds too much like *being committed to an institution.*

When people finally do settle down, they generally don't do it for positive reasons. They settle down because all their friends are married and they're feeling left out or because their dating pool has suddenly diminished with their age and they're scared of being left alone. People are pushing off commitment until the last possible moment. Then they quickly make the most of the few seconds left on the biological clock, or the few strands of hair left on their heads, and slink in with both eyes closed.

Many people don't recognize how scared of commitment they are. "I'm not commitment-phobic," they say. "I just haven't met the right person yet." These people might meet hundreds of potential mates over the course of a year—and have probably dated some of them for months or years at a time—but they won't commit. None of their dates seem good enough, so they just keep looking.

Falling in Love: A Cure for Commitment-Phobes

But commitment phobia is not incurable. It can be confronted and dealt with in a forthright, direct manner. By buying this book, you've taken the first step. And even if you didn't actually buy it, and are reading it only at the gentle, or not so gentle, insistence of a partner or loved one, you might want to read on.

What follows is a series of simple quizzes. The first will determine whether you do indeed have a problem with commitment. You may be surprised. Many people look at themselves and say, "Of course I don't have a problem with commitment! I'm always the first to fall, and fall hard! I move in with mates only a few months into a relationship. *I'm* not the one who holds back!" But there's more than one kind of problem with commitment. You can also be too ready to commit, prone to picking mates who will be alarmed by your eagerness and retreat. Or you may be drawn consistently to mates you "can't have." Sound familiar? Take the quiz, already.

Do I Have Problems with Commitment?

Grab a pen and paper and keep track of your answers. Ponder the questions and answer honestly.

1. Think about the last several relationships you were involved in. If your level of interest and your partner's (your need to spend time together, your eagerness to move the relationship along, your certainty about the relationship) were placed on either side of a balance, what would happen?

    A. My side would clunk to the ground. I was much more ready to get serious.
    B. The scale would settle right in the middle; we were in agreement.
    C. My partner's interest would outweigh mine. I questioned the relationship frequently along the way.

2. One of the most familiar images in the movies is the scene where, during the walk to the altar, at the last possible moment the bride or groom bolts for safety and escapes the marriage. When you watch a scene like that, you think:

    A. God, that reminds me of the exits of my last two girlfriends (boyfriends)!
    B. Leave it to Hollywood to create an unrealistic, melodramatic scene like that!
    C. I should watch closely and remember to keep cab fare tucked in my shoe if I ever go walking down the aisle.

3. You're set up on a blind date, and what is usually a pretty miserable experience turns out to be the most fun you've had in weeks. You return home to your apartment and immediately write in your journal, "Dear Diary, tonight I had the greatest date ever. Everything about the evening was perfect: Romantic French dinner, great conversation—wow. One thing I know for sure . . . "

   A. I will not sign the lease on my apartment next month. I'm sure we'll be getting hitched by the fall!
   B. I can't wait to see him (her) again next weekend. Maybe this time we can go for Mexican!
   C. I'm thinking I shouldn't call him (her) back. After all, nothing can be this perfect, and I'm not really sure if I have room in my life for a relationship.

4. When the idea of meeting your partner's parents or closest friends comes up in conversation, you usually feel:

   A. Extreme elation.
   B. Slightly nervous, but excited.
   C. A queasy stomach and a sense of dread.

5. You've been dating someone for weeks. He or she has already met:

   A. Your parents, your grandma, two aunts, your sister, your dog, your college roommate, and every person you work with.
   B. Your roommate, your best friend and his girlfriend, and your brother when he came through town for a visit.
   C. Your goldfish. Better to involve new people slowly in your life.

6. The woman or man you've been seeing for several weeks happens to have a family wedding two hours away next weekend. It doesn't require spending the night away but simply a drive to a neighboring town, the ceremony, and a small reception. He or she asks you to go and subtly mentions that "everyone is eager to meet you." You:

   A. Go buy a new outfit and several rolls of color film. These are the shots that you'll treasure years down the line!
   B. Agree to attend, but decline the offer to spend the entire weekend there with the family.
   C. Use the offer as a springboard for the conversation you've been

meaning to have for the last three dates: "Maybe we are getting too serious . . . "

7. In your last three relationships, the amount of time you and your partner spent together was determined by:

   A. The other person. If you'd had your way, you would have been spending five out of seven days together.
   B. A mutual agreement, based on your work schedules. Usually you ended up seeing each other two or three evenings a week.
   C. You and only you. You needed to schedule dates around your work hours, your Spanish lessons, your weekly outings with friends from college. If you couldn't commit time to these things, you'd feel cheated and resentful.

8. When you visit friends who are married and relatively "settled" in their lives, your first thought is:

   A. This is exactly what I pictured for me and Johnny (Jane). I still cannot believe that he (she) left me! I want my own picket fence.
   B. Oh, how nice. They seem really happy together. I hope that when the time comes I can achieve such peace and harmony in my life.
   C. Eccchhh. I can't imagine a more boring and lifeless existence. May I never find myself trapped in such routine!

9. You were raised in a politically liberal Jewish household, and your connection to your faith is an important element of your identity. You start noticing someone next door, last name O'Grady, whom you learn comes from a staunchly Irish-Catholic family, volunteers regularly for the local conservative caucus, and during the last presidential election campaign was sighted posting George W. lawn placards. Your first thought is:

   A. All the more romantic! Just like Romeo and Juliet, right? And anyway, opposites always attract!
   B. I should definitely introduce him (her) to O'Reilly at work! They have so much in common!
   C. Maybe I should try my luck with this O'Grady. We can just have fun together, since neither of us would expect anything long term out of it.

10. You're planning to hold a dinner party and are shopping for hors d'oeuvres. You find yourself at the gourmet shop in the supermarket selecting cheeses. Both the goat cheese with pepper and the Brie sound good. You:

    A. Stand at the cooler for twenty minutes and finally call your mother, your sister, and your best friend to see which they would choose.
    B. Decide to get both. After all, you only live once, right?
    C. Buy Muenster, which you don't like anyway. That way you won't regret choosing either the pepper or the Brie.

Any A's and C's earn you one point. Any B's get you zero. Total your score, and move on to round two:

Give yourself one point for answering yes to any of the following questions, unless otherwise instructed:

1. Have you ever been involved with someone who was married? Someone who was living with a romantic partner? *(1 point for seriously committed, 2 points for married)*

2. Have you ever had an intense crush on someone of the "wrong" sexual persuasion? *(1 point for yes, 2 points if you ever confessed those feelings)*

3. Have you ever been involved with someone who was at least fifteen years older than you?

4. Have you ever started a relationship with someone knowing that very soon one or the other of you would be moving a good distance away?

5. When you feel your partner pulling away from you in a relationship, do you attempt to fix the things you think are "wrong" with the relationship or try to make things more serious so your partner will have more difficulty breaking free?

6. Have you ever debated for more than a half-hour over whether to buy an article of clothing?

7. Do you have trouble choosing an airline, or a time of departure, for a routine air trip?

8. Do you resist making a purchase if you know that you will be unable to return or exchange it?

9. Have you changed jobs more than once a year for the past three years?

10. Have you switched living spaces more than once a year in the past two years, or does your current living space maintain a look of "recently settled" (unpacked boxes, bare walls, no curtains on the windows)?

11. Do you spend more time choosing a video to rent than actually watching it?

12. Do you ever ascribe your difficulty in relationships to the idea that "I just haven't met the right person yet. When it happens, I'll know."

Scoring

Total your points. Add one point if you're doing this quiz in pencil because you're afraid you might want to go back and change an answer at the end. Add another if you've changed any answer more than twice in determining your responses.

0–5: You probably maintain a healthy balance between giving yourself over to a relationship and maintaining a life of your own. If you still feel you need to read this book, your issues lie elsewhere; commitment shouldn't be an obstacle for you.

5–10: Commitment issues definitely play into your inability to fall in love. Continue with the quiz to determine more specifically what your issues are. Are you yourself actively resisting commitment, or do you passively resist commitment by seeking relationships with those who are blatantly commitment-phobic themselves?

10+: Look up commitment phobia in the medical texts, and you're likely to see your own mug staring back. But don't despair; read on. Clarify your MO in resisting com-

mitment (active or passive) and read on to find ways to
work on it. Rest assured, you're not alone. Have courage.
And buy another three copies of this book just to prove
to yourself that you're capable of doing it.

Commitment-Phobes Came Marching One by One

Still not sure where you fit in? Still think that despite your score of
one million you'd have no problem taking that leap of faith once
the "right person" came along? Well, here's a set of questions that
should help settle the issue once and for all. Remember, be honest.
The truth shall (ahem) set you free.

1. Are you panic-stricken when the conversation with your girlfriend or
   boyfriend turns to "where this is going"?
2. If you feel someone is becoming too close to you, do you stop calling
   him or her, and try as hard as you can to forget about the person?
3. Do you avoid romantic movies?
4. When you read Civil War histories, does the word *Union* give you a
   rash? Do you find yourself cheering for the Confederates even though
   you live in New Hampshire?
5. Do you try to find partners who will give you sex without asking for anything else?
6. Do you want to "concentrate on your career" before you give thought
   to settling down?
7. When you think of marriage, do you think of large capital expenditures,
   sticky children, a husband with a beer belly (or an ever-expanding
   wife), or do you think of connubial bliss?
8. Are you "not ready for a serious relationship right now" even though
   you're in your fifties and have never been married?
9. Have you committed to inappropriate people in the past, only to break
   up with them and leave them devastated?
10. In breaking up or turning down a relationship, have you ever used the
    excuse that you don't want to hurt the other person?
11. Have you become close to people, only to draw away from them
    when they feel that the relationship is becoming serious?

12. Do you resent the inquiries of family or friends?

13. Do you regularly cancel lunch or dinner dates with friends?

14. Do you avoid purchasing super-saver airline tickets because you're not permitted to change the date?

15. Do you find yourself pursuing and chasing an uninterested member of the opposite sex, and just as it becomes clear that he or she has become interested find yourself running the opposite way?

16. Do you regularly make promises you don't keep?

17. Do you blame your broken promises on circumstances beyond your control?

18. Do you send out mixed messages to your dates, one week calling every day, the next week not at all?

19. Do you get all sweaty in elevators? On airplanes? In an airplane hangar?

20. Do you want to date a lot before you "settle down"?

21. Do you break up relationships because of small, petty issues, like "she had a funny walk" or "he used too many exclamation marks in his E-mail"?

22. Are you more ready to shower affection on a stranger who's just in town briefly than on someone you've known for a lot longer?

23. Do you try to keep your partner separate from the other people in your world, not introducing him or her to your family and avoiding spending time together with your friends?

24. Do you refuse invitations from your partner to spend time with his or her family and friends?

25. Do you create distance between you and your partner by not speaking forthrightly about your feelings or by taking up new hobbies whenever you enter into a relationship?

26. Do you feel most strongly about partners who seem to be pulling away from you?

27. Do you have a history of being unfaithful in relationships? Are you most unfaithful to those you feel closest to?

28. Are you the one to end most of the relationships that you have been in?

29. Do you fall in love quickly, become obsessive about the person, and a couple of weeks later think he or she is completely ordinary?

30. Do you have unrealistic fantasies about people that you meet?

31. Is the activity in your relationship happening more in your head than in real life? In other words, do you dream about the person or send him or her poetry or flowers more than you actually talk together and let something real develop?

32. Are you very afraid of becoming involved with the wrong partner?

33. Do you fear losing your freedom, sexual or other?

34. Do you fear becoming bored?

35. Are you afraid of losing your individuality?

36. Are you afraid of dying without ever "having lived"?

37. Are you afraid of having someone dependent on you?

38. Do you provoke your partner into arguments because you want an excuse to end the relationship?

39. Are you afraid to say "I love you" to your partner? Do the words get stuck in your throat?

40. Instead of offering deep hugs, do you find yourself patting your partner on the back like a football buddy?

41. Do you look at friends who are married and think they've compromised themselves in some way? Do you tell yourself you'll never "settle" the way they did?

42. When you hear that a friend has gotten engaged, is your first reaction "I wonder how long *that* will last"?

43. Are you beginning to feel you're wasting your time dating, since no one you meet seems worthy of your time?

44. Are you afraid of being stuck in a boring relationship, gravitating instead toward people who are less stable but more exciting?

45. Are you addicted to bad boys?

46. Do you harbor dreams of leading a creative life—as a writer, an actor, a film director—that you've never pursued?

47. Have you changed jobs more than once a year for the past three years?

48. Are you never happy about the job you have, and are you always thinking about a change?

49. Do other people have only a vague idea of what you do for a living, because you aren't really sure what your career aspirations are?

50. Do you prefer month-to-month rent instead of signing a full-year lease?

How Am I Resisting Commitment?

Some readers may be surprised by the outcome of the quiz. They may see themselves as ready and eager to commit, and explain that the problem is not them but rather the people they choose to have relationships with. It's their partners who always resist the relationship.

But think about it for a moment. The easiest way to resist commitment is by dating people you know are inappropriate or commitment-phobic themselves. This is passive resistance to commitment, and it's just as tough a problem. Have a look at the following list of symptoms, and consider which sound most familiar:

Symptoms of Passive Resistance

💗 You have a history of becoming involved, emotionally or physically, with partners who are married or already in a seriously committed relationship.

💗 You have a tendency to "jump in" to relationships quickly, without a reasonable gestation period, leaving the relationship to root itself in fantastic ideals instead of something solid and real.

💗 You depend on romantic ideals that are not realistic or "practical," for example, a stalwart belief in love at first sight, fate, karma, or something that is "meant to be." When these elements become more important than compatibility, accessibility, and availability, passive resistance is afoot.

💗 Rather than being wary of relationship obstacles like geographic differences or a wide gap in age or interests between partners, you start rationalizing, telling yourself "it's better this way."

💗 You have a pattern of dating people who are vastly different from you in terms of ideology, life priorities, or religious or social background. Of course, couples can overcome such stumbling blocks; but when it becomes a repeated situation, it's a problem. For example, you live in strict accordance with your conservative Catholic background and abstain from drugs and alcohol, but you can't stop falling for atheist radicals who smoke a pack a day.

❤ You find yourself giving more time to your fantasies about a relationship—imagining future dates in your head, naming future children, planning a future honeymoon—than to actually making the relationship work in the present.

❤ You've given up relationships that were likely to proceed down a solid, committed path, because you suddenly questioned whether the relationship was too safe or too staid or was missing that "special spark."

❤ You find yourself attracted consistently to partners who need "work" and convince yourself that you're just the one to "fix" them.

❤ You automatically think of safe or comfortable relationships as boring, and of tumultuous or turbulent ones as passionate.

❤ You tend to want to "keep all options open" in life. Decisions that seem irreversible are frightening, at times even paralyzing you. The fear of having no way out keeps you from fully engaging with choices or decisions.

Any of these sound familiar? If more than three of these situations found you thinking, "Hey, that's me!" chances are you've got passive commitment problems, even if you think you're ready for the honeymoon. By constantly seeking commitment from impossible people or situations, you're guarding your autonomy as surely as are those avowed commitment-phobes.

If the previously listed qualities failed to ring a bell, yet you scored on the high end of the commitment-phobia quiz, chances are you're the kind who actively avoids commitment. This kind of commitment issue is easier to self-diagnose. Any of these sound familiar?

Symptoms of Active Commitment Phobia

❤ When a relationship is in the beginning phases and seems to be going well, do you ever catch yourself doing or saying things that are likely to sabotage the relationship or alienate your partner?

❤ Do you set up boundaries in your relationships, either physical or emotional, that allow you to maintain a sense of distance?

💜 Do you establish "rules" about how often you will see your partner in a relationship?

💜 Do you avoid situations that would indicate a level of seriousness
in a relationship, not even going on vacation together?

💜 Is it important to you to keep your group of friends, same-sex or
opposite-sex, separate and independent from your relationship?

💜 Do you find yourself carefully avoiding discussion of the most
private aspects of your life, for fear that after this relationship
terminates you don't want an ex knowing all your secrets?

💜 Reflecting on your history of relationships, are you aware of
causing strife or conflict in previous romances because of an
unwillingness to commit?

💜 Are you quick to notice faults and idiosyncrasies in a romantic
partner? Does this happen more frequently as a relationship
grows more intense?

💜 Are these faults and idiosyncrasies usually reason enough to dis-
continue, or put the brakes on, the relationship?

💜 Do you say and do things, like breaking dates or avoiding commitments too far in the future, that consciously or subconsciously warn your partner not to expect too much from you?

💜 When assessing the pros and cons of a relationship, do you tend
to see the sacrifices overshadowing the benefits of pursuing the
relationship?

The preceding tendencies are characteristic of someone who
actively avoids committing to a serious or long-term relationship.
It's simple enough to recognize which of these qualities ring true in
your situation. It's not so easy to determine why you do this. Fear is
a major factor in the development of commitment issues. Opening
yourself up to a true covenant with another human can be scary
indeed. It involves giving something up. It means working to maintain communication and understanding. It means weighing someone else's needs and desires as well as your own when progressing
through life. It means exposing yourself to the real possibility of getting hurt or feeling rejected. But you're reading this book, so you
must know that the prospect of falling in love is worth a little risk.

Breaking the Patterns

There are a number of practical suggestions I would offer to all those fearing commitment. Try to find ways to incorporate them, one at a time, if necessary, into your life. If you find yourself repeating old patterns, don't be so hard on yourself that you give up altogether and resign yourself to a lifetime of six-week relationships and lousy first dates. Just keep trying.

Take Responsibility

The problem is yours, and you need to face it. You can make no positive changes in life without first acknowledging a need for change. To help you muster the inspiration for change, think a few years down the road. Do you really want to come home to an empty apartment for the rest of your life? Close your eyes and imagine what that would be like. Take a virtual tour of a potentially lonely future. You arrive home after a grueling twelve-hour day (you live for your work). In the fridge is nothing but half a lemon that's growing a green beard and an open bottle of Coke with no fizz. Your company for the evening is Danny DeVito on *Letterman* talking about how he burned his lasagna. Strewn all over the bedroom are old, dirty socks. You try to pick them up, but they're stuck to the carpet. You cuddle next to your little pooch, who promptly relieves his bladder over your business suit. You put it on the next morning anyway.

Quit the Excuses

Blaming your parents' constant fighting, your first boyfriend's heartless breakup with you, or the time you caught your college roommate making out with your fiancée will get you nowhere. Habits like that just keep you in the past. Move on to tomorrow. It's not true that you haven't met the right person yet. You've dated fifty people, for goodness' sake. You just haven't thought seriously about making a life with any of them.

Be Aware

Be mindful of the tricks and tactics you use to maintain distance. Think about the patterns of inappropriate partners in your past. Get over your fixation of dating only guys with pierced eyeballs. Be aware of the moment in a relationship that in the past has caused you to flee commitment. Then stay alert when you're at risk of repeating the pattern. Don't let your history repeat itself.

Commit to Yourself

The first step to learning how to commit is to commit to the one person who is certain to be a part of your life, always: you. Invest, not necessarily money but time and energy, into making your life as complete as it can be. Do not wait for a relationship to fix your life and fill your holes. This is not what commitment is about. Rather, practice commitment in other areas of your life: career, friends, artistic passions, outdoor activities, volunteering, learning. When people ask you out for lunch, go. When you need to fly to L.A. for a meeting, just book the darned ticket, even if it's a month in advance. Of course, I'm not suggesting you substitute these other pursuits for a romantic life. Rather, I believe that engaging in the development of self, by constantly making commitments and honoring them, will make it all the more fulfilling and natural to share this life with another human being.

Don't Get Hung Up on the Little Things

I know, easier said than done. If it means restricting the time you can spend musing over shopping choices or studying a menu, then do that for a while. The thing to remember is that you have the power to effect change. Very few decisions are permanent, and those that are, like marriage (ideally, at least), are choices you must make without knowing the future. This is about faith. Take the leap, make the choice, believe that it will all work out for the best. Practice making decisions. Choose just one E-mail address. Don't run from a job when it's not fulfilling; *make* it fulfilling. Try doing things that aren't always fun but are rewarding, like volunteer work.

Practice Saying No

This is a toughie for many people. It is yet another way to avoid resolution. Say maybe, and you can always turn back. Avoid the question, and you avoid someone's resenting your *no*. But you know when *no* is your honest answer. Use it.

Live in the Present

Stop thinking about next week or next month or next year. To do justice to a relationship, you must live in the here and now. Don't allow your imagination to carry you away to all the problems the two of you will face down the road. There are exceptions, of course, times when the future must be considered. But for many true commitment-phobes, this goes too far, for example, picturing your future children's orthodontist bills when the woman you really like confesses she wore a retainer. Stop! Don't let yourself go there. Blot out any and all thoughts that unreasonably pull you away to the big, scary future. If you must, think about next week. Or better yet, think about ordering dessert.

Keep Your Promises

The best way to get into the habit of committing is to do it daily, in small ways as well as large. When you tell someone you'll call at 8:30, don't wait until 11:00. This goes back to the first suggestion on this list. If you are the kind of person everyone expects to be late, and thus have granted yourself a permanent pardon for tardiness, break the habit.

Give Up on the Elusive Paradigm of Perfection

Perfection is appealing in part because it's elusive. And it's elusive because it doesn't exist. If you continue to wait for the "perfect relationship" that will instantaneously inspire you to commit, you'll be waiting for a very long time.

Date Someone You Don't Like

Every third relationship, make a point of asking out or accepting a date from someone you wouldn't normally be attracted to. You'll be surprised. The very idea that you can commit to even one date with someone you don't like can help you overcome inner resistance and thus your fear of commitment. And who knows? You might just find out that the person is amazing.

Stop Chasing the Unavailable

When you catch yourself breaking dates to spend more time with your married boss; when you take a detour at work to pass by the beautiful man with the picture of his boyfriend on his desk; when you know you're traveling down that well-worn path of geographically or emotionally doomed relationships, stop yourself. You're not going to be the one to fix, move, heal, solve, motivate, or inspire him (or her) to change these things. Move on.

Delight in Reality

Real relationships with real, available people aren't always easy. They're not always fun. Real people can be frustrating, difficult, emotional, and confusing, and sometimes they have cellulite. But they are there to hold you, and to listen, and to argue with, and to laugh with. In the flesh. That's what you're after.

6

The River, the Kettle, and the Bird

Remedies for Loneliness

Love takes off the masks that we fear we cannot live without, and we know we cannot live within.

—James Baldwin, *The Fire Next Time*

One word frees us of all the weight and pain of life; that word is love.

—Sophocles

The reason why all men honor love is because it looks up, and not down; aspires and not despairs.

—Ralph Waldo Emerson

The Jewish Talmud, in a story that predates Rip Van Winkle by several millennia, tells of *Honi Hama'agal*, Honi the Circle-Drawer, who once went to sleep under a fig tree and woke up seventy years later. Seeing that his whole generation had perished, that he was left without even one contemporary, he turned his eyes heavenward and proclaimed to God, "Give me companionship or give me death." (Patrick Henry, too, came much later.)

Ideally, love vanquishes loneliness. Through the absolute union of two people, through the utter intimacy the Bible refers to as "becoming one flesh," those feelings of aloneness—of not being recognized for one's unique qualities, of not being truly understood—dissolve, and the pain recedes.

But how?

Throughout my teenage years, I had vivid and colorful dreams. I always wondered what they meant. In fact, the very first book I wrote, in my early twenties, was about dream symbolism and interpretation. While researching this book, I came upon something from the Talmud that, for reasons I was never sure of, stayed with me for many years. Now I know why.

The Talmud says that he who dreams of three things—a river, a kettle, and a bird—will find love. When I started thinking more and more about relationships, I came to understand this piece of Talmudic wisdom on a much deeper level. These three images connote three different types of relationship, each representing a more profound level of intimacy than the last. Every good relationship goes through these three ever-deepening phases. They represent a progression from close to closer to closest.

The cure for loneliness can be found in these three styles.

The River Relationship: A River Runs Through Us

The first kind of relationship, the river relationship, may be the most common in our society. Sadly, it is also the most superficial. In this image, the two partners are like two cities, two independent worlds, whose only connection is a river that runs between them. That river represents their marriage: their mutual affection, their kids, their mortgage payments. But the marriage goes no deeper than that. Indeed, the partners don't want it to be any deeper. They are happy the way they are. They cherish their independence. Theirs is no deep soul connection. In fact, these two people barely know they have a soul, so what's to connect? Their stock portfolios?

What connects them is the river, in other words, their relationship. Or their *version* of marriage. Otherwise, they are two different beings, separate worlds altogether. They have their own interests and keep their own schedules; they are complete, independent.

Each of these two sister cities has its own commerce, its own industry, its own emergency systems. Each city is self-contained, fully
able to function without relying on the other. Nonetheless, being
sensible members of the modern political world, both cities have
realized that their alliance has its practical virtues. After all, two
working together can accomplish more than one alone. So their
ships go back and forth between each other's port, participating in
trade and exchanging cultural gestures. The purpose of the commerce is entirely pragmatic, the connection between them entirely
functional. If trade breaks off, it will be a practical loss but no big
deal. Only a few extra conveniences will go by the wayside. After
all, there are other cities farther down the river. Neither city *needs*
the other to preserve its integrity, its identity.

The same is true of a man and a woman in a river relationship.
In practice, the two coexist comfortably enough; they go to movies,
dine together, socialize. But their interaction is superficial; their
conversation never delves below the surface. What absorbs them is
the functional side of their lives. They talk about movies they've
seen, coworkers who annoy them. They have their own lives and
their own sources of livelihood, their own friends, their own hobbies. They even make love functionally. Mad, passionate lovemaking is utterly foreign to them. They prefer to be in control. They
love each other, but they're not in love. They probably never did
fall in love; they're afraid of falling. This is love with two steady
feet.

In many cases, one half of this passionless partnership is a career
woman who prides herself on taking fulfillment from her work
rather than from a man. She's also been disappointed so many times
previously by men that she has cultivated a studied indifference
toward relationships. Though she expects to get married, she cannot give herself over completely to a man. Her heart is still her
own; her soul and person are still closely guarded possessions. The
other half? Perhaps a man who's been single so long he's built his
own emotional infrastructure. He may have become involved in the
relationship because he thought it might be a nice amenity in his
already full life. Sure, he gets lonely, and he welcomes the warmth
and comfort of a female companion. But his real moments of ecstasy

come in closing a big deal or making a killing in the market, rather than in holding a woman's hand or making love to her. His woman is peripheral to his life rather than central. She is one of the things that he does, and he is one of the things in her life, slightly more important than her therapist.

Still, the benefits of a relationship and marriage cannot be denied. So this man and woman build a river of a relationship between them, and eventually they are married. Their relationship may appear successful from the outside to family and friends; the couple themselves may even see it as "working." And from their superficial perspective, it is. They produce two or three children, own a four-bedroom house, and carry a hefty mortgage. They take the family on a two-week vacation every year to one of those resorts where he can play golf, she can play tennis, and the kids can be shuttled off to day camp. Their lovemaking sessions echo the national average: twice a week for about fourteen minutes at a time.

Functionally, he and she remain two separate individuals. Their relationship is tangential rather than integral to their lives. Theirs is not the unburdening kind of love, where you turn yourself inside out like a sweater, unafraid to show the seams. Deep emotional intimacy is not their goal. They don't intertwine; they never become fully enmeshed. Whether or not they sign a prenuptial agreement, whether or not they establish joint bank accounts, whether or not they take each other's names (or even hyphenate them) is of little consequence. What matters is that they don't deliver their hearts and souls to each other. Independence is far more important to them. They enter the relationship fully clothed and never get naked, even when they undress. They always know where the escape hatch is. They love each other, but they don't *need* each other, not in any existential sense. The deep divide of that river remains between them, and it causes loneliness and lack of fulfillment. Even if they say they never feel lonely, it's because they have become incapable of recognizing their innermost needs.

The river relationship, perhaps not surprisingly, is often pervaded by lies, not the *I did not have sex with that woman* variety of lies, but lies of the heart. In a river relationship a man and woman make love to each other, but each often thinks about someone else.

Each member may harbor well-suppressed, unspoken dissatisfaction with the relationship, but they persist in the belief that this is as good as it gets and find displaced contentment in confiding and complaining to close friends or relatives. Both are afraid to talk about past relationships for fear they will incite jealousy. One party never finds the courage to mention the other's nasty and annoying habits, and the other wouldn't have the strength to change anyway; the two continue on, blinded to each other's feelings, socking away a lifetime of unspoken resentment.

Also typical of the river relationship is the near absence of passionate kissing. These couples peck each other on the cheek rather than really kiss. That would be far too intimate, far too scary. They hardly ever kiss with their eyes open; that would also be too real, and the same for eyes-open sex. Lovemaking, at the river level, is a game of tuning out your partner. Here they are, in the closest physical proximity possible between two people, and they're closing their eyes! Focusing on their own sensual experience. It's as if what they really want to cry out to each other in the course of lovemaking is "Would you kindly get the heck out of here? I can't enjoy this with you around distracting me." Eyes-open sex is difficult for many people; studies show that 94 percent of women cannot climax with their eyes open. (For open-eyed lovers, that eye contact is an ultimate connection, like a surge of energy passing between the two.)

The vast majority of relationships I have encountered, especially among professional men and women, follow this model: men and women with a river's difficult passage running between them. Consider how many couples today date and date throughout their twenties, without a serious thought of ever marrying or having children. When they break up with each partner, their hearts quickly mend, distracted by "infotainment" overload and a merry-go-round of dating. Tonight, throughout the world, millions of couples will get physically naked, without ever having gotten emotionally naked. They will take off their clothes and have sex but never once remove their inhibitions, expose their vulnerability, truly make love. After a while, I have found, people in river relationships lose the capacity to make love, or even to feel love. Instead, they make peace with their loneliness by burying the deeper parts of their soul under a mountain of material goods. After all, if we fill all the empty spaces, we can convince ourselves that our lives are "full." If you don't know yourself—if you don't expose yourself—how can anyone else know you? Worse, if you become so satisfied with your surface existence that you lose touch with your deeper self, how can you ever share your innermost heart with your beloved?

The Kettle Relationship: Not Quite Boiling

One level up on an ascending scale is what I think of as the kettle relationship. The kettle model is built on the understanding that men and women are opposites, like fire and water. Fire and water are two elements of nature that appear to be incompatible: Water can extinguish fire; fire can evaporate water. And yet here's the rub: Put a kettle between them, and they can produce hot water for a warm bath or a boiling cup of coffee; they can produce steam to supply power and heat. In a kettle relationship, much the same happens between a man and a woman.

Though the clashing characteristics of the two genders might suggest that they couldn't live together, that they would cancel each other out, men and women in kettle relationships both become productive, with the kettle as their medium. They are able to negate their differences and build (cook, wash, heat) something together that they could not alone. The kettle helps them maintain balance and achieve common goals.

Whereas the cities in the river relationship merely coexist under a kind of mutual political arrangement, couples in the kettle relationship have actually taken a step closer to true harmony. They share a deeper understanding, a closer connection, in part because their connection involves the admission that they need each other. They perceive that they need each other to get things done, to improve their lives. If they want children, they need each other. If they want an active sex life, they need each other. If they want the emotional support that a relationship provides, they need each other. And the practical conveniences also present in a river relationship—social standing, a two-paycheck income—don't hurt either.

But there are limitations to the kettle relationship. While partners in such a relationship do love each other and long for connection, they're nonetheless held apart by their conflicting genders. Because they still cling to their individuality—and identify themselves primarily as *man* or *woman*, not *lover* or *soul mate*—they must have a kettlelike arrangement to preserve a certain distance between them, or their chemical interaction will fizzle like a fire doused in water. Just as fire and water need the kettle between them in order to be productive, so the partners in the kettle relationship will always suffer from a certain gap in intimacy. The partners in such a relationship have not completely merged. In fact, in some respects they feel greater intimacy with members of their own sex, who seem to understand them better. To be sure, like opposites that attract, kettle couples are deeply pulled toward one another, but they remain aware at all times that they are different from each other. He might get a thrill from the sex between them but still value a night out with the boys just as much. She might grit her teeth as he snores through the night, looking forward to a Saturday afternoon out shopping with the girls. At best they can only bridge their differences; they cannot transcend them. They never overcome their gender differences, merely find a way to work around them.

Given the way I describe it, this might not seem that tempting a model to follow. Yet I'd contend that the kettle relationship has been widely championed in the last decade or two as the ideal model for modern romantic relationships, perhaps most famously in the Mars-Venus theory of the writer John Gray. Gray, of course, sees men as from Mars, bringing fire to the relationship, and women from Venus, bringing water. He counsels that the only way to build a successful relationship is to work around those differences. And what is the kettle in their relationship, you might ask? Well, it's John Gray's own books. Couples can at best offset their dissimilarities, neutralize their differences. There can never be complete harmony; respect for difference is as close as these couples come.

Modern kettle couples, bolstered by advice like Gray's, believe there's no point in "working" on their relationship, trying to transcend each other's differences. It's the boys-will-be-boys approach. When men retreat into their caves, unwilling or unable to explain themselves, women are led to believe that there's no point in trying to cajole them out and get them to talk; on the contrary, women learn to leave them alone for the time being. What about the potential for building a deeper intimacy in such a vulnerable moment? Fuhgeddaboudit! Men just aren't built like that, or so the kettle logic goes. It's the same for women. They'd rather complain to a girlfriend about their men than confront the man and work out their differences.

So each retreats to his or her gender-specific neutral zone. That way, neither has to feel rejected or misunderstood. "Women—can't live with 'em, can't shoot 'em," he jokes to his buddies. "It's a guy thing," she moans. Gray and others like him are only teaching the tricks that many in kettle relationships already use to cope with their imperfect relationships. Kettle men know they don't have to worry about being problem-solvers; they just have to lend a sympathetic ear when their partner's had a bad day. As long as they understand when to say "too bad" or " uh-huh" or "It's all right, honey," they don't need to understand the problems that underlie the complaints. And kettle women accept that when their men feel dejected they don't need to talk about it; what they need is to spend a night out with the boys, blowing off steam, and then to return to a conversation-free night of hot sex.

To my mind, the greatest problem of the kettle relationship is that it involves permanent frustration. You try hard to get close; you transcend the dry coexistence of the river relationship. But then you come up against this impenetrable, natural barrier. Venusians can breathe only on their planet, and Martians are limited to theirs.

Many of the kettle relationships I've witnessed involve couples who've been together for a significant stretch of time, say ten years or so. She loves her man and feels close to him. He comforts his woman, knows her "like the back of his hand," as he always tells people. They practically finish each other's sentences. But she still discusses the real issues in her life—problems with a colleague, worries about her health, concerns about her aging parents—with her girlfriends rather than her husband. Why? She doesn't have to prove anything to her female friends; she can let her hair down. She doesn't have to look pretty; she can be cranky, even bitchy, and her fellow Venusians will understand and commiserate. Getting away from Martians like her husband, in fact, is a relief. He, meanwhile, has stopped trying to teach her the rules of basketball, would rather not admit that he fears his company's in trouble, and doesn't share his concerns about aging with anybody. They understand each other's limitations and accept them. They don't fault each other for them. But neither do they turn to each other in their greatest moments of crisis.

My friend George is in a kettle marriage. When his small company started to tank, George kept it all inside. But I could see that his spirits were sagging—everybody could—and we all knew it was over his finances. When I spoke to him about his dejection, rather than give him business advice, I first asked, "Have you discussed this with your wife?"

"Yeah," he responded. "She knows."

"But that's not what I asked," I continued. "Have you *discussed* it with her? Have you told her how frightened you are? How you never wanted to fail in life, how you're terrified that you may not be able to support your family, how you don't want to let her down or lose her respect? Have you told her any of that?"

He hadn't, he admitted. "This is business stuff. She wouldn't understand the business, and she certainly doesn't understand this part of me. She'll just worry. Why should I get her all worked up?"

And yet what is a partner or soul mate for, I wondered, if not to be there in darker moments like these, as well as in the moments of triumph? What George needed, first and foremost, was to be comforted. He needed to be reminded that money wasn't what made him, so its loss could never break him. And that kind of comfort could come only from the woman who loved him.

Isn't it sad how so many of us deprive ourselves and never get even close to maximizing the potential of our relationships? After a while, the kettle marriage hardens just like a real iron kettle, imprisoning our hearts and deadening our spirits. If men and women are so different, can never become one flesh, can never be joined at the hip, then why bother at all? It's a compelling question that for too many people today doesn't have a compelling answer.

So they choose to opt out, remain single, rather than live in a kettle relationship. They deny themselves passion in the process. The fire of the men will never be tempered by the tranquillity of the women. The men will never set down roots; they'll work and work, and leave their fortune to some charity or university. The women will never have their cold water heated up by the embers of passionate male energy. They may find some temporal satisfaction in their lives, but they will never achieve that sense of fulfillment that men and women alike can find only in a deep and trusting relationship.

The kettle relationship, then, is incomplete. Kettle men and women never end up enriching each other, needing or being needed by each other. At most, they learn how to avoid grating against each other. And we all deserve more than that.

The Bird Relationship: The Sky's the Limit

The highest level of relationship is one that relatively few achieve, but it is the most rewarding of all and any of us can attain it if we only strive for it. Those who don't reach it rarely know what they are missing, but those who do are blessed with true bliss.

To understand the bird relationship, it's crucial to recognize that all relationships are fraught with contradictions that must be overcome if the relationships are to flourish. The most prominent is the conflict between passion and intimacy. Most relationships begin with a certain degree of physical and emotional passion; yet as the initial electricity fades, and the couple grows more emotionally intimate, that spark has a way of diminishing. As we grow together and become best friends, we often become quiet or complacent as lovers.

An ideal relationship, on the other hand, involves a delicate balance. Two must become one, while remaining two. A man and a woman become one unit, in other words, while at the same time they remain individuals; they become one flesh while retaining their distinct personalities. That, in essence, is the underlying meaning and message of the biblical story in which Eve is formed from Adam's "rib"—not, as many feminists argue, that woman was an afterthought, but that Adam and Eve are different entities derived from the same source. More on that mistranslated story later.

It's the remarkable balance between self and other that creates the alchemical magic of an ideal relationship. If two partners morph into one another completely, obliterating their separate identities—if they come to know each other so well that all mystery disappears—they will inevitably come to bore each other, to grow tired of each other's company. Their relationship will die a of monotony, the plight of too many, as I've seen. In the best kind of relationship, on the other hand, the two partners are able to maintain their individual selves. They never bore each other; their lives never grow monotonous. Paradoxically and mysteriously, that doesn't stop them from sharing total intimacy, from creating a relationship with no limitations or barriers. Any other scenario predicts a lesser level of relationship.

How can two lovers achieve this delicate balance, drawing close enough but never too close for comfort? I find the solution in the image of a bird.

A bird is a creature with two wings, two equal, yet opposite, limbs. These wings are located on either side of the bird; they work together to propel the bird forward and aloft. The fact that they're placed in opposition to each other is no accident. If both wings were on the same side, the bird would fly in circles or never leave the ground.

In the same way, I believe, men and women are meant to act as a pair of wings, their carefully balanced efforts lifting their relationship off the ground and into the sky above. The wings, of course, are different, but their powers are equal, and they embrace that difference and use it to carry them forward and aloft, together.

A bird relationship involves mutual trust and cooperation. A couple might not always agree, but they will never run from their differences. They enjoy complete communication and absolute honesty. Men and women in bird couples can be almost childlike in their innocence, their emotional openness. They are as naked, as devoid of emotional armor, as two kids who never grew up. Infinitely curious about each other, they play a lot. They still tease and flirt with each other years after meeting and marrying. They laugh openly and often, especially in bed, where they make love with eyes and lips and hearts wide open. If there's a TV in the bedroom, it's no longer on when the clothes come off.

When he hurts, he tells her. And she doesn't judge him the worse for confessing his weaknesses. When she just wants to be held, it's not because she is holding back sex in some manipulative way. And he is there for her, without resentment. They are there for each other, in any way they can be. They need each other, know it, admit it, actually revel in the fact. When they are together they are never lonely. Even when they are alone, on a business trip, for example, they carry their partner with them in their heart.

Bird couples, I've noticed, tend to talk with each other constantly—in the kitchen, in the car, in the bedroom. They never lie to each other; even if they wanted to, they couldn't. Their natural honesty is born of intimacy, and that honesty in turn only enhances their intimacy. Truthfulness becomes their credo, the wedding vow they renew every day. They use it to learn from and about each other. They practice what I call *radical honesty*. For example, if one partner is momentarily attracted to a stranger, as naturally happens to all of us from time to time, there's no shyness about mentioning it. And if the confession is met with jealousy, it's no more than a moment's controlled attention, with the heat of a warm fireplace rather than a raging inferno. Indeed, it can often serve to fan the flames of their passion for each other. Radical honesty means: "I want you to know me as well as I can be known. I want you to know the me I thought might *never* be known."

When the prospect of a bird relationship opens up before us, it is a moment of magic. It's a *Eureka!* experience, often suffusing us with a Zen-like sense of well-being. The relationship flows naturally, as the bird's wings flap in perfect rhythm. And the couple feels the rush of their relationship moving forward. Each new year brings new insights; all sense of threat disappears; possibilities seem infinite.

The gender differences that have so preoccupied our generation are not merely overcome. In a bird relationship, they are transcended. Instead of ignoring or counteracting their differences for the sake of the "partnership," the couple will find that their distinct personalities are enriched through mutual exposure. Standing alongside each other, they see that their doubled strength and commitment help them reach the stars.

How River, Kettle, and Bird Relationships Combat Loneliness

These three images—the river, the kettle, and the bird—illuminate the ways that we as individuals and lovers can help alleviate the loneliness that visits us all.

A river relationship, despite its shortcomings, can help assuage the basic loneliness we feel when we are without the company of others. In the earliest stages of such a relationship, the two people simply enjoy each other's companionship. They meet for coffee, dinner, or a movie, doing things together that they had been doing alone. Though there's nothing profound going on, such simple surface interaction can be enough to rescue us from our sense of isolation. Walking trails together we once walked alone, we savor the difference. We experience things anew, seeing familiar sights through a new pair of eyes. We revel in reviewing the day's events together, enjoy bouncing thoughts, ideas, and feelings off each other. Since neither party would risk a display of vulnerability—after all, each separate city treasures its independence—neither feels any pang of disappointment at the lack of intimate comfort. River relationships may be all about surface feelings, but they're much more enjoyable than living each day alone.

Loneliness is allayed on a deeper level through the closer mutual dependence of a kettle relationship. Kettle couples offer each other more than just comfortable companionship; the two partners learn that they can depend on each other, that together their relationship can become more than the sum of its parts. Each partner offers the other a home base, an oasis in the desert of loneliness, a soft spot in a hard world. And they do things for each other that no one else can do. Couples in a kettle relationship are more interactive, and much more passionate about each other's company, than those in a river relationship. The partners feel more whole, more complete, and less lonely in an existential sense, because now there is someone who knows them wholly, completely, inside and out. But something deeper remains untouched.

It is only when a relationship reaches its full potential, as an intimate merging of two beings in common pursuit, that our deepest, most universal loneliness can be assuaged. Working together, like the wings of a bird—I like to picture a dove—we can strive toward true empathy and, therefore, true love. Is this an idealistic image? Yes, certainly. But without ideals we would have no inspiration, no aspiration, and no way to search for happiness or recognize it when we find it.

Another word for the belief in ideals, of course, is faith. If you are longing to create this deepest kind of relationship with a partner or soul mate, I suggest that you look to your own faith for inspiration. Whether you think of yourself as religious or not, you are probably aware of some power that evokes the vastness of the universe. Call it what you will—Mother Nature, the Force, universal consciousness, God—but you may be surprised to find that belief in a higher power can serve as a profound bond, bringing you and your mate closer together, and helping in a unique way to ease the stubborn pain of loneliness. Acknowledging a power greater than yourself can be the very thing that enables you to overcome doubts about falling in love. Make a practice of your faith, through reflection or meditation or prayer. Ascribe to the higher power the ability to know and understand you in ways that perhaps even you don't understand yourself. As a rabbi, I have always believed that the need for prayer is not just religious but deeply psychological. You may find that, as ancient Jewish tradition holds, God has it in his power to answer one of humankind's most profound prayers—by sending you a soul mate.

Are you . . .
Sister Cities?
Elemental Opposites?
Flying High?

What kind of relationships have you been in? What kind are you in now? How can you improve the situation you're in? The following pages offer a glance at how river, kettle, and bird couples behave in different situations. If you recognize yourself, your dating partners, or your mate consistently in any one role, you may just learn something about yourself.

On a First Date

River

It takes Brad and Buffy, who were introduced at a trade convention, two weeks to negotiate meeting for coffee at a Starbucks near their offices. Both come dressed in full-business-attire body armor. She tries to assess his assets; he can't take his eyes off hers. Their conversation revolves around the joys of booking hotels on-line and how long Madonna and Guy will stay married. While Brad takes an "important business call" on his cell phone, Buffy scans the room for eligible bachelors. Words like *marriage* and *relationship* are conspicuously missing from the dialogue. When they discover they're both into squash, the two arrange a mixed-doubles date with work colleagues. Later, each calls a best friend and reports on the date. "What a pair of . . . eyes!" Brad boasts. "He had on the best-tailored suit," Buffy gushes. He E-mails her to set up the next date.

Kettle

Marv and Vera, who met at a wine-tasting course, go for a drink one night after class. She wears flowery Laura Ashley; he wears his favorite Jets sweatshirt. They discuss therapists in a general sense, neither admitting having his or her own. They both mention that they'd like to settle down eventually; the "c" word (*commitment!*) even graces their banter. He invites her to a basketball game. She invites him to a ballroom dancing class. Both pretend they have other commitments but agree to a second date. He calls to set the date; she screens the call and waits the *Rules*-prescribed three days before calling back.

Bird

Kenneth and Barbara are introduced at a party by mutual friends. Kenneth calls Barbara on Tuesday. They meet Saturday morning at the local park. Both wear blue jeans and black shirts; they laugh at the coincidence. He likes blondes, and she's a brunette; she likes tall men, and he's exactly her height. Nonetheless, they like each other immediately. Though they don't seem to have that much in common, they find plenty to talk about. They laugh a lot. A single mother, she proudly shares details of her daughter's science project. He tells a funny story about almost flunking chemistry in high school. By noon, she asks him if he's free for lunch. Later they call each other—at the same time!—to plan their next get-together.

At a Restaurant

River

After checking a *Zagat*, Brad and Buffy agree on a restaurant that's convenient to both their offices. While Brad picks a wine (clueless on the topic, he plays it safe by ordering the most expensive), Buffy scans the room for potential bachelors. Buffy orders the caviar appetizer, studying Brad's reaction. Brad orders the melon, studying hers. Both order the house special, without asking anything about it. He talks about the latest deal he's closing; she has trouble getting a word in edgewise. With great bravado, Brad grabs the check. Buffy never intended to pay.

Kettle

Marv suggests a little bistro nobody knows about; Vera doesn't let on she's been there three times on dates. While Marv looks over the wine list (clueless on the topic, he asks the waiter for a recommendation), Vera checks her blouse to make sure she's got some cleavage showing. He orders steak; she orders fish. She talks about a conflict with her mother; he listens and tries to help problem-solve. He alludes to his painful past; she doesn't press him. He insists on picking up the check. She pretends to object.

Bird

Neither cares much where they go, aware that "it's the company that's important." They spontaneously end up at a low-key Italian restaurant in the neighborhood. While Kenneth orders wine (he tells the waiter he's clueless, and the waiter makes a recommendation), Barbara can't seem to take her eyes off him. They decide to share a couple of dishes. She talks about raising a child alone; he says he wishes he had children. They both comment on how easy it is to talk to each other. He offers to pay; so does she. They agree to go dutch.

In Bed

River

Brad folds his clothes neatly; Buffy undresses in the bathroom. The timing is always the same: right after Leno's opening monologue. Foreplay is perfunctory, if it happens at all. They rely faithfully on the missionary position. Lights on, TV on, eyes (and hearts) closed, in silence. A few quick pecks on the lips; no deep kissing. Neither reaches orgasm; she fakes it. By the time she gets back from the bathroom, he's asleep.

Kettle

Marv dons his English Leather, Vera her Victoria's Secret teddy. They home in on what they know turns each other on, and return to it every time. He whispers sexy lines he read in *Men's Health.* She tells him how manly his biceps feel. Once, when they are feeling especially adventurous, they make love in the kitchen. Neither reaches orgasm; both fake it. They cuddle for ten minutes, by which time he's snoring.

Bird

Kenneth and Barbara start taking each other's clothes off before they get to the bedroom, in whatever room they happen to be turned on in. They alternate pleasuring each other. There is tickling, fondling, kissing all over their bodies, frequent talking and giggling, passionate and patient lovemaking, sometimes exuberant groaning and screaming. Both reach orgasm, sometimes simultaneously, sometimes not. They fall asleep in each other's arms.

Celebrating an Anniversary

River

Brad nearly forgets, has his secretary send flowers. Buffy, having checked her PalmPilot days before, buys him a gift certificate to Home Depot.

Kettle

Marv gives Vera a gift certificate to Victoria's Secret. She makes him his favorite dinner and dons the Victoria's Secret gift for him the following weekend.

Bird

Kenneth and Barbara take each other to the park where they met for their first date. They bring a bottle of wine, pâté, and bread. Each brings a handmade card for the other.

On Vacation

River

They go to Hawaii so that he can take advantage of the time difference and work at night while his East Coast office is still humming, and she can boast to friends that they stayed at Waikiki's most famous resort. He spends the day on-line; she spends it working on her tan. He reads the *Wall Street Journal;* she flirts with the sailing instructor. When they get home, they get back to work wallpapering the den.

Kettle

They go to a Club Med, where he goes scuba diving and she can play backgammon near the pool. At night they meet for dinner and dancing. Next day, same thing all over again.

Bird

They decide to tell all their friends they've gone to Paris. Instead, they stay home, ignoring the phone, the mail, and the E-mail. They go to restaurants; make romantic dinners at home; drink cognac in front of the fireplace; talk about their past, present, and future; and make love all over the house.

Parenting

River

The au pair wakes, dresses, feeds, and bathes the kids and shuttles them to dance class and soccer matches. After Pilates class, Buffy spends quality time with the kids watching Disney videos. Brad, who works late, rarely has dinner with the kids. But they've all got the latest designer clothes, own the hottest toy every year, and have their parents wrapped around their fingers.

Kettle

Marv and Vera check the schedule to see whose turn it is to wake, dress, feed, and bathe the kids and shuttle them to dance

class and soccer matches. Dad is at the head of the table for
dinner every night; Mom serves. On Saturday the whole family
goes to the planetarium together. Mom shouts all day, "Wait till
your father comes home!" When they find out that their
teenager's smoking pot, Marv broods and Vera goes into denial.

Bird

Kenneth wakes the kids while Barbara gets breakfast going. The
kitchen is chaos central, but somehow they all get to where
they're supposed to be. There's lots of physical affection, as well
as verbal expressions of love. The parents share the burden of
disciplining the children. The kids pick a weekend activity the
whole family attends.

Financial Matters

River

Separate back accounts. Separate investment portfolios. Prenup
city.

Kettle

He earns; she spends an hour each day E-trading; they both spend.

Bird

Joint checking, joint savings. All financial decisions by mutual
agreement.

Career Setbacks

River

After being fired, Brad puts on his suit and tie and leaves the
house each morning for the next two weeks before he can tell
Buffy he's been let go. When Buffy gets reprimanded at work,
she seeks the advice of every friend she has, except Brad.

Kettle

Marv tells Vera his job's being eliminated, but he makes it clear
he doesn't want to talk about it. When he comes up with a new
plan, he tells her about it. When Vera loses her job, she tells
Marv right away, and he upsets her by giving her career advice.

Bird

When Barbara is downsized, she and Kenneth sit around the kitchen table for hours. When they talk about their options, they both come to the same solution: looking for work in another city. Kenneth offers to seek a transfer.

Caught Being Unfaithful

River

Each turns a blind eye toward the other's ongoing affairs (they've both had more than one). What they don't know, they tell themselves, won't hurt them.

Kettle

When Marv is caught he admits it, blaming it on work pressures and midlife crisis. He is genuinely contrite. When she is caught she's equally contrite, blaming it on his inattentiveness. They go to counseling, renew their commitment, and press on.

Bird

N/A

On Their Twenty-fifth Anniversary

River

Brad and Buffy throw a big, fancy party, with the right caterers, a band no one likes, and lots of speeches. Later, they go home and make love. She fakes it.

Kettle

Their immediate family rents a private room at the little hideaway where Marv took Vera for their first date. Marv and Vera give special toasts to each other. Later that night, they both fake it.

Bird

Kenneth and Barbara have two celebrations. One is an all-afternoon open house, potluck. Their family and dearest friends offer individual toasts. For the other, they take a picnic basket to a park and reminisce—alone. Later that night they make love, slowly and tenderly.

7

The Union of Opposites

We two form a multitude.

—Ovid

The day will come when, after harnessing space, the winds, the tides, and gravitation, we shall harness for God the energies of love. And on that day, for the second time in the history of the world, we shall have discovered fire.

—Pierre Teilhard de Chardin

Dear Rabbi Shmuley,

My husband and I have this typical man/woman thing. Whenever we argue, he wants to kiss and make up, while I can't do that until we talk the problem through. Of course I admit that this can sometimes lead to more fighting. But is it better just to sweep problems under the carpet?

—Needlessly Neglected

Dear Rabbi,

I have been dating Lucy for two years now, and she still baffles me at times. For months leading up to her birthday, she warned me that if I tried to do anything to commemorate the day, she would run and hide. Even flowers delivered to her desk at work would be too embarrassing. This is a *direct quote! So I didn't do anything special for the day, and treated it like any other Tuesday. Now suddenly she won't speak to me! I don't get it! Why is a woman so hard to understand and so demanding?*

—Perplexed in Peoria

If those two E-mails, one right on the heels of the other, don't sum up the predicament, nothing does. How can men and women fall in love when they can't even understand each other? When he's all about action, and she's all about feelings? When he can't figure out what she's feeling, and she has no idea what his actions mean? The gender gap can make the Grand Canyon seem like a pothole. And if we are so fundamentally different from each other, what hope is there of finding common ground? What hope, and what point?

John Gray, and those who followed him, did a valuable service in shifting our focus onto gender differences at a time when we as a culture needed to reexamine them. But I believe we have moved well beyond that time. Now that it's been reestablished that men and women are indeed different—isn't it amazing that we ever convinced ourselves otherwise?—I propose that we take this knowledge and embrace it, rather than simply trying to work around it. In place of the gender-neutralization tactics of the Mars-Venus crowd, I recommend a course in gender enrichment, a different approach that should help you and a potential mate turn your differences into advantages.

To get to the heart of the problem, let's take a short diversion on the subject of dualism. We all know the first words of the Bible: "In the beginning God created heaven and earth." (Genesis 1:1). A few lines later: "God said, 'There shall be light' and light came into existence. God saw the light was good, and God divided between the lightness and the darkness. God named the light 'Day' and the darkness He named 'Night.' It was evening and it was morning, one day" (Genesis 1:3–5).

And so begins the world, in dualism. In light and dark, in day and night, in heaven and earth, with everything divided into two. *Dualism*, a philosophical principle developed three millennia ago by the Persian philosopher Zoroaster, is the belief that everything in the world has its opposite, and that this vast network of equal but opposing forces gives our world a universal sense of balance. Good and evil, light and darkness, mind and matter, intellect and emotion— Zoroaster saw these all as forces in eternal, yet benign, opposition. The universe as we know it will always be fraught with conflict, and yet this conflict, he argued, keeps the world in a state of healthy equilibrium. Trillions of dollars have been made in Hollywood on the basis of this thinking. How exciting would a movie be if the good guys weren't challenged and balanced by bad guys? It's easy to see how the influence of Zoroastrian dualism became so pervasive.

One reason is that dualism seems to be echoed everywhere in our daily lives. Night *does* follow day; there *are* good guys and bad guys (and not just in the movies); heaven *does* tower over earth. And our internal worlds reflect the same dualism: We have an inner moral compass of good and evil, whether we follow it or not. We distinguish between body and mind, heart and soul, intellect and emotion. Zoroaster prophesied a never-ending conflict between the forces of good and evil in the world, and that idea became one of the foundations of Greek thought. From the Greeks, dualism found its way into Christianity. Much of Christian lore is based on strong dualistic themes, from God's eternal battle against Lucifer, to Jesus' temptation by the Devil, to the eternal conflict between virtue and sin. It isn't hard to see why dualism has become such a common lens through which to view the world, and why even today we're so often eager to break down every question into two sides.

Despite the influence of dualism, there have always been those who believed in a higher vision, who saw the hidden within the obvious, the esoteric within the revealed—the mystics. The great and holy Kabbalists of old, the Jewish mystics, looked deeper. They peered beneath the hood of creation to check out its engine, and what they found was not dualism but unity. The mystics introduced the concept of monism, which holds that everything emanates from a single, indivisible source. That's why the mystics were always joyous, while the frustrated and pessimistic Greek dualists wrote heartbreaking tragedies. The Kabbalists saw unity at the core of existence and, further, saw love as the underlying force within the universe.

What has this got to do with me, Shmuley? you may be asking. *How is this going to help me fall in love?* Bear with me a little longer, and you'll see. Where this philosophical digression gets interesting is in the matter of men and women.

The dualist philosophers, right on down to John Gray, point to the two sexes as the ultimate proof of their worldview. *Why, even humankind is governed by the dualistic model!* That's why the Greeks posited the existence of a male god named Zeus and a female god named Hera. Men and women actually emanated from disparate sources, these thinkers believed. Sure, they can make momentary peace; they can negate their differences and get along for a while. But there is nothing that can ever meld them from two into one.

To the mystics, however, the existence of two sexes proves just the opposite. Men and women, they believe, are two distinct energies that stem from a single source, not conflicting systems but rather two aspects of the same life force. They *are* the underlying unity of the universe. The proof: When man and woman join in the most sacred of unions, sexual intercourse, they create a single, indivisible life. And in the process they themselves become one flesh.

The union of male and female makes for an impossible and suprarational equation that demonstrates their unity:

$$1 + 1 = 1$$

It's perhaps the only case in all of mathematics in which the whole is neither equal to the sum of its parts, nor more, nor less.

The Jewish mystics weren't the only ones to recognize this universal truth. The mystical tenets of all the world's oldest religions and cultures rejected dualism and saw union at the core of existence. To these thinkers, the oppositions we recognize in the world all emanated from a solitary, indivisible source. Male and female are not two opposing forces, but rather two dimensions of a single energy. In Chinese Taoist typology, the receptive female force *yin* is balanced by the inextricably linked active male force *yang*. In Hinduism, the male god of *Siva* is known as the Destroyer, and *Shakti* is the mother goddess who stands for all aspects of nature from birth to death. In Indo-Tibetan art, the unification of male and female sexual energies is symbolically depicted by the female goddess seated on the lap of the male god, called the *YabYum*. Buddhists distinguish *samsara* (suffering, considered male) from *nirvana* (blissful enlightenment, female). And in Kabbalah, *zah* is the provider (male) and *nukvah* the recipient (female). The medieval Christian scholar Nicholas of Cusa summed it up well when he referred to the masculine and feminine blending in harmony in what he called the *coincidentia oppositorum*, the "union of opposites."

Love: A Religious Experience

It still sounds easier said than done, right? It would be reasonable to ask: How do two people who appear to be so incompatible—how do any man and any woman—find the middle ground?

For that answer, we need to look back even further than "In the beginning." We need to look at God Himself. (Stand back, it's theology time. You didn't think a rabbi like me could get through a whole book without it, did you?) Remember when I suggested that we could think of a relationship as a religion? It's an image with intriguing implications: The man and the woman are its two gods, the home is the temple, the marital vows are the doctrine of faith, the bedroom is the sanctum sanctorum, and the bed itself is the altar in which the act of sexual intimacy is sacrosanct, the most spiritual expression of that faith. As our look at the bird relationship might suggest, this religion of romance serves a crucial role: to create a balanced accord between male and female, which allows these two gods to thrive together in harmony.

One of the deepest secrets of the Jewish mystical discipline of Kabbalah is that God Himself has a male aspect and a female aspect. After all, doesn't God seem to have a dual nature, a feminine side and a masculine side? On the one hand, there's the stern disciplinarian, the ultimate judge and jury, the King of Kings, the masculine God of strength and revelation. This is the God of history and miracles. Like a vector, He descends from the heavens and into our world, rewarding the righteous and punishing the wicked. This side is most manifest early in the Bible, in Genesis and Exodus, as God reveals himself to the inhabitants of earth, displaying his awesome powers, laying waste to false gods, deftly wielding His stick of obedience, to get human beings to turn away from their foibles and embrace a sanctified life. Everything about this side of God is linear. He wields a kindly scepter, proclaiming Himself as sovereign over the earth, and uses a stern rod of justice to punish iniquity and reward righteousness.

But as the biblical story unfolds, a different side of God emerges, a side in which God's behavior, even presence, evokes our common sense of the feminine. This is the nurturing side of God, who is cloaking Himself behind the hidden veil of nature. To the prophets, God is no longer visible but becomes instead a disembodied heavenly voice. By the time of the later scriptures, He has retreated completely into silent whispers of time and space. In the book of Esther, for instance, God redeems His people through natural circumstances, no longer using the strong arm of miraculous intervention; the name of God never appears once. He allows man to find God behind every colorful leaf and every brilliant sunset. This is the part of God that nurses us in His bosom, always with us, surrounding and comforting us at all times, through all of our travails. This is the side of God that hovers invisibly above all of Creation, that cannot be seen but only experienced, cannot be heard but intuited. This is God of creation, whom the philosophers call the Transcendent God. This is the side of God whose representation is a circle, whose voice of inspiration is always beckoning to man to better himself and reach higher. This is the female, Merciful God, who delivers not justice but compassion, not sternness but love. Cloaked behind the curtain of nature, this is the side of God who sometimes goes by the name of Mother Nature, a protecting angel, patient even in the face of human corruption and darkness, awaiting man's repentance and embracing of the light.

What the Kabbalists illuminated for us is that these forces are not two Gods, not two visions in conflict, but rather two aspects of one God. The Jews are credited with introducing the radical theological concept that there is only one God, indivisible, not broken down into a trinity or a duality. And the Kabbalistic vision of how these two sides of God emerged is remarkable. In the beginning, they say, there was only God, endless and limitless, a light that filled the infinite expanse. Nothing else existed. But God wished to create a world, filled with finite and limited creatures like you and me. And so He decided, as the story goes, to withdraw his light from the center, to make space within Himself in order to create the worlds. In Hebrew, this was known as the *tzimtzum*, "contraction" or "condensation." That space, "a cavity within Himself," as it translates, is a circle. Into that space, that circle, God then sent a thin ray of light, finite—not infinite like the light that preceded it—to animate and illuminate His creation. The light that surrounds and envelops creation is circular, feminine—powerful enough to create and sustain the universe, like a mother. And the light that radiates into creation, the face of God that interacts with our universe, is linear and finite. Though it cannot create, it can animate, like a father who helps develop the character and potential of the children born to him by his wife.

This mystical story is perhaps the most important concept in the Kabbalah, which itself has become quite trendy these days ("trendy" being defined as something Madonna has suddenly grown interested in). And it's not hard to grasp why. We can see its themes played out every time a man and a woman fall in love. The image of one God, whose two aspects—focused and all-embracing, linear and circular—define all creation, helps us understand why men and women need each other. Once we recognize that men and women, like these two different lights, have a common origin in one God, it is easier to understand that male-female relationships are meant to be complementary, not conflicted. They are meant, in other words, to be like the two wings of a single bird.

The Line and the Circle

Let's reduce this to the most basic terms.

Men are lines.

Women are circles.

It's a simple notion, I admit, but I believe it can be profoundly useful in helping us grasp the difference between the sexes. For if we want to find lasting love, we must first understand why we're drawn to each other and how we can use that knowledge to build a bridge to love.

What are the characteristics of a circle? It is round. It surrounds and embraces; it envelops, protects, nurtures. It is endless. If you follow it, you find that it is constantly renewed. A line, on the other hand, is one-dimensional. It is focused, directional, rigid, unbending. It has a beginning and an end. Structurally, a circle is stronger and more pliant than a line, which is vulnerable to breakage. Masculine energy moves in a linear progression; female energy emanates like an aura. Men are almost always either moving forward or retreating, while women are opening or closing, making themselves more available to intimacy or less available. Of course, there are obvious anatomical parallels to be drawn as well. The male organ is linear and external, while the female is internal, cyclical. In the sexual act, male energy expresses itself in a linear thrust. The woman embraces the man's energy, encircles it, receives it.

The same is true in the broader dynamic of male-female relationships. Men are logical, sequential, and goal-oriented; they are best when going from point A to point B in a straight line (unless, that is, they don't know the directions, which they are genetically predisposed not to ask for). Men work toward an end. *Where are we going, how are we going to get there, and how long will it take?* They like to tackle a problem, solve it, and then move on. And the truth is that women like this in men. As countless surveys have shown, most women are attracted to a man who is self-confident, who knows what he wants from life and pursues it vigorously. When such a man comes along, a woman will open herself up to him, taking him into her arms and into her world. Men who reveal themselves to be weak or pliant, on the other hand, quickly lose their appeal.

Whereas men are preoccupied with ends—destinations, goals— women are concerned with means. For them, the journey is the reward. That's why women love foreplay; every step along the journey is significant to them. Their patience is infinite, and they don't mind asking for directions. *Why are we going, where can we stop along the way, and how will we feel when we get there?* They're much more flexible, able to change course when things don't go according to plan.

Men are direct, obvious, blunt; they speak loudly and forthrightly. Women are subtle, ambiguous, diplomatic, and mysterious; they speak softly. Men are overt, women covert. Men are generally more aggressive; they like to take charge. Women are more likely to be thoughtful and cooperative.

The way men and women behave in romance bears out this description in almost every way. For women, dating is a game of cat and mouse. They circle around their male prey in a pattern of approach and avoidance. There's an old saying that men fall in love with their eyes, while women fall in love with their ears. In truth, women fall in love with all five senses, with everything that surrounds them. Men pursue dating in a linear fashion. From the first date, they proceed single-mindedly to their end goal, most often, the bed. (Sorry, guys, it's true.) They love the thrill of the chase. From the moment the woman succumbs, it's an uphill battle for a man to maintain his interest. This is one of the inherent difficulties with the male-female dynamic: Men get claustrophobic. They feel trapped by the circle. For women, on the other hand, that moment is when the story really begins. The idea of commitment isn't as likely to make them feel trapped. They're more interested in exploring depths than pursuing goals.

The male focus on goals helps explain why so many men grow bored prematurely in relationships. In fact, in the many interviews I've conducted with single men, I've found that their number one fear in relationships, the single factor that prevents them most surely from committing to a woman, is the fear that monogamy will lead to boredom. Men have trouble renewing themselves; it's easier for them to start off on a new search, a new line, than to stay put and find fulfillment in one place. Women, on the other hand, want consistency and continuity. The female need for attention has rarely found a match in the male attention span.

I hasten to add that it isn't all bad. If men and women were truly mismatched, after all, none of us would be wasting our time trying to find a partner to fall in love with. (For that matter, we might not be here at all; the race would have died out a long time ago.) It remains the case that the line and the circle naturally attract each other for the very same reasons that their relationships sometimes run aground. For example, women thirst for the directed, focused passion men naturally exude. It brings excitement into their lives. Women are good at fostering intimacy and stability, at closing the circle, but their lives can become so consumed with responsibility that they forget to have fun. On the other hand, men, who have a greater talent for passion than for intimacy, treasure a woman who can ground them. They love finding someone who can help them absorb the regular shocks that come with their more aggressive approach to life.

What each sex is looking for, in other words, is to be rescued—to find the balance, the refuge, that only the opposite sex can provide. Men want a woman who soothes the pain of constant aggression, who loves them for who they are, not what they do. Women want a man to give them focus, to add a sense of direction and excitement. Women teach men to be natural, to take comfort in the world around them without feeling under constant pressure to change it. And men show women how to exert control over their world, to bring action and even surprise into life.

Some of the great fears that keep us from successful relationships have their roots in these differences. Despite all their self-confidence, for instance, men spend a lot of time—much more than they acknowledge—worrying that they won't measure up. And it's not (just) penis envy I'm talking about here. Men realize, deep down, what women want from them, and they feel the pressure intensely. *Will I be successful enough? Exciting enough?* The great male fear is that the woman will be difficult to please, that as often as he performs miracles for her, all his tricks will fall flat. And women have their worries, too. The main female fear is that, one day, Mr. Right will lose interest. Very often, in our surface-obsessed society, what attracts a man in the first place is attributes—looks, basic personality, happiness—that are too intrinsic to be easily controlled; what a woman fears is the moment when those strengths suddenly fail her, when she takes off her clothes and his only response is to pick up a new section of the Sunday *Times*.

Yet the best relationships succeed, as we have seen, when these opposing forces balance each other out. From the woman, a man receives affirmation of his masculine attributes. When his male traits please a woman—when he makes her laugh, or makes her feel great in bed, or makes her feel protected—it makes him feel like a man. And the man, in return, offers his woman corroboration of her femininity. When a man is captivated by her beauty and her company, when he longs to hold her, be with her, and confide in her, when he moves mountains and strives to accomplish in order to impress and please her, she feels special and desirable. She feels like a woman.

Are You a Line or a Circle?

It's true. The entire world, and everything in it, belongs to one tribe or the other. Rock stars (Madonna is a line, Sarah McLachlan is a circle), politicians (Hillary is a line, Bill is a circle), foods (curry is a line, melon is a circle), countries (Germany is a line, Italy is a circle), historic events (the bombing of Pearl Harbor was a line, Woodstock was a circle). The list is endless. Once you get the hang of it, you should be able to come up with some examples yourself. Here are a few categories to get you started:

The Line Lover

Brushes teeth before making love.

Rips clothes off—if they come from JCPenney.

Takes off clothes and hangs them up—if they come from Barney's.

Sees sex as a destination.

Is visual and orgasm-centric.

Makes love with the lights on.

Has mirrors on the ceiling.

Has a video camera for motion, digital camera for stills, Internet webcam connection to share the experience.

Closes eyes during sex. Thinks of latest *Baywatch* episode.

Thinks of foreplay as a prelude to the real event.

Goes right for the genitalia.

Doesn't talk or laugh during sex.

Utters four-letter words as though reading them from cue cards.

Rolls in opposite direction and goes right to sleep afterward.

Speaks boss's name while sleeping.

The Circle Lover

Enjoys sex in the afternoon.

Takes your clothes off very slowly, then throws them across the bed.

Sees sex as a journey.

Is sensual and experiential.

Puts plenty of time into kissing, hugging, and foreplay.

Turns off the lights and makes love by moonlight.

Giggles, tickles, massages, fondles, arm-wrestles, and speaks soft words of endearment.

Keeps eyes open during sex and stares deeply into yours.

Has a slow hand that touches your whole body as though it were velvet.

Holds you until you fall asleep together in the spoon position.

Speaks your name while sleeping.

The Line Worker

Gets in early to get a beat on the competition.

Spends a couple of extra minutes in the staff kitchen to find out whom to suck up to after the new corporate restructuring.

Reads *Unlimited Power* and *Awakening the Giant Within*.

Takes work home every night, whether he gets to it or not.

Has set five-, ten-, and twenty-year career goals.

Philosophy: "Make your money, the love will follow."

Plays squash after work with the VP of marketing to build solid alliances upstairs.

Works hard to move up the ladder.

Drops tidbits of malicious gossip to push others down the ladder.

Gives cell phone number out to all business contacts.

Works twenty-four/seven.

Attitude: If you're not working, you're not living.

The Circle Worker

Gets in early to help squeeze in time for exercise later in the day.

Spends a couple of extra minutes in the staff kitchen finding out who's been fired after the new corporate restructuring, so he or she can send condolence cards.

Careerwise, follows passions and interests.

Reads Hawking's *A Brief History of Time* and Moore's *Care of the Soul.*

Philosophy: "Follow your love, the money will follow."

Goes for a drink after work with the VP of marketing in order to establish a real friendship.

Works hard for the pride of a job well done and appreciates the unfolding of his or her potential.

Uses cell phone for outgoing calls only and gives the number only to immediate family and special friends.

Takes work home, but only when on deadline.

Almost always takes off a full weekend, but works when necessary.

Attitude: At death's door, no one ever says, "I wish I'd spent more time at work."

The Line Politician

Says anything that will get him elected.

Kisses babies for photo ops.

Kisses interns for the real thing.

Makes promises he has no intention of keeping.

Screws rich donors out of their money.

Screws campaign aide just before important debate.

Holds wife's hand whenever a reporter is in the vicinity.

Spins and respins all news until no one knows what he stands for.

Becomes all things to all people; says what everyone wants to hear.

Gets elected and holds resolutely on to power.

Becomes a fanatical micromanager; alienates his staff.

Staff leaks damaging stories to the press.

Gets resoundingly defeated in next election.

Publicly repents mistakes; plans comeback.

Secretly harbors resentment and contempt for the public.

Justifies ruthlessness because he is from Mars and "all men love power."

The Circle Politician

Articulates his beliefs clearly, despite political risk. Refuses to pander.

Helps the down-and-out; kisses lepers and others with contagious diseases.

Respects all campaign staff; is personal but professional.

Promises only what he thinks he can deliver.

Goes to the people for financial support and doesn't focus only on rich donors.

Hugs his wife just before important debates.

Holds wife's hand even in privacy of the campaign airplane.

Grants complete access to the media. Admits it when he's wrong, without spin.

Speaks with conviction to the people; genuinely feels their pain.

Manages by delegating authority and empowering his staff.

Staff is fanatically loyal; protects him from an aggressive press.

Wins reelection by a landslide.

Public lauds him for his virtue; an equestrian statue of him is erected.

Continues after office as elder statesman who loves and protects the public.

Ten Things You'll Never Hear a Line Say

1. "No, stay in the bathroom as long as you like."

2. "Can we just cuddle a little more before we have sex?"

3. "Can we just cuddle a little more after we have sex?"

4. "Of course, I'll support your decision to have breast reduction surgery."

5. "Sit, I'll do the dishes."

6. "The hell with *Monday Night Football;* let's watch this video, *Martha Stewart: Live from Suburban Connecticut.*"

7. "Can I borrow your Barry Manilow CD?"

8. "We've only been dating six months; sex is something that shouldn't be rushed."

9. "Sure, we can sell my tickets to the Knicks-Lakers game and visit your mother instead."

10. "I was thinking of pastels for our wedding colors, too."

Ten Things You'll Never Hear a Circle Say

1. "Spending last weekend with your fraternity buddies turned out to be so much more enjoyable than that weekend I had planned at the oceanside B&B."

2. "No, leave it on. I prefer having sex while you're watching the game over my shoulder."

3. "I'd *love* to stay home tonight with the kids while you go drinking with your buddies."

4. "I wish we'd bought the stuffed moose head instead of this wicker rocker."

5. "Can we *stop* talking about it now?"

6. "Please let go of my hand—I'm trying to hold the remote."

7. "I love the World Wrestling Federation!"

8. "Of course it's all right with me if you think about another woman in bed."

9. "Why should we get married, when I can live with you until you get bored of me and then find a younger replacement?"

10. "How thoughtful: a washing machine for our anniversary!"

The Esoteric Made Practical

The concepts I've been discussing can help, on a practical level, in improving relationships. Let's start by revisiting the Kabbalists' image of God as He opened up a space within Himself for creation. That process of *tzimtzum*, that opening of a cavity—a gesture of generosity and self-sacrifice for a greater goal—suggests a spirit that men and women alike should bring to the start of a romance. When you're eager to enter into a relationship with someone, you must first make space within yourself for that person to enter. If every bit of the space around you—emotional, spiritual, even temporal (in your Day Planner)—is already occupied, how will anyone find a way into your life? Too many of us haven't committed to making room for love in our lives. Some of us are so preoccupied with ourselves that we've forgotten how to love, like the self-absorbed writer who asks, "But enough about me; what do *you* think of my book?" To embrace another, you must open your arms and show him or her the way in.

A model can be found in that image of *tzimtzum*, that gesture of contraction that is necessary for every relationship. In order for two people to get along, they must first contract themselves enough for the other to be present and thrive. If, for example, you find that you're doing all the talking on your dates, it might be useful to take a step back and listen for a while instead. Ask questions, and wait for the answers. And when those answers come, avoid the urge to jump in too quickly with your own "What *I* do is . . ." counterpoints. On early dates, especially, too many of us feel the responsibility to fill the silences, to keep the conversation going. But listening is at least as important as talking, and it's doubly appreciated. The greatest gift you can give someone is your undivided attention.

The idea of *tzimtzum* can be helpful for singles who are just beginning to date, but it can also be a useful image for people who are worried about preserving the comfort level within a relationship that's already under way. Many men and women in longer-term relationships, for example, complain from time to time about not being able to read each other's thoughts. "I can never tell what he's feeling," a woman recently confided to me about a man she'd been dating for a year. "Getting him to emote is like pulling teeth." Ironically (or not), the man in question took me aside at around the same time. "Sometimes my girlfriend can be so moody and distant," he said. "I never know where I stand with her." The problem here, I could tell, wasn't that these two weren't connecting; they knew and loved each other well. It was that they weren't leaving each other enough space to be themselves, to keep some thoughts and feelings and pursuits to themselves.

To achieve the delicate balance of love, the partners in a couple must be in a constant state of *tzimtzum*—contracting, then expanding—as they make room for each other. Think of the relationship between parent and child. Parents must provide constant attention and guidance to their children, but a parent who smothers his or her children with too much love or supervision will handicap them. Likewise, in a romantic relationship each partner must leave the other space to breathe. For some, this is counterintuitive; their whole objective in entering into a relationship is to spend time with someone else, to fill up the space. But a healthy relationship is a process of mutual self-discovery, and self-discovery requires time spent with the self. You know that you've made an extraordinary contribution to your lover's life when you help him or her toward greater self-awareness. That's why the best relationships help us find untapped reserves of creativity and strength within ourselves that we might never have found on our own. A successful relationship is one in which our partner helps us to discover and manifest our every potential.

The Superiority of the Feminine

As you may recall, the image of *tzimtzum*, the opening of a space within, is essentially a female image. It is a gesture of quintessentially feminine virtue: comfort, generosity, welcome. It is also, I believe, the indispensable gesture in human interaction. This observation leads to a message that may come as a welcome surprise to many of my readers: I believe, as Judaism has always held, that the feminine principle is superior.

In the traditions and culture of Judaism through the ages, there was never any talk of the equality of the sexes. Women were always thought to be superior. They are God's infinite energy made manifest, while men manifest only the finite ray of God's light. More than five hundred years ago, Rabbi Isaac Luria, the greatest Jewish mystic of all time, wrote that the Messiah would not come until husbands began listening to their wives. What he meant was that society will be perfected when the feminine principle is predominant: when men and women seek love rather than sex, when people learn to connect rather than dominate, when the spiritual is superior to the material, when subtlety replaces vulgarity—when the embrace of a circle tames the aggression of a line.

This conception in no way denies men their role in human life or suggests that the masculine is unimportant. What it does mean is that raw masculinity, untempered by the feminine virtues, can be unproductive, even destructive. Look at our culture of businesspeople of both sexes, who work and work but have no feminine force in their lives to ground them. As one of them told me, "On Wall Street, Shmuley, we single guys all play two kinds of games. The day game is accumulating as much money as possible. And if you succeed in the day game, then you're ready for the night game, which consists of accumulating as many women as possible. Earn enough money, and you can start earning women." Need I say more?

The story of civilization bears out my theory. In the ancient world, and through to modern times in the form of countless military dictatorships, unchecked brute force has been at the center of the great crises of history. Yet today we have come full circle, as it were, and it's the feminine principle that dominates society. The great heroes of history, the Caesars and Alexanders, the Shermans and Pattons, embodied masculine aggression. But today's heroes are people like Mahatma Gandhi and Nelson Mandela, political figures who buried the cudgels of war in favor of peace. The most respected men and women in the world today are winners of peace prizes, not battlefield medals. The same is true even in modern American politics. Whereas George Bush the elder, the last president of the World War II generation, made his greatest mark as commander in chief of the Gulf War, his son George W. Bush got elected as a "compassionate conservative," a political affiliation that might take as its symbol a line tempered by a circle.

Within the microcosm of romantic relationships, the same progression is also apparent. Despite the lingering influence of feminism, most relationships are still initiated by men, with the active, direct gesture of a phone call, or an E-mail, or a pickup line at a party. The truth is that most women I know prefer it this way. Does this mean that the man is naturally in control? Think again. In fact, by making the first move, he becomes the supplicant, the one who has to ask for a sign before proceeding. The woman, on the other hand, gets to be the gatekeeper. She gets to brandish the sign: *Wrong Way* or *Go Slow* or *Welcome to Linda*. The longer a man pursues his goal, the more receptive the woman feels able to be, and the closer he gets, the softer he gets. He allows his emotions to emerge. His line begins to curve to her circle.

It's a process that can be traced in a hundred different little behavioral changes. At first, when they're still nervous, each member of a couple might put some aggressive energy into trying to impress the other: trying to make each other laugh, suggesting exceptional restaurants, fretting over what to wear. They're performing miracles for each other. But as time progresses and they become more and more comfortable around one another, that single-minded, heat-seeking mindset is subsumed by a gentler, more embracing energy. The emphasis on destinations is replaced by an immersion in the journey itself. Overt and superficial romantic gestures (flowers, half a dozen calls a day) give way to deeper, less blatant signs of love (conversations about disappointment and vulnerability, the most intimate words of affection). Couples create rituals, then observe and repeat and build on them, returning to a favorite restaurant, revisiting the story of the first time they kissed. The energy that once was spent on winning each other over is replaced by an interest in deepening the relationship, in fostering intimacy. And before they know it, their embrace has become a circle: rounded, all-encompassing, and complete.

The Balance of Passion and Intimacy

If this all comes so naturally, Shmuley, how come it's been so hard for me? Why have so many of my relationships fizzled out before they could get off the ground? And why do even the good ones seem to go sour? Where's my completed circle?

The answer, for almost everyone, is in the balance. The embracing feminine energy of the circle may suffuse the best relationships, but relationships wouldn't exist at all without the focused masculine energy that propels any couple into joining together. Love requires both line and circle, both fire and water, both passion and intimacy. Neither can sustain a relationship on its own. Left untended, the fires of passion can wane. Couples blessed with nothing but a mellow kind of intimacy may find themselves succumbing to boredom. And a couple whose attraction is all animal passion, without true intimacy to give it context or meaning, will consume itself and burn out.

In the time I've spent counseling couples, I've found that the challenge of maintaining this balance often leads relationships onto rocky shoals. And among those who don't succeed, many abandon ship too early, taking either the easy way or the chicken's way out.

Two Ways to Cop Out

At twenty-nine, Karl is already a successful high-tech whiz kid. But he hasn't yet been successful at love, because he's too content with his utilitarian, dualistic approach to relationships. We met through his boss, a friend of mine, who encouraged me to talk to Karl about his love life.

"Are you having trouble finding someone?" I asked.

"Not at all," Karl said matter-of-factly. "In fact, I'm dating several women right now. The problem is, I get bored too quickly."

Why? Because, it turns out, he's compartmentalized his love life, dividing the duties between two women he's dating. With one of these women, he is able to satisfy his craving for emotional intimacy; with the other, his desire for physical stimulation. In this respect, Karl is no different from the kings and noblemen of old, who looked to their wives for pedigree, procreation, and joint rule, and to their mistresses for fire and excitement. The first woman he sees twice a week, for dinner and conversation. "We have nice talks," he says, "but I don't have romantic feelings for her. In fact, we'd both be disappointed if something physical happened. It would just complicate things. She's just a good friend. I can confide in her. She makes me feel comfortable and secure." But the idea of a long-term relationship—or marriage, God forbid—leaves him yawning.

The other woman is very attractive, though not quite as smart as the first, and not as emotionally available or attentive. "I don't love her as much, either; we have great sex," Karl says. But then he confides, "Even that's getting boring, though. Frankly, I could take it or leave it. There's always someone else. If I had a choice between the first friend and the second, the cuddling and the sex, I would choose the first any day of the week." Sex, this intensely passionate act, has become no big deal to him.

As we talked, I discovered that the relationships that truly sustain Karl are those he shares with his close male friends. Karl and his pals go to games together; they go camping for weekends; they sit around and talk about the women who don't satisfy them. They are the male equivalent of the women in *Sex and the City.* "I feel closer to those four guys than to anybody else. To me friendship is everything, and my guy friends and I understand each other," he said quite passionately, quick to assure me of his heterosexuality. "I could live without the women. But I'd be devastated if I were to lose those friendships. I've known these guys since I was in elementary school."

In recent years, as I've listened to singles like Karl describe their lives, I've realized that there's a whole new sexual arrangement that's becoming increasingly common among people who have been unable to find both passion and intimacy in one place. These nonsexual relationships, most often among same-sex singles, stand in for intimate romantic relationships in every way but sexually. It's not surprising. It makes perfect sense that members of the same sex, whose experiences and perspectives are so similar, would find it easy to reach a basic level of emotional intimacy. If it means that romance drops to the bottom of the priority list, well, that's just one less problem to worry about.

Having lined up part-time caretakers for all his diverse needs, Karl has convinced himself that he's happy. In his mind, he has no need for a long-term romantic relationship. He relieves his sexual urges with a quick fix and has plenty of friends to confide in.

Thoughts of starting a family have apparently not yet entered his mind. In moments of honesty, he admits being jaded. He even seems to recognize that his dependence on close male friendships may be keeping him from falling in love. But Karl can't yet find his way out of the trap he's built for himself. "Love lets you down," he complained recently. "It has the power to make you feel head over heels, but you can't sustain it. Friendship doesn't let you down. So what do I need a woman for?" He hasn't developed the faith that he can find one person to satisfy all his needs.

Now meet Melissa, also twenty-nine. At this point, she seems to have opted out of the search for love altogether. An aspiring actress, a bright woman who hides her good looks behind old-fashioned glasses, she makes ends meet as an assistant graphic design artist for a Manhattan art-house newspaper. When we met, she wasn't involved in a relationship; she dates intermittently, but briefly. Having been burned twice by men who broke things off with her, she was cautious, to say the least. On the other hand, men who seemed capable of developing emotional intimacy with her soon "grew tiresome" to her, she told me. "They would seem too comfortable, and invariably I would hurt the person and lose the friendship."

I asked her what she was looking for now, passion or intimacy.

"That's a good question," she replied tentatively. "It's *the* question. I grew up thinking you were supposed to look for passion. I waited for the signs: the nervousness and apprehension you don't have with someone who's just a friend; the trembling and sweating when your new crush is nearby. I've gone for passion and hoped that everything else would develop out of that. But it's never worked out. So now I'm trying the other approach: to start with a friendship and let the passion develop. I'm wary of any relationship that doesn't start that way, or indeed that doesn't end that way. I'm now friends with all of my exes."

While she's waiting, Melissa is seeing an old male friend from time to time. She also finally gave up obsessing over a guy whom she had a crush on but who didn't make any kind of move to ask her out, after she found she couldn't get up the nerve to ask him out herself.

"So are you happy now?" I asked her recently. "Or just resigned?"

"Relatively happy, I'd say. Yes, yes, I'm happy."

But methinks the lady doth protest too much. To me, it's clear that she's still in a quandary, struggling to keep faith in her ideal, which is to find a man she can feel both passionate and intimate with, yet sabotaging her chances through her behavior. Like Karl, she's divided the duties of a lover, rather than holding out for someone who can bring everything to the table. Having close male friends gives her a semblance of male companionship, but her appetite for passion remains unsatisfied. As she admits, "By now I'm afraid I can't fully commit to someone who's there for me emotionally, because I'll always regret not pursuing some other man who lights my fire." So she waits and waits, too embarrassed even to acknowledge how lonely she is.

Women Behaving Badly

I have every hope in the world for young women like Melissa. The fact that she still forms innocent crushes, even though she's too shy to act on them, reassures me that when her best chance comes, she'll find the courage she needs to take the plunge.

But there's another kind of problem I've seen cropping up among young single women that worries me much more, a problem that involves the worst kind of imbalance between the masculine and feminine energies, between the line and the circle. If there's ever a worldview that will keep you from falling in love forever, this is it.

Let me tell you an unhappy little story that will show you what I'm talking about. I have a friend who's an up-and-coming playwright. He's a do-gooder in the best sense of the phrase, a man of the highest values who fights for social causes, and not just in his plays. He gives up holidays to volunteer in soup kitchens; his heart bleeds daily for those less fortunate than he. If he weren't so charismatic, talented, and funny, he might be impossible to be around. At thirty-five he is still not married, holding off for a woman who can completely "unhinge" him, in his words, that is, who can rock his world. Finally, one evening over dinner, he told me he'd met her: The One. From the moment they met, there were sparks. She was a successful entrepreneur, the head of a software manufacturing company that worked specifically with minority groups. They both fell headlong in love, or so it seemed. Then, while they were lying in bed one night, she steered the conversation around to the future.

"So how much can you expect to make as a playwright?" she asked.

He estimated that if everything went well, he could expect to make six figures in a good year. This stopped her cold; hers was already approaching seven. "But I've worked so hard! And I want children! And when I stop working I don't want to compromise the lifestyle I've been able to afford up till now as a single woman." She paused for breath. "Now you want me to reduce my income by six hundred percent so you can run around writing your do-gooder plays? How about helping us, right here, in this relationship?"

But devoting himself to social commentary and reform was his life's ambition, he said. As an artist, he'd be able to help improve the lives of so many people who'd been disenfranchised. He couldn't drop everything and become a banker just to ensure her of the comforts she'd grown to expect. "Look, on my income we can live in a good house with a nice lifestyle. So we won't take big exotic vacations or have a big household staff. But we'll have each other, and our love will help so many other people."

"Well, then, I guess that's that," she said abruptly. "We really have no future together."

He was in shock. "You mean it's *over*? As in *over* over? I'm not going to make enough money, so that's it?"

"Yeah, that's exactly what I'm saying. Our life's ambitions are not compatible."

With that he got out of bed, got dressed, and, with great embarrassment, frustration, anger, and pain, left her home at two o'clock in the morning. He was devastated; this was the first woman he'd ever been in love with. A few weeks later, she called to tell him she had some of his things and would be sending them back. When the package arrived a week later, among the items was the ultimate insult: another man's underwear.

I have no doubt that my friend will eventually find that woman who "unhinges" him—in the right way. He's lucky he didn't get any further with this cash-hungry false alarm. She would have unhinged him, too, and sent him to the nuthouse—or the poorhouse.

But I do worry that too many women suffer, in one way or another, from the delusion this woman was under: that success or status or money is more important than love. It may sound like the biggest cliché in the book, but you'd be surprised how many women even today think it's in their interest to eliminate honest, decent, caring men just because their wallets don't (yet) measure up. Instead of having faith in the superiority of the circle's embrace, these women have taken all the old excesses of masculine behavior, of the untamed line, and co-opted them for their own ends. But there is no reward in this behavior. They may end up rich, but they will definitely end up unhappy, quite likely with men who are just as heartless as they are.

And the men they turn down? *They* will inherit the earth.

Smart Men, Wise Women

Despite my concern about women who are adopting the worst of men's behavior, I have to put my faith in the opposite trend: that women will trust their intuition and that men will learn from them. The higher virtues—kindness, generosity, understanding, love—are all virtues of the circle. They are part of the feminine spirit. There's an old Talmudic saying: *Men are smart, women are wise.* This concept is reflected in the strongest advice I can give to singles of both sexes who are looking to fall in love: Men, in dating, look to your woman for guidance, for signals. And women, look into yourselves, trust your hearts, and work with your men.

Even among the supposedly mature, self-aware singles of the twenty-first century, the leading role in building a relationship still falls naturally to the woman. Men look to women to be bold and break the ice when it comes to matters of emotional intimacy. Men usually aren't comfortable enough, adept enough, to start that conversation on their own. Women must be receptive, not judgmental; they must be patient, not pushy.

I know this may seem like an uneven division of labor, but I believe (and history supports me) that these qualities come naturally to women. And there's reason to believe it won't be as hard as it used to be: Believe it or not, men are improving. According to a recent survey by *New York* magazine, more men than women are saying they would choose an intimate relationship over casual sex. After all, the values of the circle—sensitivity, sensuality, emotional nakedness—are not alien to men; they simply come more slowly. Men who take a moment to remember how badly they wanted the affirmation and faith of a woman in the first place will be better able to build a relationship.

The ultimate "enabler" in this quotient, though, is the admission that we dearly want to be in love, that we need love. In the next chapter, we'll look at how you yourself can proudly declare your dependence.

8

Dependence Sets Us Free

I think a man and a woman should choose each other for life, for the simple reason that a long life with all its accidents is barely enough time for a man and a woman to understand each other and . . . to understand is to love.

—John Butler Yeats

Occasionally in life there are those moments of unutterable fulfillment which cannot be completely explained by those symbols called words. Their meanings can only be articulated by the inaudible language of the heart.

—Martin Luther King Jr.

When you realize you want to spend the rest of your life with somebody, you want the rest of your life to start as soon as possible.

Billy Crystal, *When Harry Met Sally* (1989)

When Pia, a late-thirty-something account executive for a public relations firm, came to my New York office one day recently, she had intended to discuss a project I was working on. But the subject quickly turned to relationships. Finding nice men who would commit wasn't her problem; it was committing to the nice men she found.

"I've been the dealer of pain many times, and it's starting to really tear me apart," she confided. "I'm attracted to nice guys. I know that's a good thing. But I dangle them, because I'm never sure I'll ever marry. I know it's a terrible thing to do; I guess I do it because I think I can convince myself that this guy will be the one. I've ended every relationship I've been in because of my fear of waking up one morning and feeling miserable that I'm lying next to a guy I'm not in love with. I'm dating a guy now; he's everything on my checklist, plus! I know he wants to marry me. And, you know, when I let myself go and say it's okay, things are great. It's just that I'm afraid of finding out that I'm not truly in love. I find myself holding back from telling him things I really want to tell him."

Then there was Sheila. When I first met Sheila, she was a twenty-three-year-old graduate student at Oxford. She had it all, or nearly. She was pretty, athletic, superbright, practically a genius. And she was a very strong feminist. She had started coming to Oxford L'Chaim, the student organization I had started, after losing her father. A staunchly independent woman who took issue with almost everything I said in my lectures about singles, she vehemently accused me of being a chauvinist. Eventually, and not surprisingly, she broke up with the guy she was dating and returned to her native South Africa, where she went on to earn $1 million a year with an investment banking firm. When I visited Cape Town several years later to give a lecture, Sheila got in touch with me. Now thirty-one, she had undergone a complete metamorphosis. "Don't remind me of anything I said at Oxford—I'd be embarrassed," she said. "I'm so lonely. I really want to meet somebody. I live on airplanes. My home is a hotel room. I never have time for relationships. Men tell me I intimidate the hell out of them. They never invite me out again. All that ranting I used to do about feminism? Now I realize that the thing I want most in life is a man. I am so lonely I could cry. My job doesn't satisfy me the way it used to. I would quit tomorrow for the right relationship. I want to feel like a woman."

Another Oxford connection was Paul, who was twenty-seven when I first met him. Paul was a man of generally stellar character, a giving man who could tell right from wrong, but he fancied himself a modern Don Juan, and he spent far too much time acting out that delusion. For some reason, women fell all over themselves for him. He wasn't rich; he wasn't brilliant; he wasn't even particularly handsome. But he was so earnest and paid such focused attention to them—who wouldn't want a best friend and lover like that? The only trouble was that Paul was a commitment-phobe. Coming from a dysfunctional family (his mother had died when he was young; his father was no kind of role model; his brothers and sisters all had troubled relationships), at least he recognized his problem. But Paul could never resist the next woman, and for years he'd felt unfulfilled.

Even when he finally met a woman and found himself falling for her, Paul resisted calling it love. "I've gotten used to her," he told me. Though he conceded that he couldn't live without her, he also couldn't live with her, that is, with her alone. He would cheat with as many as three women a week, all behind his girlfriend's back. When she found out, she threw a fit and dumped him. Not long after that, he happened to see her with another man at a restaurant; the incident so upset him that he went to her house and begged her forgiveness. "I've got to have you back," he told her. "You're the first woman that I truly miss." And he meant it. As she tried reasoning with him, her date for the evening waited for her in another room. When Paul heard the other man calling her, he told her that if she went back to him he didn't know how he could go on living. "I was a fool, and I'm not going to lose you again," he cried. It was like a scene from a movie. When they realized how much they loved each other, this couple forged their commitment on the spot. (Leaving them alone together, her date made a quiet exit.)

What changed Paul's mind? What made him realize that he loved this woman, even though the word *love* didn't come easily to his lips? It was the revelation that he'd come to *depend* on her. Even with his blinkered view of love, he realized that they had become part of each other, and he couldn't think of his life without thinking of hers as well. He needed her, and she needed him. She had become his grounding force. After the two were married, he got an even better surprise: His career and his enjoyment of life both grew as a result of his happiness. The stability of married life removed him from the ranks of nomadic desperadoes. And this young man, who once told me he wanted to be dead by age thirty, was now, at thirty-seven, the head of a family with three lovely kids and a devoted wife. Dependency had turned his life around.

Pulled from Both Ends

People like Pia and Paul are struggling with two seemingly contradictory forces, the two primal needs that pull us in opposite directions from the moment we are born. One is the need to be cared for. It begins as a biological necessity. From birth we are literally helpless, completely dependent on loving caregivers. Even before birth, we are safely in the womb, protected from cold air, loud voices, harsh lights, and the harsh realities of fending for ourselves. Who in his or her right mind would want to emerge from that warm enveloping environment, in which all bodily and emotional needs are automatically fulfilled, into a world where people have to fulfill their own needs? Who voluntarily wants to go out into the cold? Later, we experience that same dependency, at the other end of our existence, when the circle of life closes. The elderly, deemed dependent by society and their own failing bodies, need the care of family and often of health care workers, to see that their daily needs are met.

In all those in-between years, we feel the need to strike out on our own. This is the second need we are driven by: to take care of ourselves, to be independent. Even while in the womb, like the salmon that must swim upstream, we itch to get out on our own. Eventually that warm womb becomes stifling and too small. We're curious to see what other worlds there are to conquer. At about the age of two, the "terrible twos," we're suddenly possessed by the need to assert our separateness. At that age every kid is a Thomas Jefferson, those constant cries of "no" and "mine" all early, single-syllable declarations of independence. Young kids start feeling embarrassed about showing their own mothers affection in public. They go from calling them Mommy, to Mom, then finally to Ma, as if dropping letters will shorten the umbilical cord. Later, teenagers go through a wholesale rejection of all things that smack of authority and control. In those preadult years, young people, with their music and their pierced *everything*, draw a clear line around themselves, saying to all who might cross it, "This is *my* world, not *yours*. I don't need you anymore!"

Psychologists call the steps young people take to separate from their parents individuation. They say that individuation is a healthy developmental stage that we all must go through to reach a mature sense of self, otherwise known as adulthood.

Meanwhile, along with the psychological tug-of-war, the pull toward independence is being reinforced by the cultural influences that surround us. Men get cues from almost everywhere that independence is more masculine than dependence and thus, in our culture, stronger and more desirable. Strong, silent role models have always been rampant in the media, from John Wayne and Gary Cooper to Clint Eastwood and Arnold Schwarzenegger. Think of James Bond, the quintessential emotional nomad, taking pleasure in any bed he might. These maverick individualist stereotypes perpetuate the sense that excess emotional display is weak and superfluous. And men no longer have a monopoly on this problem. Since the 1960s, women have fought for the right to assert their own strength. From "I am woman, hear me roar" to "What's love got to do with it?" and from *The Mary Tyler Moore Show* to *Thelma & Louise*, since the 1970s the media has presented female role models who seem to get along fine, thank you, without a male partner.

The High Price of Independence

We pay a price for insisting on self-reliance. At the same time that we are expressing our individuality, every one of us is also searching for connection, both generally and specifically. In broad terms, we're always looking for a community of like-minded people, friends on whom we can depend, who form a net that can catch us when we fall. We call that a support system. And at closer range, we are desperately seeking that one like-minded person who will be there for us no matter what. We call that person a soul mate, the love of our lives—eventually our husband or wife. What we are looking for is someone to lean on who can also lean on us.

When we find that person and fall in love, we want to feel free to trust each other as soul mates, to depend on one another. Yet those mixed messages—that lifelong push-pull between dependency and independence—tell us not to surrender, not to admit our vulnerability, not to face one of life's fundamental facts: that as humans we need each other. This has been especially true in the last thirty years, as baby boomer values, with their emphasis on business success and the accumulation of wealth, have threatened our instinctive understanding of what is good for us. The lure of big money, whether on Wall Street or on the information superhigh-way, has only bolstered the acquisitive mind-set that can wreak such havoc on our values.

The *Other* Four-Letter Word

The film that best captured the compulsion to chase wealth was *Wall Street*, in which Michael Douglas's voracious trader, Gordon Gekko, spoke the line "Greed is good." As I mentioned earlier in this book, I have a more radical suggestion. If you're looking for happiness in life—if you're looking to fall in love—you've got to stop treating your search for a soul mate like the search for a good investment. Whether you're a woman or a man, you must realize that building a successful relationship isn't like building a successful business. You can't worry about whether you're shopping wisely. Love isn't about self-interest; it's about selflessness and self-sacrifice. It's about opening yourself up, exposing your vulnerabilities, and creating a space where you and a lover can grow together.

It's about realizing, in short, that *need* is good.

Need has become the four-letter word of relationships. It's the dirty little secret that no one wants to admit for fear of being called "needy," an adjective that ranks right down there with "clinging" and "desperate" among the biggest turn-offs to both sexes. To need someone is to acknowledge being weak. It's to concede that we are inadequate and incomplete in some fundamental way.

At lectures all over the world, I ask women in the audience to raise their hands if they "need" a man. At first they pretend to be puzzled by the question. This gives them more time to respond. "Need a man for what?" they ask. "Just *need* a man," I answer. "For-get about 'for what?' Just please raise your hand if you *need* a man. And the emphasis is on *need*. Not 'like a man,' not 'enjoy a man,' not even 'can *stomach* a man.' It's simple: How many of you *need* a man?" Typically, out of a thousand women in the audience, no more than four or five hands will go up. And those go up only about two or three inches, as if I'd asked the audience to acknowledge having a sexually transmitted disease. Of course, the rest of the women in the audience stare daggers at these women for breaking ranks with the sisterhood. No lecture goes by without an outcry against the rabbi's attack on their very femininity.

No surprise. What's amazing is what happens next. "All right," I say. "Now how many of you need a refrigerator?" And all the hands go up. The triumph of technology: A steel and plastic device designed to cool one's food has superseded masculine flesh designed to warm the female heart. GE brings good things to a woman's life, after all; all the average guy brings is the odor of gym socks. A *man?* *Who needs a man?*

The truth is, dependence has been linked in our culture to weakness. The word *dependency* has become inextricably connected with drug and alcohol abuse. And relationships are said to be "codependent" when one partner's behavior inadvertently or unconsciously reinforces the other partner's dependence on bad habits, from drinking or drugs to gambling or other forms of psychological addiction. Such associations, universally familiar even to those with no such abuse in their families, have infected our ideas about romance, discouraging people from admitting they need anyone else.

I frequently hear people telling their friends, "The reason you don't fall in love is that you want love too badly. You're desperate; people can *smell* the need on you. Love won't find you until you stop looking for it." My friend Leslie once told me, "I used to go to parties and all these dreadful singles events because I wanted to find a man. Now I've finally grown out of that. I'm happy being alone. If some guy comes along, great. But there is no way I will ever humiliate myself like that again."

Sound familiar? Looking for love has become something to be embarrassed about. You don't hear people talking about employment this way: "I used to go to job interviews, looking to get hired by law firms. I found it absolutely humiliating, having to cozy up to the partners to get them to give me a job. So I decided I will never go for an interview again. I'll just live here on the streets, with no money and no food. If some guy comes and offers me a job, I'll take it, but I will never search for it again." That kind of "independence" doesn't seem all that alluring. But is a big empty apartment and no one to snuggle with at night really that different?

We all must remember, after all, that one of our goals in the search for romance is to find someone who needs us. Imagine how you would feel if your lover one day told you, "I love you, but I don't need you. I admire you, but I can live without you." The only way to find love is to embrace that sense of mutual need. If you truly want to fall in love—to build an open, emotionally fulfilling relationship with another—you must let go of the posture of independence. No one can find love by pretending to be entirely satisfied with the single life. You can convey that you're happy; there's nothing wrong with that. Just don't pretend you're not looking.

Need Requires Maturity

I'm not suggesting that single men and women become wailing martyrs to loneliness. Nor am I arguing that we should be so needy that we allow ourselves to become doormats in relationships. What I'm talking about is healthy need, which is the product of strength, not weakness. Love is powerful, ultimately, because it's about affirmation, and being needed by a lover is the highest form of affirmation. It makes us feel special, important, indispensable. It reminds us that we serve a valuable role in at least one other human being's life. More profoundly, it reminds us that our existence was purposeful and necessary, not accidental or capricious. To be responsible for another, to feel his or her full weight on our shoulders, is a precious gift. Consider this: When a leader runs for president, we understand that it's not because he's insecure, because he needs Air Force One and the Secret Service in order to feel important. It's because he knows he has something valuable to offer his country, and he wants to serve.

Healthy need is also liberating, because it involves making an honest and accurate assessment of our own limitations. When we fall in love, we throw away our delusions of arrogant independence and replace them with a sense of our equality and balance as a couple and with the strong conviction that our own identity involves both gifts and needs. And the beauty of a relationship is that it is the perfect solution to both. It's the way we humans were designed to live.

But, Shmuley, you may be thinking, *I've heard so many experts say that we have to love ourselves before we can love anyone else.* I know psychologists say that you shouldn't enter into a relationship from a state of dependency, but I believe that this is a shallow and misleading idea, because it presupposes that people can be strong and special on their own outside the context of a relationship. It is a disempowering and imprisoning philosophy that confines the individual within the cage of his or her limitations. To me, the higher truth is that what makes people special is the unique contribution they make to their environment and their society. In that sense we are all of infinite significance. The trick is to find a relationship in which that special gift is appreciated and reciprocated.

No Risk, No Reward

Many of you may be thinking that what you're afraid of isn't just the appearance of weakness; it's the possibility that once you throw yourself headlong into love, once you allow yourself utter reliance on another human being, love won't be there to catch you. *Will the net be pulled? Will I fall flat on my face on the cruel hard ground?* And everyone can point to terrifying examples. I asked my friend Linda, who'd been living with Alex for five years, if they had any plans to marry. "Not if I can help it," she quickly replied. "Alex has asked me a few times. But all the married people I have seen are either divorced or miserable. They all look so bored, as though they've been watching too many *I Love Lucy* repeats over and over again. The fact that Alex and I *aren't* married is what keeps us together. This way he can't take me for granted."

Surveying a landscape like this, full of boredom and broken hearts, it's easy to fear abandonment, whether actual or just emotional. Nothing hurts so much as risking trust and then being disappointed. It's like plunking your head down on a soft pillow, only to find out the pillow is made of concrete. Such heartbreaking disappointment can have the power to destroy faith: faith in another person, in our own judgment, in love, and, most disappointing, in faith itself.

So we pull back. We withdraw our hearts and redirect our faith to all the old familiar gods: the gods of 401K, of StairMaster, of Neiman Marcus, of Hefner's bunnies. But those gods are no more dependable than the others. Once you lose the job and the savings plan, lose the battle of the bulge, lose the unforgiving fashion contest, Miss February dumps you. These are conditional lovers, fair-weather friends, sand-castle memorials to so-called independence. In a moment's notice, without loyalty or even warning, they're gone with the wind. The Rutgers National Marriage Project, in its Next Generations Program's recent study *The State of Our Unions 2000*, found that "the singles mating culture may pose obstacles to reaching the goal of soul-mate marriage." The report echoed my firsthand observations of singles today: "We found that women are just as committed as men to making it on their own and getting a place of their own before marriage. Indeed, compared to their male peers, these women are even more fiercely determined to 'take care of myself.' . . . Today's twenty-something [culture] is not oriented to marriage, as it has been in times past, nor is it dedicated to romantic love. . . . It is perhaps best described as a culture of sex without strings and relationships without rings."

Almost in passing, the report noted what might have seemed, superficially, like a contradiction between these singles' beliefs and their behavior. "The young men and women in this study," the report noted, do "expect their future marriages to last a lifetime and to fulfill their deepest emotional and spiritual needs. . . . [They] want to marry a best friend and 'soul mate' who will share and understand their most intimate feelings, needs and desires." Though the report went on to say that "young people, and especially young women, are not confident they will achieve this goal," I believe a different, more optimistic message can be drawn from their findings: that despite the rampant cynicism of our culture, despite our distrust of authority and tradition and our fear of getting burned, somehow single men and women have preserved their faith in marriage as an ideal, as a goal. In other words, deep down we are all still closet romantics. And that is the best news I have read in years.

Do you need anybody?

It's time to get in touch with your inner needs.

Before undertaking any of the following exercises, set aside a little time alone in your room to prepare mentally. This will take only a couple of minutes. Turn off the phone, or turn the answering machine on low, so you won't be interrupted. If it's daytime, close the shades. If it's night, turn off the lights. Get undressed as though you were going to sleep, lie in bed in a fetal position, close your eyes, and pull the covers up over your head.

Imagine yourself stripped of all your worldly possessions, all your accomplishments, all your family and friends—in effect, egoless. Then think of the person to whom you are closest: a husband, wife, girlfriend, boyfriend, child, parent, best friend, relative, bloodhound—the single person without whom you cannot imagine living. Now imagine this person out of your life. Gone completely, as if you'd gotten divorced or fallen out of friendship or out of contact. Think of the things you've done together, good times and bad, things you've said to each other, things you've confided that no one else knows, ways you make each other feel—never again to be experienced. Think deeply about the loss. Internalize the vacuum. Hold on to that feeling of loss and abandonment, feeling the empty space no one else can fill the way he or she does, until you almost feel you're in mourning. Hurts, doesn't it?

You see, you're not such an independent character after all.

Next, still in the fetal position in a darkened room, contemplate the most embarrassing thing you've ever done: the shoplifting you got away with as a teenager, the porn your boss caught you downloading from the Internet at work, the affair you had outside your marriage, the lie you told to get hired, the malicious gossip you spread about your best friend, the time you slept with your best friend's boyfriend when you got drunk, the vicious names you called your mother when you lost your temper. Whatever it is that constitutes your deepest secret, the most embarrassing thing you ever did, imagine that it got out. Imagine that the story went public. You're caught with your pants down, with your hand in the cookie jar, cheating the government of revenue or being unfaithful in a relationship. Imagine the humiliation, the total loss of face, as you're naked and stripped of your dignity. Imagine being hated by your coworkers, fired by your company, divorced by your spouse, abandoned by your friends, shunned by your community. How vulnerable do you feel right now? Is the first emotion that comes to mind your strength and independence, your ability to "stand on your own two feet," or would you do anything to have a caring man or woman by your side for support?

Do you need the people around you to love you, or do you simply not care?

Here's a more practical exercise. If you still believe you don't really *need* intimate companionship, try cutting yourself off from others altogether for a little while. For some, this might mean a forty-eight-hour weekend alone at home. For others, two nights alone might be just about all they can stand. Set your own time limit, and during that time don't make or answer phone calls or send or read any E-mail. Don't even open your snail mail. If you really want to be tough on yourself, don't watch television or listen to the radio, though listening to some favorite CDs or tapes is okay. Use this time for reading, introspection, meditation, prayer, and perhaps some light exercise or stretching. See how long it takes before you begin missing the people who normally fill your days.

To push the exercise to the next level, try playing with the other kinds of needs that are part of all our lives. Go on a food fast of twenty-four hours or longer, if you can handle it. Or try a verbal fast: Don't talk to *anyone* for twenty-four hours. In Hebrew it's called *tzom dibbur*, a fast of speech. When you end your fast, you'll be amazed at how precious words suddenly seem, how rich your food tastes, how meaningful your social contacts are, how dependent you are on all of it.

In the end, you should begin to appreciate your own natural hunger for human company in the same way that you recognize your hunger for food.

Freedom Through Dependence

Can dependence really set us free? A surprising number of people offer the sorriest of excuses for not taking a chance on love. "This love thing," they say, "it's going to rob me of my freedom to do, even think, what I want when I want to. There's no guarantee that it's going to work, and there's no guarantee that I'm going to be happy. And it's going to take up a lot of my time and attention, not to mention money."

While no one has done a study to corroborate this, I would wager that single men and women spend—I could say waste—inestimable hours planning dates, wondering when (even whom) to call, sitting there waiting for the phone to ring, and strategizing about how to get the attention of the man or woman of their dreams. Then they spend hours more in postmortems, talking endlessly with their friends about how they fared. They throw away thousands of dollars on dinners, flowers, cards, movies, cologne, clothing, phone calls. I believe that it's not marriage but the "single mating culture," as the Rutgers study put it, that imprisons the body, the mind, the spirit, and the pocketbook. It limits and confines us.

Remember my friend Henry, the wealthy real estate agent I introduced at the start of the book, who's got a bowling alley in his basement but no love in his life? Henry typifies the single man trapped by his own "freedom." He has often told me that wealth bought him freedom, that the only true blessing of being filthy rich is that you can do what you want when you want to. But Henry failed to realize how surely his wealth vacuum-sealed him into his risk-free universe. Imagine trying to keep up with half a dozen women you're dating, all at once. (Perhaps some of you can relate; the rest of you, of course, may be thinking *Lemme at 'em!*) Think of the time spent juggling a week's worth of dates, all the while trying to ensure that no one woman ever learns about the others. Consider trying to keep track of the lies you'd be forced to tell—and to wriggle out of when you get caught. Once, Henry told me, he'd double-booked—set two dates for the same night. Worse yet, both women were celebrating special occasions, so no rain checks were allowed.

I cared less about how he got himself out of that jam than about how much discomfort and inconvenience he was causing them and himself.

I've discussed at length with Henry my belief that falling in love, or declaring your dependence, as I sometimes like to think of it (more on that in a moment), actually frees you on many levels. It enlarges rather than diminishes you, because the most important freedom in life is the freedom to maximize your human potential, to take whatever gift you have on the inside and make something of it on the outside. When we are deprived of this freedom, we live in pain and disillusionment. Although according to Jewish Sabbath laws, no work can be done from sundown Friday to sundown Saturday, one of the exceptions is that a cow can be milked if its udder is full; otherwise the animal will be in terrible pain. We human beings are the same way. When we have no one to draw us out, the pain we experience is terrible. Love enables us to bring out that interior gift.

Many young married couples fear that having children will rob them of their freedom. They won't be able to pick up at a moment's notice and go to a movie, or spend a week in Paris, or make love in the living room at midday. Nevertheless, the gift parents get in return releases them from something much greater: the weight of adulthood. Having children liberates the playful, innocent side that gets trapped by the seriousness and rigidity of everyday life. People love children because they feel free around them, free to laugh, cry, or literally go fly a kite. Loving your children—sitting with them on the living room floor, playing together, watching them learn about and master the world around them—frees your own inner child. (See? I do think we have something to learn from psychology after all.) Parents often tell me that while having kids is exhausting, it also invigorates them, making them feel reborn. Why? Because seeing the world through a child's eyes frees us from seeing the world as we have come to see it. It allows us to recapture our sense of innocence.

John Lennon was one writer who understood the process of discovery that can lead to embracing dependence. In the lyrics of his song "Help!"—once dismissed as a movie theme but now appreciated as a deeply personal statement—Lennon described his own

progress from line to circle, from self-assurance to emotional inter-
dependence. "My independence seems to vanish in the haze," he
sings. "I know that I just need you like I've never done before."
There's a suggestion of pain here, but the song is sung with such a
sense of rhapsodic release that we're left with no question. Realizing
what's missing in our lives, he seems to say, is half the battle.

Sign On!

Overcoming the fear of dependence is crucial to establishing a fulfilling relationship. So crucial, in fact, that, with apologies to the
founding fathers of the United States of America, I have adapted
the American Declaration of Independence and created a Lovers'
Declaration of Dependence. Drafted by Thomas Jefferson in June
1776 and presented a month later on July 4, the original Declaration of Independence is America's most cherished symbol of liberty,
its "self-evident truths" recognized worldwide as a consummate
blueprint for human rights. The Lovers' Declaration of Dependence
speaks to the self-evident truths that are the heart of commitment;
they form the solid foundations on which any serious relationship
should be built. Read it, sign it, and then pass it along to potential
lovers to read and sign. Ask the guy or girl you're dating to sign the
Declaration of Dependence, so that you can weed out the commitment-phobes before you waste your time. (Though you might want
to wait until after dinner, so you don't get stuck with the check
when he bolts for the door.) Let this document serve as a symbolic
demonstration of your shared willingness to admit, and submit, to
this most basic of human needs.

Declaration of Dependence of the United State of Love

A Prerequisite to Committed Relationships

When in the Course of human events, it becomes both necessary and desirable for two people to dissolve the emotional barriers that have separated them from each other, and to exercise the right to have the loving and committed relations to which the Laws of Nature and God entitle them, a decent respect to each other requires that they should declare the causes and needs which impel them to such a unification.

We hold these truths to be self-evident, that all men and women, while created equal, are nonetheless created with unique and distinct differences, thereby rendering them capable of enriching each other in an intimate and nourishing relationship; that they are endowed by their Creator with certain unalienable Rights, and that among these are Life, Love, Liberty, and the pursuit of Happiness within a secure, healthy, and satisfying relationship. That to secure these rights, open communication, vulnerability, and honesty must be instituted between men and women, deriving their just powers from mutual consent, freeing them forever from game-playing and manipulation. That whenever any new dating theory or social trend becomes destructive of these ends, it is the Right of Men and Women to alter or to abolish it, and to institute new practices, laying their foundation on such principles that guarantee their Happiness within their relationship. Prudence, indeed, will dictate that behavior patterns long established are not easily changed; and accordingly all experience hath shown that man- and womankind are more disposed to suffer from the fear of vulnerability as they have not allowed themselves to approach another with guard down and heart open in many, many years. While these evils are sufferable, it has also been shown that righting them can only be done by toppling the walls that have protected people's emotional insecurities.

After a long train of abuses and failed relationships, invariably the result of following a despotic heart's misguided temporal temptations, it is our right, it is our duty, to throw off such wasted efforts, to free ourselves from the tyranny of fear—be that the fear of intimacy, the fear of boredom, or the fear that John Gray will be crowned King of Relationship Theories—and to provide new ways and means for their future loving relationships.

Such has been the patient sufferance of modern singles; and such is now the necessity that constrains them to alter their former Systems of Relating. The history of the present pattern of dating and relating is one of repeated dead ends, commitment-phobic men, cynical women, runaway brides, broken and numbed hearts, all leading to their own emotional tyranny and emotional Constipation.

At every stage we have petitioned for redress in the most humble terms. Our repeated attempts at rehabilitation have been answered only by a repetition of the same stupid patterns. A Prince or Princess whose character is thus betrayed by his or her own actions, despite his or her best intentions, is unfit to be a true lover.

But recovery is always possible for those who repent and express sincere willingness to change. We have reminded those wayward souls who have gone astray that the ties of our common kindred are in jeopardy and that refusal to agree to these terms could inevitably interrupt our connection.

I, therefore, as a representative of the United State of Love, by the authority of all the good people still hoping to fall in love, solemnly publish and declare that all lovers ought to be free to declare their dependence; that, once done, they are absolved from all allegiance to the legions of single people who will resent them for breaking rank; that all connection with exes or current hangers-on unwilling to declare their dependence ought to be totally dissolved; and that as free and dependent lovers, they have full power to levy love, promote peace and harmony, contract emotional alliances, establish the free trade of heartfelt sentiment, and to do all other acts and things which dependent lovers may of right do, including marrying, making love, and raising a family. And for the support of this Declaration, with a firm reliance on the protection of divine Providence and the romantic leadership of the one and only Love Prophet, we mutually pledge to each other our Lives, our Fortunes, our sacred Honor, and most of all our undying commitment.

_____   _____
Your Name Here   Your Lover's Name Here

_____

_____

_____
Names of Past Lovers Here

_____   _____

9

The Archetypal Couple

Everything I Know About Falling in Love I Learned in the Garden of Eden

God [thus] created man with His image. In the image of God, He created him; male and female He created them.

—Genesis 1:27

Although I conquer all the earth,
yet for me there is only one city.
In that city there is for me only one house;
And in that house, one room only;
And in that room, a bed.
And one woman sleeps there,
The shining joy and jewel of all my kingdom.

—From *Poems from the Sanscrit*, translated by John Brough

Monday. This new creature with the long hair is a good deal in the way. It is always hanging around and following me about. I don't like this; I am not used to company. I wish it would stay with the other animals. . . . Cloudy today, wind in the east; think we shall have rain. *We?* Where did I get that word?—I remember now—the new creature uses it.

—Adam, in Mark Twain,
"The Diary of Adam and Eve"

History and culture have offered us countless couples as role
models: David and Bathsheba, Antony and Cleopatra, Henry VIII
and Anne Boleyn, Romeo and Juliet, Rhett and Scarlett, Ozzie and
Harriet, and John and Yoko, just to name a few. So familiar are they,
so embedded in our psyches are their relationships, that we can talk
about them in shorthand without even using their last names. But if
the present disappointing state of affairs of the heart is any indica-
tion, we may have been following the wrong leads.

If we truly want to understand relationships—how we got to where
we are, and how to get where we want to be—why not go to the source?
And the source, ladies and gentlemen, is the story of the world's first
couple: Adam and Eve. In the biblical story of the love affair between
the first man and the first woman, we have the archetypal relationship,
replete with ups and down, better and worse, temptation and redemption. In examining this great love story, we can dissect and discern the
necessary ingredients of the falling-in-love recipe.

Here were God's Everyman and Everywoman. Adam was all
man, Eve quintessentially feminine, and it worked. That old magic
of magnetic attraction was evident right from the start. Adam saw
Eve, and she took his breath away. There was no objective evaluation on his part, no comparing her to prior paramours, no disappointment in the size of her chest, no frustration over the size of his
wallet. Adam and Eve were *meant to be,* as we might say now. They
were soul mates. They had eyes only for each other. And in each
other's company they found paradise. Granted, they didn't have a
heck of a lot of dating choices, but that's the whole point. They
didn't feel the need; they weren't missing anything. And the pull
that grew between them was so strong that they were willing to
transgress God's commandment to enjoy and share with each other
all the pleasures of the Garden, even the forbidden ones.

To see how far we've come from the ideal, imagine Adam and
Eve meeting and assessing each other by modern standards. They'd
meet at a fern bar in a trendy Garden neighborhood. She'd be
impressed with his very expensive oxen and wonder to herself if he
was truly able to commit. He'd try to imagine how she would look
on his arm at the agricultural fair and think, "If only she were a
blonde. Too bad this garden is in Mesopotamia." They'd look

around, notice how lousy their options were, just the way we do now, and "settle" for each other, all the while wondering who else God might get around to creating. If they'd approached dating the way singles today do, we might all still be a twinkle in God's eye, hanging around waiting for that couple down on the dance floor to get on with it and "become one flesh."

The point is that, in the beginning, Adam related to Eve as a unique woman, not as just another date. He was attracted to *wom-ankind*, not to one particular kind of woman. In the beginning there was no judgment, just the raw attraction between masculine and feminine, like two poles that cannot help being pulled toward one another. And that is just one of the lessons we should take from the first couple's union. In fact, a careful reading of this timeless love story reveals eight attributes, or virtues, that constitute the essence of love. After all, theirs was a love that endured for more than nine hundred years, all the while retaining its passion. (We know this because they gave birth to their son Seth in their six hundredth year; evidently something was still in working order.)

In this chapter I outline the eight essential virtues:

❤ An admission of loneliness

❤ An ability to go naked before each other (emotionally as well as physically)

❤ A willingness to return to a state of innocence together

❤ Preservation of a sense of wonder for each other

❤ A true compatibility based on strong values

❤ Selflessness

❤ A respect for each other's differences

❤ A rich shared history

I suggest that we all look to these attributes for guidance in our search for ways to reawaken the possibility of love in our hearts and lives.

The Power of Eight

That there are eight essential attributes, I believe, is no accident. In the ancient Hebrew mystical texts, the number seven represents the natural order: seven days of the week, seven heavens. The number eight, then, represents that which goes beyond the natural order, that which transcends nature. For example, there are eight days of Hanukkah, the Jewish Festival of Lights celebrating the "great miracle" that occurred when a tiny bit of Temple oil that should have burned out in a day lasted eight full days. Another eight-day Jewish holiday, Passover, honors the most famous miracles recounted in the whole of the Bible, including the ten plagues against Pharaoh and the parting of the Red Sea, allowing the Israelites to escape from Egypt.

One of the ancient Jewish prophecies is that with the building of the Third Temple and the arrival of the Messiah, new music for the traditional seven-stringed harp will be written for an eight-stringed instrument, symbolizing that the miraculous will be the natural order.

Other Nuances of the Bible

There are a great many such nuances to be gleaned from a close reading of biblical texts. For example, it's also important to note that the Hebrew word for man, *adam*, is collective, referring not to an individual but to men as a whole. *Adam* also means earth and signifies the fact that all men derive from the earth's clay, which God formed into man, breathing into him the breath of life. (Indeed, many women enjoy the corroboration that the male's origin is the slime pit.) Similarly, *eve* translates as "mother of all life"; we need no more justification for looking to these two types as signposts for all of human behavior.

The Eight Essential Virtues

Now let's go back to the Garden and take a closer look at the essentials of the model couple. All the material I use is drawn from Genesis 1:26 to Genesis 3:22. My citations come from *The Living Torah*, by Rabbi Aryeh Kaplan, an excellent modern English translation of the Five Books of Moses, but any Bible will do. These biblical verses offer a compelling blueprint for falling in love.

1. The Pain of Loneliness

Although he is immersed in the beautiful paradise that is Eden, the very first feeling Adam experiences is not ecstasy but loneliness. It is the first direct observation God makes about Adam and the first thing noted as bad in the Bible: "It is not good that the man should be alone" (Genesis 2:18). It is then that God decides: "I will make him a helper fit for him." Loneliness, in other words, is a primal condition of man, in fact, the premier pain of man. And its cure is the company of another who is right for him.

Though immersed in verdant Eden, where sensory pleasures surrounded him on all sides, Adam was consumed with that one need, a need as palpable as hunger or thirst or the instinct for self-preservation. He needed a companion. Neither the angels nor the animals of the Garden relieved his loneliness. None of the glories of the kingdom God had created, full of trees and plants and all sorts of distractions and attractions, sufficed.

In fact, before God thinks of Eve, He first introduces Adam to "every beast of the field and every bird of the air" (Genesis 2:19). Adam names them all, "but for Adam there was not found a helper fit for him" (Genesis 2:20). This doesn't mean that God was trying to hook Adam up with animals; it emphasizes the important distinction between man and animal, and the human dominance over the animal kingdom. The main difference between animals and humans is that humans think, feel, and have values. Animals are interested in sustenance, not significance; in survival, rather than soulfulness. An animal makes no demands on us; its needs are not our needs. Even the names they are given speak to the distinction. The animals are named as groups: oxen, deer, horses. It was only when God created an equal for Adam that He used a unique name: Eve. The very act of love, after all, is an act of equalization. It is a statement that you have found someone worthy of you. When you love someone, you raise that person up to your level. You can be a king marrying a commoner, but in the act of being loved and married, she becomes a queen.

When Men Act Like Animals

In our time, the man who I believe has done most to undermine and replace the biblical lessons of Adam and Eve—that man and woman must "become one flesh"—is Hugh Hefner. I harbor no personal ill will against Hefner; indeed, *Playboy* even published an extract from my first book, *Kosher Sex*. Still, there can be no doubt that Hefner's magazine, and the "*Playboy* philosophy" touted in its pages, has contributed to the animalization of womankind. After all, its great contribution to culture is the Playboy *bunny!* Ages after the first man, Adam, found himself profoundly dissatisfied with his potential animal partners, craving instead an introspective and communicative human like himself, Hefner issued an alluring invitation for both men and women to revert once again to the level of all mammals. Whereas Adam felt lonely and wanted to be loved, the *Playboy* man feels horny and wants to get laid. Whereas Adam, by loving Eve, gave her distinctiveness and raised her from the level of the animals, the *Playboy* man, by seducing anything with a pair of breasts, reduces women to a form of chattel created to service the male libido. Whereas Adam found that the animals were not special enough to take away his loneliness, the *Playboy* man finds that ordinary women are not special enough to participate in his fantasies. To Hugh Hefner and others like him, women are hardly equals; they are simply means to the end of sexual self-satisfaction. The revolving door of the Playboy mansion, with bunnies hopping from bed to bed, is the modern inversion of Eden.

What's sad is that so many men have taken Hefner's message to heart. Take my friend Jerry. For months, I pointed out to Jerry that he treated women as appendages to his lifestyle. He chose to date women who were beneath him intellectually, socially, and spiritually; the one thing they had was ravishing beauty. But Jerry's inability to master his libido, and to channel it into a higher form of communication, sabotaged his relationships from the start. Many of his girlfriends, perhaps the majority of them, had their interest piqued first and foremost by his wealth. "You can't love someone you don't see as your equal," I would tell him. "You're unconsciously incapacitating your relationships from the beginning by choosing women who are inappropriate.

They will never challenge you to grow. They won't bring out your best." Several weeks later he would dump his latest girlfriend, complaining she wasn't good enough for him. "Gee," I would say. "I thought that was why you were dating her." He was caught in his own emotional catch–22. And I could easily imagine a closetful of old *Playboys* in his room.

A Hunger for Companionship

Adam needed to experience the pain of loneliness—needed, in fact, to have it called to his attention, like many men and women today—until God showed him how to find love and ease the pain. And so, from a rib of Adam, God created woman (Genesis 2:22). Enter Eve; exit loneliness. Adam is one happy guy: "This at last is bone of my bones and flesh of my flesh," he says (Genesis 2:23). No more fern bars for him.

Many women take objection to the suggestion that woman was fashioned from Adam's rib, as if she were a less substantial afterthought. But what's at fault here is merely the translation. The line reads: "And God caused a sleep to fall upon Adam . . . and He took one of his ribs and closed up the flesh in that place. Then God formed the rib which He had taken from the man into a woman" (Genesis 2:21–22). But the traditional Jewish interpretation of these verses in Genesis suggests that the word *tzela*, usually translated as "rib," actually means "side." Adam, in other words, was a hybrid of both male and female; when he fell asleep, God removed his feminine side, made it an entity unto herself, and left the two of them together to keep each other company—or, as Jerry Maguire would put it, to "complete" each other.

Thus Adam and Eve recognized each other not only as like beings but also as two halves of a whole, a powerful image too easily dismissed in an age when we're all persuaded we must be "whole people" ourselves before we can fall in love. In truth, a person who derives too great a sense of worth from his own self-regard, a person who can feel "whole" through simple self-satisfaction, can look upon a new partner only as a distraction, an extra limb, easily severed if it causes more pain than pleasure.

There's a story that perfectly illustrates this point. It's about the entrepreneur who tries to make a living selling third arms. When he approaches a man walking by, the man says, "I'm not interested. I already have two arms. Why do I need a third?" The salesman makes his pitch: "Just think of all the possibilities. You could dial the phone, eat a sandwich, and slap the kid all at the same time. You could carry more groceries into the car from the shop. The possibilities are endless!" Intrigued, the customer agrees to give it a try. The first month everything goes well. The third arm really is a tremendous convenience. But after a few weeks, some glitches appear. One morning it won't wake up at all, complaining it's too tired. The next morning it's temperamental, grumping all the time that it's not appreciated enough. The third morning it even has the audacity to slap its new owner in the face, reprimanding him for being mean and uncaring. "That's it," says the customer. "I've had enough." And he returns the arm to the salesman.

Too many singles today view marriage as if it meant acquiring a third arm: *I'm doing just fine with what I've got, am I not?* When people view their partners as superfluous to their essential being, it's no wonder the divorce rate is so high. But the story of Adam and Eve completely rejects this outlook. Questioning whether we need a "helpmate" betrays a lack of self-understanding; it bespeaks an arrogance that's antithetical to happiness. Adam's example demonstrates the importance of recognizing the need for love.

2. Nakedness

"The man and his wife were both naked, and they were not embarrassed by one another" (Genesis 2:25). Nakedness is perhaps the most famous element of the Adam and Eve story. So critical is this virtue that it's mentioned four times in the short text of Genesis alone. The repeated references underline the importance of three metaphorical levels of nakedness—intellectual, emotional, and spiritual—as well as the physical level. Not coincidentally, the progression moves down from the head, through the heart and soul, to the sexual organs, a line of love that then circles around again and again. Each level is required, ideally in that order of appearance, for a fulfilling and loving relationship. Adam and Eve are lucky enough to have attained all four, and all within two verses (Genesis 2:23–25), which in modern times would probably be equivalent to about four absolutely perfect dates.

What do I mean in using the word *nakedness* in this context? The image symbolizes a thousand things: openness, honesty, innocence, trust. When I say that Adam and Eve shared an intellectual nakedness, for example, I mean that there was no pretense between them; there were no self-protective facades, no secrets. When Adam says, "Now this is bone from my bone and flesh from my flesh," we can sense his relief. Here, finally, was a woman with whom he saw eye to eye, a being with whom he could share what he knew about the world, limited though it may have been at that point. "This is my kind of woman," he thought to himself. Their repartee must have been sparkling, for theirs was a free mind-to-mind exchange, untinged by anxiety or shyness. They were free from the fear of being judged. They felt free to be themselves around each other.

Imagine for yourself what this must have been like. Adam had no mental checklist to use in judging Eve: no Julia Roberts filter, no Charlize Theron filter, no Pamela Anderson filter. Eve hadn't dated and bedded every guy in the garden. If you were to ask her, "Are you attracted to him?" she would not have said, "Well, kinda sorta. He's no Matt Dillon. He's not even that baboon that came on to me this afternoon." She would have said, "He's a man. Naturally I am attracted to him!" There was no "he's my type" or "she's not my type." There *were* no types, only a pair of archetypes. The senses were fresh; the heart was not yet jaded. These were the days when the opposite sex *was* a big deal.

And what was the result? Here is a lesson to take with you: These two young lovers told each other, from the very start, exactly how they felt about each other. They acted with no pretense and certainly with no manipulation. They had no agenda, nothing to hide. They were practicing the radical honesty I discussed in chapter 6. Each had an opinion and voiced it; each allowed the other that opinion. They looked at each other and saw through naked flesh to the soul beneath.

Emotional nakedness is the next, deeper level, the level on which

Adam and Eve were completely comfortable revealing their feelings. Adam and Eve were uninhibited, utterly transparent, and frank. Whereas most of us need a translator on dates to detect the meanings that have been carefully hidden to protect ourselves, Adam and Eve understood each other immediately. Recognizing that neither was complete without the other, they gladly declared their dependence on each other. "I've been lonely here in the Garden," Adam would have confessed to her. "I'm so glad *you're* finally here."

Neither Adam nor Eve felt insecure around each other. She wasn't worried that he might develop a roving eye if she put on a few extra pounds. He knew she wanted him even if he wasn't the best gardener he could be. There was no fear of rejection. They were able to talk about their vulnerabilities and deepest fears of abandonment. There was nothing to be ashamed about. "It's so easy to talk with you," Eve would have said, over an organic veggie lunch. "I feel I can tell you anything." There was no shallow small talk, no need to impress each other.

Spiritual nakedness occurs quite naturally, as well, after the layers of intellect and emotion are stripped away. For Adam and Eve were true soul mates. Would you expect less from their Matchmaker? If there was any doubt in their minds, the adversity they faced later—in getting a cosmic eviction notice, but forging ahead together; in going on to raise a family and live to a ripe old age— merely confirmed what they knew from the first. This was the love of a lifetime, a love that had literally no antecedent.

As it is written, "A man shall therefore leave his father and his mother and be united with his wife, and they shall become one flesh" (Genesis 2:24). For Adam and Eve, discovering their spiritual connection must have felt like déjà vu, as it does when two people who've just met feel mysteriously attracted to each other, as though they've known each other a long time. It's a feeling many of us have experienced, that a part of us, once missing, is now retrieved, making us whole again.

Once Adam and Eve had exposed so much to each other, physical nakedness was a foregone consummation. And "becoming one flesh," the physical expression of that union, was the highest form of communication. We can only assume the earth actually did move that first night they spent together.

The physical act of lovemaking was the experiential, or worldly, expression of their spiritual love. Like the rivers that emerge naturally from the spring, and like the smile that comes innately to the face when the heart is gladdened, their physical love was the organic outgrowth of their emotional closeness. After intellectual, emotional, and spiritual nakedness, it was the breaking down of the last barrier between them. They were making love to the whole person, not just the sexy body of the most eligible bachelor in the Garden. Sex was the manifestation of the union they had achieved.

It's well known, of course, that words like *sex* or *making love* never appear in the Bible. Indeed, I find the oft-cited euphemism *knowing*—"in the biblical sense," as high school kids call it—to be a telling expression of the level of nakedness Adam and Eve had reached. Now they knew each other on every level, and the physical act was the obvious and natural outgrowth of that knowledge. The *Zohar*, which is the principal work of Jewish mysticism, says that sex is the highest form of knowledge. When practiced correctly, it says, lovemaking involves a three-pronged unity, merging spirit, soul, and body. Making love with your eyes open, you open your soul to your partner. Kissing passionately, you exchange the breath of life, thereby becoming one spirit. And twining your limbs and bodies together, you become, ultimately, one flesh. One soul, one spirit, one flesh—the result is a completed circle of unity.

Couples who experience these levels, ideally in the order I've presented them, become joined together into one. To take the opposite course, from the groin up, makes everything much more difficult.

Stripped of Virtue

After these first few instances, the next time the word *naked* appears is after Adam and Eve have eaten from the Tree of Knowledge and are on the lam in the Garden. "And the eyes of both of them were opened, and they suddenly knew that they were naked," the text reads, "and they sewed fig leaves together and made themselves covering." Later God calls to Adam after tracking him down. "I heard Your voice in the garden," Adam explains, "and I was afraid because I was naked so I hid" (Genesis 3:10). In this passage, we watch Adam and Eve go from one type of nakedness to a radically different variety: from blamelessness to shamefulness, from innocence to guilt, from transparency to opacity, and from virtue to deficiency. They went from being naked because they had nothing to hide, to being naked of virtue, feeling empty and bereft of redeeming qualities.

In that one line, I hear the voices of singles I counsel all the time. Though they put it in different terms, what they're really telling me is: "I'm hiding from commitment, hiding from rejection, hiding from loneliness." Rather than admit any of that, they hide behind their successful careers, their perfectly toned bodies, their self-help gurus, their repudiation of marriage. Whereas Adam and Eve rushed to put on clothes, people today put on airs: "Did you see my Porsche?" "I graduated from Harvard." "Want to come to my beach house for the weekend?"

What Adam and Eve had was a taste of independent judgment. Good and evil had been external criteria; into their subjective paradise, the harshness of objectivity had intruded. Suddenly, nakedness meant insecurity and deficiency. The fruit of the Tree of Knowledge—Hef, are you listening?—had instilled limitless desire in their hearts, and all at once nothing was good enough. They became insatiable.

From this point on, things might start sounding familiar to anyone who's been dating awhile. Now, after the first blush of dating, so to speak, Adam sees Eve's blemishes. As soon as they commit this cardinal sin, then, Adam and Eve both run to put on clothes. The woman, Eve, puts on makeup, not to highlight her beauty but to cover her nakedness; she puts on clothing, not to showcase her curves but to cover her flabby thighs. And the man, Adam, runs around helplessly, looking for a Ferrari to compensate for his own inadequacies.

All at once, Adam and Eve started to feel they no longer needed each other. The easy harmony and attraction that once existed between them was undone. They went from a complementary relationship to one of combatants, from two individuals who felt naturally drawn to each other to individuals who had to be suspicious of each other. And thus was born the war of the sexes. Now finger-pointing and blame become part of human relationships. Remember the very first thing that Adam did when God asked him why he sinned? He blamed Eve. In turn, Eve blamed the serpent. God punished the whole lot of them (Genesis 3:12–14).

Anyone in a relationship lives with this curse of objectivity. It is the anxiety of a woman who takes off her clothes in front of her new man, worried sick because she knows he's probably seen fifty female bodies already and will be more than happy to judge whether she's an eight or a two. The divorce rate, the overemphasis on looks and fashion, jobs, and other status symbols—these are all the direct result of shame at our nakedness, physical, emotional, and other.

God, of course, understood the problem. When He asked, "Who told you that you were naked?" (Genesis 3:11), what he meant was "Where did you get all these insecurities? How did your healthy nakedness get transformed into this unhealthy shame? How did you lose your innocence?" As if He didn't know. But His question was an invitation to self-reflection, a suggestion that should send all of us, as it did Adam and Eve, on an introspective journey. In fact, His question might be phrased in another way: "Who said you couldn't fall in love?"

The loss of healthy nakedness between the sexes is felt at every turn in our lives. It's the source of our shame, of our fear. But it can be recaptured, as we shall see.

3. Innocence

What is the most attractive thing about any man or woman? The sense of innocence, no doubt. And is it any wonder, given Adam and Eve's experience in the garden? Who wouldn't want to return to that blissful paradise of subjective love? Innocence is irresistible; we yearn for it the way we do for our own childhood.

Every day we get dressed, leave our homes, and spend eight hours trying to manipulate the world to our own advantage and reap the rewards. Then, when we come home, we want to feel we can take it all off and reclaim our innocence. Is this difficult? Of course. But unless we can find a way, in our private lives and relationships, to retain our innocence, we have indeed lost the ability to love.

The love affair between Adam and Eve was quintessentially innocent. Eve, of course, was not simply the first woman Adam dated, but the first he had ever seen. He was able to love her unconditionally because he had no one to compare her with. Rather than judge her against other points of reference, he saw her for what she was, beheld her beauty as a thing unto itself. He brought no previous experience to bear in evaluating her; in other words, he loved her from a position of complete innocence.

Adam and Eve pranced around naked in the Garden because they had done nothing wrong; they had neither warts nor iniquity to conceal. They *needed* no clothes. They felt that they were beautiful just the way they were born. The pristine luminescence, the sheer purity, of their souls shone through, and their bodies did not mask it. In this couple there was complete synthesis between body and soul. They were *homo spiritus*, Godly beings without sin; nothing obstructed their closeness to God or clouded their dignity.

On a broader level, innocence is about more than simply nakedness or sin. It is about preserving a union between our outer and our inner selves. If we are innocent, we are in complete harmony. There are no aspects of ourselves that we find disagreeable and therefore necessary to conceal. Innocent persons radiate even as they walk down the street, because the light of their soul illuminates their entire being. They don't embellish their status on dates; they don't drop names; they don't sport gaudy makeup and push-up bras. Among the innocent there is no disconnect, no game-playing, no hypocrisy.

But there is another dimension to innocence. Much as we appreciate innocence in our lovers, we also yearn for the loving gaze of the innocent. We yearn to feel that we are significant, that we have knowledge that can make a difference to them. There is no better way to experience this than to feel that we have been a formative influence in someone else's life. Like the first couple (and I don't mean George W. and Laura), we treasure the innocence of our lovers because it reveals their difference from us, even as we yearn to share knowledge about ourselves with our own lovers, thus closing the circle and completing each other.

Whom Do You Trust?

Trust is a big component of innocence. Adam and Eve's relationship began with trust. They had no reason *not* to trust each other. Innocent couples bring out the best in each other, because they don't suspect each other of manipulative behavior. When Eve tempted Adam into the sin of tasting the forbidden fruit, she in turn felt she'd been manipulated by the serpent. And so began the "begats" of blame.

Perhaps the most destructive force in dating today is manipulation. Men and women have become master manipulators. We've gone way beyond unsubtle ploys, like getting pregnant to force a guy to marry or sleeping with an ex-girlfriend's best friend to make her want you back. Modern manipulation is much more sophisticated. It's dating a new guy to get over the last guy and then telling the last guy about it just to make him feel bad. It's "sharing" stories about abusive parents just to win sympathy and love. It's sighing as if you cared, just to make it easier to get her into bed. And most troublesome of all, it's saying "I love you" when you know you don't.

This kind of manipulation, it should be evident, cannot lead to love. If you spend all your time engaging in this kind of strategic warfare, you'll be far too engaged in pushing someone's buttons to allow something as embracing as love to sweep you off your feet. How can you "fall," after all, when you're holding on so tight? And no matter how you slice it, playing this kind of game always involves lying, whether outright lying, lying by omission, or simply withholding the truths of your heart. And where there is lying, there can be no trust. Weary of being used, we've all developed our B.S. detectors to guard against being duped. We've been trained by the consumer movement, among other things, to look for the lie. And this in turn has created an atmosphere of defensiveness around all of us as we begin dating, making it nearly impossible to be natural—innocent—while on a date.

Today's men and women pride themselves on being the opposite of innocent. They are worldly, streetwise. But I have found that if "a little bit of knowledge is a dangerous thing," as the saying goes, then with regard to dating and relationships, a lot of knowledge is even more dangerous. Everyone is a relationship expert these days. Everyone's got a theory about why this relationship didn't work, why that one is still hanging on, and why the other one—well, *they* shouldn't have gotten together in the first place! Trained in these hyperrational times to judge everything and everyone with a cold, dispassionate eye, we find weak links in every chain, and in our search for a flawless mate we all too often end up lonely and dissatisfied.

Hipper than Thou

Smug and savvy, we as a culture have grown accustomed to looking down our noses at what we think of as naïveté. To call people naive is to condemn them for being ignorant, in other words, not as cool as we are. The naïf may not be among the ranks of thieves, rapists, or murderers, but to us he is up there with the fool. Yet those of us who come from a Jewish perspective find this curious, since in our tradition innocence is the highest of values. In the Kabbalah, one of the highest descriptions of God is *peshitut ha'atzmut*, the Ultimate Simplicity. And every year, on the Yom Kippur, the Day of Atonement, it is that simplicity and innocence that we are trying to rediscover for ourselves.

Naïveté—innocence through a lens, darkly—seems bad only because our superhip culture says it is. In truth, to be naive is to be open to the world. The naive are the people who most often seem happy, while the street-smart rogue scowls away, cynical, suspicious, negative, doubtful. The difference is simple: The innocent believes in goodness. The one who blushes still believes in love. Before the world was corrupted, before Adam and Eve dropped the ball, innocence and naïveté were the natural order. In fact, the only thing that makes naïveté such a liability is that there are unscrupulous people out there in the world, ready to take advantage of innocence. But what is the best remedy for this state of affairs? That all the naive and innocent people become scoundrels or that the naive hold on to their innocence and try to influence others by example?

No matter how worldly and experienced you are, no matter how many times you have eaten of the forbidden fruit, I believe that you can redeem your innocence. You can recapture what I call your *mental virginity*. By cleaning the slate, emotionally speaking; by letting go of past heartbreaks; by breaking the habit of dating inappropriate people; by ending on-again-off-again relationships; by refusing to chastise yourself for being alone; by resisting the temptation to overevaluate, compare, and judge—you can attain the pristine soul you had before you became too experienced for your own good.

Another biblical story that has become Jewish rabbinical legend, recounted in the Midrash (the ancient rabbinical discussion of hidden stories and meanings within the biblical text), may shed light on how those who feel they've lost their innocence can regain it. After the Jews built a golden calf and were expelled from Egypt, God asked His people to repent by building a golden tabernacle, which they did. But where did that gold come from, asked the sage old rabbis, if the Jews had used it all to build the golden idol? The ancient rabbis explained that every man had kept a little gold in his pocket, a sort of spiritual Swiss bank account. That's why the tabernacle was considered so important; it shows that the Jews were prepared to give up even their secret stash of gold. The Midrash goes on to say that that gold represents our innocence—the innocence that can't be compromised, tread upon, or lost. We can always access that account and redeem our innocence.

Our innocence, in other words, is our soul. If our skin gets torn, a scar is left. But the soul, as a spiritual entity, cannot be damaged. It is always transcendent. No matter how we try to deface it, the graffiti never sticks. And by tapping into our soul, we experience the art of renewal. We are all always capable of reinventing ourselves, of looking at every experience as if it's happening for the first time. We're all capable of finding something new and magical in every moment of life. And we're all capable of recovering from our wounds, overcoming negative experiences, and finding love.

4. Desire and Wonder

In all the years I've been counseling men and women about relationships, what mystifies me the most are these recurring questions: "Shmuley, why do you make such a big thing about love? It's no big deal." "Shmuley, why do you make such a big thing about sex, call it 'the highest form of knowledge'? It's no big deal." "Shmuley, why do you make such a big thing about the opposite sex? They're no big deal."

What confuses me is this: If love is no big deal; if marriage is no big deal; if sex, especially, is no big deal; then what is? Making money? Going on vacation? Shopping? Doesn't this sound to you like a certain world-weariness? Are we living in a world that has grown tired of love and decided to move on, to try to find bigger and better things?

I wonder what Shakespeare would think if he heard this. "Hey, Will, all those love sonnets you wrote, get over it, man. Love ain't no big thing." And King Solomon. "Hey, Sol. That Song you wrote about erotic love. Got anything snappier?" Indeed, what if we went to the Beatles. "Look, lads, how long can you guys keep on with this 'love is all you need' stuff? Can't you work in something about profit-earning ratios?"

What would today's men, who look at a woman and see nothing but a potential conquest, say to all the great romantic poets, from Ovid to Keats, who looked at women as a *really* big deal? In a woman they saw a goddess, the embodiment of God's creative energy, a colorful flower, a fascinating being deserving affection and admiration. What, too, would all these figures say to us? They would wonder, I think, what happened to one of love's central qualities: wonder.

The attraction between Adam and Eve was motivated by something more precious and complex than simple animal magnetism. They were drawn by *wonder*. In encountering the opposite sex, they thought, "Here at last is a fascinating creature." Eve was not a beast, but neither was she exactly like Adam. Remember the scene from *West Side Story*, when Tony and Maria meet at the dance at the gym? That's what it must have been like when Adam and Eve's eyes locked at the pond where they both took water.

When I was studying to be a rabbi, engrossed with all my classmates in our studies, none of us in our all-male seminar dated any women. In fact, we had very little interaction with women. Rather, we were satisfied contemplating the feminine ideal in our minds, as creatures of infinite mystery. They had about them a sense of magic and wonder. When I studied in Jerusalem in my late teen years, there was a women's seminary down the hill from us, and every morning we watched from afar as seven hundred girls made their way into the school building. Sure, they proved a pretty serious distraction to our studies. And sure, we occasionally lifted our heads from our giant Talmudic tomes to look as they passed (always making sure that the head of our academy didn't notice).

The amazing thing that I remember about that time was that we looked not with lust but with wonder. We longed not to conquer or acquire these women but to discover them. There was about them a sense of delectable mystery, almost otherworldliness. We were infinitely curious about them. Who were these incredible creatures passing by us every day? We knew they could enrich our lives in some way, even if we weren't quite sure what that meant. For us, a woman was a superior heavenly creature. Sex was the supreme act of knowledge by which the mystery of this creature would become known to us, and a relationship was the medium through which the man and the woman could connect, become whole, and be sewn together as one flesh. I was always amazed at how all of us so desperately wanted to marry. To us, finding a woman was the source of all blessing, and a life without a woman was a life bereft of enchanting beauty and filled with loneliness. We all married, therefore, in our early twenties. And each of us felt honored when a woman accepted our proposal of marriage.

There were no commitment-phobes in our seminary. How could there be? For us, life *began* when you married. The fear of marriage that I sensed around my more secular peers always confused me. Sleep around before you marry to get your wild oats *out* of your system? Hold on! What if your *wife* wanted those wild oats? Weren't you supposed to get crazy with *her* in bed? Wasn't the source of your connection and closeness the passionate lovemaking the two of you would surely practice in your youth? For us, marriage was the highest form of liberation, not only because it freed us from loneliness, but because it freed all the love we had inside.

Familiarity Breeds . . .

Today, with the gradual neutralizing of masculine and feminine energies in our society, men and women are more familiar with each other from childhood on, and that sense of mystery and wonder is rapidly disappearing. Instead of exciting wonder in young men, women elicit judgment. The sight of a woman transforms a young man into not Cyrano de Bergerac but a kind of Chief Justice of the Court for Feminine Studies. Immediately, his mind gets working: "nice eyes, chest a bit too small but compensated for by stunning long legs." This is a tragedy, and its major consequence is that our sense of wonder is dwindling, our very attempt to narrow the gap between the sexes is actually widening the gulf.

I still remember once trying to introduce a young man at Oxford to a special young woman who had just arrived as a graduate student. He told me not to bother unless she was stunning. Luckily, she was, or at least I thought so. After their first date, he called me up. "Look, Shmuley, you're my rabbi and you can teach me about God any time. But I need to teach you about women. That girl wasn't attractive at all." I was startled. To me she seemed very pretty. So I said to him, "You want to tell me she isn't beautiful? Are you blind?" He answered, "Sure, her face is beautiful. But did you see her body?"

That was the first sign I had, though certainly not the last, that these days men judge a woman's looks on the basis of her body much more than her face. I know this sounds naive, but coming from a Yeshiva background I had no idea how universal a practice it had become. I thought you looked into a woman's eyes and saw her beauty. That men today were being subtly trained to look right past the eyes, straight to the body, was astonishing to me.

Men examine women today as if they were butchers sizing up a cut of meat. And as the mystery wanes, they grow more and more bored. We have become so totally familiar with each other that tampon and Viagra commercials have become common viewing for both sexes. When I hear about women who undress casually in front of their husbands every night, whether or not they're going to have sex, I am puzzled. "Don't you realize," I tell them, "that if you undress casually every night and he sees every hill and valley, even if you are married, then one night when you undress *in order to elicit a response,* it ain't gonna happen?" If we are to preserve the sense of wonder that has been at the heart of romantic love since the beginning, we must work to ensure that we balance our openness and honesty with a sense of mystery.

Putting Your Best Face Forward

Once, in a restaurant, I overheard a conversation between a thirty-something man and woman that left no doubt that wonder was a thing of the past. "You seem really irritable tonight. What's wrong?" he asked. "Well, not only am I having my period," she said, "but I also have a yeast infection, and do you know what it's like to experience a cottage cheese discharge? No, I didn't think so. So give me a break."

Oh, yuck! Was she nuts? Couldn't she have said, "Sorry, honey, it's a woman thing. I'll be more chirpy tomorrow"?

Contrast this with how God created Eve. Notice that the Bible says He first put Adam to sleep (Genesis 2:21). Only then did he take one of Adam's ribs and create Eve. Why this way? This was a question that the daughter of a Roman emperor asked of Rabbi Joshua. She said, "Your God is a thief, for he took Adam's rib when he was asleep. He could have done it when Adam was wide awake and with his permission." Rabbi Joshua, who was in Rome at the palace at the time, said, "You are asking a very good question. But before I respond, let me tell you that I am very hungry. Let's first go to the royal butchers, choose some heifers, let them slaughter and prepare them before our eyes, and have a barbecue."

And that's what they did. When it was time to eat, Rabbi Joshua said to the emperor's daughter, "Aren't you joining us? Why have you suddenly lost your appetite?"

And she said, "I sat there watching these animals being slaughtered, skinned, chopped, and cooked. Do you really think that I feel like eating?"

"Ah! And now you know the answer to your earlier question," Rabbi Joshua told her. "This is exactly why God put Adam to sleep before he took the rib and created Eve. Had Adam witnessed how Eve was created—the flesh, blood, and sinews all being brought together—he would have despised her."

God saw the importance of wonder, of having Adam always look upon Eve as though she had magical, angelic qualities. Hence God has given us all radiant skin to cover all of our seams.

But when they later sinned, Adam and Eve lost the sense of wonder. How else to explain Eve's interest in the Tree of Knowledge (Genesis 3:6), a metaphor for the temptations of the material world? Soon both Eve and Adam were distracted from their own love by the alluring tree, and before long their growing dependence on the material pleasure of the Tree of Knowledge of Good and Evil had subverted their idyllic romance. They became more interested in acquisition than love, in having than in being, in owning than in sharing, in purchasing coverings than in continuing to be naked. It's a lesson we should all take to heart, especially over dinner.

It's a Wonder-ful Love

Those of us who are looking for romance today must beware of the same scourge of familiarity. Instead of treating a new romantic prospect as a potential conquest, or just another conversation partner, we must find a way to recapture that sense of wonder at the potential for romance. Love should inspire within us the noblest of emotions: awe, selflessness, consideration, a curiosity about the other that transcends one's preconceptions or expectations. Curiosity is the very engine of life. This thirst for knowledge is the single most important ingredient in any healthy male-female relationship. So long as a man and a woman still want to know each other, their relationship is healthy and strong. But the moment they think they can predict what the other is thinking, for all intents and purposes the relationship has suffocated.

In the Book of Ruth, the Jewish nobleman Boaz shows unusual kindness to the Moabite (and thus foreign) woman Ruth by granting her special agricultural privileges. Ruth turns to Boaz and asks, "Why have you made an effort to recognize me, when I am a stranger?" But the words literally translate as, "Why do you claim to know me when I am unknowable?" Indeed, this is the greatest offense. To claim to know someone is to claim to have him or her all figured out, when what we all want is not to be sized up and patronized but to be explored.

To sustain novelty in our modern relationships, it's important to introduce new sides of ourselves to our lovers on a regular basis. Some ways of accomplishing this are straightforward. Others are more creative. Once a middle-aged widow told me what had kept her marriage so vibrant for so many years. "I had one great secret," she confided. "I always gave my husband something to look forward to. Not just year to year, or even month to month, but day to day. For example, I used to go to his office a few times a week, for no good reason at all. Just to close the door behind me and start kissing him and sitting astride him, telling him I had a surprise in store that night when he got home. Sometimes the surprise was nothing more than a sexy outfit I had bought. Other times it was a rare bottle of wine. Once I even arranged for us to go skinny-dipping in a local hotel, late at night, where no one would see us but where it was still dangerous. These were little things, but they always gave him something to look forward to. Understand?" You bet I understood.

Eve, of course, went a bit too far in trying to keep things interesting. If only she had taken Adam skinny-dipping, we might still be living in the Garden.

Mastery, "Munchery," and Mystery

Here's another way of looking at wonder. We humans have three responses when faced with an object of true beauty: mastery, munchery (yes, I invented the word), and mystery. Mastery: As soon as we see something spectacular, we have to have it, to know all about it, to conquer it. Munchery: We have to enjoy it, consume it, partake of its pleasure, and use it to our advantage. Mystery: We're compelled to stand in awe of the spectacle and allow it to move us. I would argue that the most soulful response when we are confronted with anything awe-inspiring is simply to behold it in wonder. When Moses sees God in the burning bush, his first reaction is to remove his shoes and turn away. He dared not defile the wondrous sight he was witnessing.

Imagine hiking through a wintry forest and coming upon a majestic, snow-covered mountain vista. How would you see it? Would you see it as a climbing challenge, as a great place to build a ski resort, or simply as a gift for your eyes to behold? Indeed, I believe that these three reactions are the product of three different human mind-sets: insecurity, selfishness, and holiness.

The insecure person sees the mountain and immediately is overtaken by his insecurity. He feels small in its presence and experiences an immature desire to prove his superiority over it. The selfish person sees the mountain and asks, "How can I derive enjoyment from it? How can I make it serve my ends?" For him the end goal to everything is always his own pleasure. He is the classical aesthete; so long as he can partake of its pleasures without bringing harm to it, he is satisfied. But when the third person sees the mountain, his response is not to think of his insecurities, nor even to think of himself. He thinks of the *mountain*. He isn't threatened by it, nor does he need to exploit it. He is just joyous that it *is*. Here is a person who responds out of a sense of wonder and holiness. He is moved by the splendor of the world, by its magic and mystery. Watching a beautiful sunset, he allows the sun's rays to illuminate his soul; walking through a luscious garden, he drinks in its beauty; hearing a beautiful melody, he allows it to permeate his being.

Let us extend the analogy to the world of contemporary dating. Seeing a beautiful woman, a man can have the same three responses. The first might be a compulsion to have her. Her beauty makes him feel insignificant, so he has to conquer her. He shows off to get her, and then when he gets her he shows her off to others. It's his way of saying, "You cannot outshine me. I'm better than you. If I want something, I have the power to get it."

The second response is subtly different. Spot a beautiful woman walking by, and our friend the aesthete might also desire to sleep with her, but not so much to conquer her as to pleasure himself. To him she is an object that can provide pleasure. He doesn't have to have her so much as use her; after sex he's happy to let her go on her way (he may even be glad to be rid of her).

But in the third response, a woman of great beauty—whether physical, intellectual, or spiritual; this man is attracted by all three—will only elicit awe, not acquisitive desire. He may want to be near her, to interact with her, but it is never his desire to *have* her, to dominate or use her.

Awe, majesty, and rapture are essential to falling in love because they mean that one is capable of stopping in one's tracks and becoming transfixed by the virtues of another. Those who are always lunging forward, trying to make an impression, to make their mark or possess someone else, cannot fall deeply in love, because they have never devoted themselves to selfless appreciation. Without wonder, you will be one of those cynics who forever complain that no one is good enough for them.

The wonder of the attraction between men and women is just that: It is full of inexplicable and unpredictable mystery, awe, magic, and miracle. As such, it can sweep you away. As a force that defies rational explanation, love has the ability to overpower you, to make you fall, and gladly.

Wonder breeds many other positive reactions: respect, gratitude, joy. Wonder is what rescues you from the superficial and gives you perspective. And the very act of standing back in wonder, literally but also metaphorically, allows room for another person to join you in your space. Those who can never stop playing the role of the chaser, the examiner, the judge, or the inspector are doing themselves in. They're preventing themselves from being impressed and leaving no room in their lives for anyone but their own cold, calculating selves.

5. Compatibility

Dear Rabbi Shmuley,

My dear baby brother just announced his engagement to a woman he has known for just short of three weeks. What is he doing? Could there be anything more ruinous to his bright and shining prospects for the future? He knows so little about this woman—and she is fairly religious, so she refuses to live together for even a week before the marriage. They haven't even had sex, for goodness' sake. How can they possibly know if they are compatible, both sexually and otherwise? I just worry about him! What if he marries her and then realizes that she is not the one?

—Suspicious Sis

Suspicious Sis might well have been Adam's older and justifiably concerned sibling. My response to her was just about the same thing I'd have written back to Adam's sister. Here's my letter:

Dear Sis,

First of all, I am one of those strange people who actually believe that all men and women are overwhelmingly compatible. To be sure there are exceptions, but they just prove the rule. By and large, the basic attraction between male and female—not the particular qualities of any one man or woman—is what ensures that the sexes still gravitate toward each other. The mere fact that one is male and the other female is the strongest possible sign of compatibility.

I know this idea isn't in vogue. I know that if you ask the average woman, she will deny that it's simply his manhood that draws her to him. It's rather his kindness, or his devotion, or his Paul Newman blue eyes. Men, particularly, will say that they are attracted to a woman's looks, and that therefore not every woman attracts them. One man will say that only a woman with big assets attracts him, another that he dates only younger women.

Suppose a woman marries a man, call him Daniel, citing his calmness, gentle nature, and youthful good looks as the reason for her love. And suppose Daniel then goes through ten years of terrible business misfortune, rendering him no longer calm, rather less gentle, and old before his time. Is his wife still likely to love him and remain married to him? The answer, in most cases, would be yes. Most of the fine women I know would persevere and remain devoted to their husbands in situations like this, helping them through their problems. Now consider this: Instead of a troubled career, imagine that Daniel is successful in business and that he and his wife lead a blissful life together. Then, one day, he arrives home in a skirt and bra and tells his wife, "Honey, I have a surprise for you. I'm no longer Daniel—call me Danielle. I've become a woman, but I still love you, and I want to remain married to you." Would his wife stick around, with her calm, gentle, devoted partner, who now has an hourglass figure to boot? You know the answer. Every woman you know would be out the door. In the end, it wasn't Daniel's kindness or concern that won his wife over. It was the fact that he was a man.

My second point is this: There is no such thing as the "best" person to marry. Every human being is special in his or her own way and is of infinite value.

The issue of sexual compatibility, which has become so important a question in modern-day relationships, is, to me, positively absurd. Conventional wisdom says that a couple must have sex before marriage to discover whether or not they are sexually compatible. Even more preferable, it's said, is for each to have sex with various partners before marriage, in order to ensure that they're both making an informed decision. But those who make this claim are wrong. Why? Because in the end we are all sexual creatures. It is only the comparison that causes the problem. Do we make tests to ensure that couples are eating-compatible? Breathing-compatible? No. Nor do we need such tests for sex. Rather, a couple like your baby brother and his fiancée should grow into their sexual life together, learn from each other, and create their own compatibility, their own language.

The reason so many people, especially men, complain of sexual incompatibility with their wives is that too many men don't take the time to build sexual intimacy in their marriages. We are all different, but within every one of us there lurks the potential for sexual passion and excitement. Too many husbands opt for quick, uninteresting sexual fixes. Whenever I meet a man who complains that his wife isn't interested in sex, I tell him, "If you don't take the time to heat up the oven, don't complain when the dish is half-baked."

So stop worrying about whom your brother is dating and contemplate the kind of person he is. When each partner in a relationship is leaning inward toward the other, when both partners' desire is to please each other and make each other feel intensely desirable, a marriage is sure to flourish. Tell him to be a good husband, attentive and devoted to the woman he marries, and you will see that he and his wife will always be happy.

Hoping to see you at the wedding and then with the nieces and nephews.

Rabbi Shmuley

There's nothing wrong with hoping for compatibility in love, but as my letter suggests, the preoccupation with compatibility has led us in the wrong direction. We obsess over superficial similarities, finding someone whose tastes in music, film, fashion, food, or finance match ours; whose tax bracket or body type or sexual fetishes mirror our own. But all this emphasis on our tastes, tastes formed before we met this potential lover, is both distracting and degrading. When we use ourselves as the standard by which we judge the opposite sex, we are engaged in a pointless exercise. Instead of looking for a joyful complement to our own personalities, we're looking for a stunt double.

In our narcissistic age, it's no surprise how easily we've fallen in love with ourselves. If your primary concern in finding a mate is compatibility, the best thing I can suggest is that you spend less time trying to replicate your old ways and devote yourself instead to opening yourself up to someone with new ways that will broaden your own. As long as a couple share a set of basic, dearly held values—whether they include social conscience, religious conviction, a passion for learning, or love of the arts—they are well on their way to soaring together.

Another key is having a shared vision of the future. Whereas many people talk about past and present sources of compatibility—we're both from Connecticut, we both have demanding and compelling jobs—I find more reason to be hopeful for a couple who both want children. Where you've been and where you are now aren't nearly so important as where you want to go together. Call it shared destiny or the promised land, but it's your vision of the future that needs to be in sync if in twenty-five years you want to be looking back happily together.

I came to this understanding of compatibility late. At one point while Debbie and I were dating, I became distraught by the thought that we might not be compatible, because we seemed so different. Matters came to a head when I took Debbie on a helicopter ride in Miami, which I found exciting but she found positively terrifying. So I sought the counsel of a trusted rabbi friend. I said, "I like her, but there's nothing in common. I mean, zero. I'm talkative. She's quiet. I'm adventurous. She's reserved. For example, she's afraid of helicopters and I'm not."

He eventually interrupted my callow list of complaints. "So you still haven't told me why you're not compatible. Didn't you say you want to be rabbi to students and that she wants to work with you with students too? You said that after your parents' divorce, the most important thing for you was building a joyous and stable family life. Didn't you say she wanted the same thing? And that having kids was more important than the freedom to run to Paris on weekends? Sounds pretty darn compatible to me.

"Of course," he added, "if you break this relationship because of the helicopter thing, I will completely understand. We can all see the importance of husbands and wives taking regular helicopter flights together." So I left his office with my tail between my legs and married Debbie shortly thereafter. We have been married now, thank God, for thirteen years and have never again needed to be on a helicopter together.

When God created Eve, he was creating for Adam a compatible partner, bone from his bones, flesh from his flesh. They were not identical but complementary. There has to be that dynamic tension we saw between the line and the circle. Otherwise, why would we need each other in the first place? We might as well all be lines or all be circles, and let's see how far civilization advances that way.

If you're to build a loving relationship with someone, the person you choose must also be your equal. Love without a feeling of equality is always tinged with compassion (at best) or pity. It can even be an excuse to wield power and control. Love with someone you perceive as lesser inevitably creates a caste system within the relationship, and the inevitable result will be revolution. Similarly, if you try to forge love with someone you feel to be your superior, you're certain to spend a lifetime battling insecurity, misery, and pain.

What we're all after is love with an equal, a fascinating, awe-inspiring equal. In other words, two wings can lift the bird only if they are equal in strength.

6. Selflessness

In many respects, the central theme of Adam and Eve's love story is selflessness. Selfishness kills our ability to fall in love, because those who are full of themselves have no room for another in their lives. More specifically, the story is about how the serpent of selfishness manifests desire and seduces our egos to focus our attention inward rather than outward. It's selfishness that draws Eve to the fruit. She wants, as we all want, to have the wisdom of God, to be God. We want *more*. But in the end that desire is insatiable.

The serpent tempts Eve with an irresistible offer: In eating the fruit from the Tree of Knowledge, not only will she taste immortality—"You certainly will not die!" (Genesis 3:4)—but she can be omniscient. "Really, God knows that on the day you eat from it, your eyes will be opened, and you will be like God, knowing good and evil" (Genesis 3:4).

Her eyes, indeed, are opened to the distinction between the self and the other. Suddenly she, like God, can distinguish between good and evil. Now the world turns from objective to subjective: from the way it is to the way *I* see it. Before she partook of the fruit, attraction between the sexes was based on virtue rather than beauty, character rather than personality, a good heart rather than good skin. Before the sin, Eve would look at Adam and ask, "Is this a good person that I can share my life with, and can I see the two of us together for the next, say, seven or eight hundred years?" After the sin it became, "Is this someone whom I will have fun with and who will make my skin tingle this Saturday night? And will my friends approve?"

Eve's total submission to the subjectivity of her senses is conveyed in the next verse. Eve "saw that the fruit was good to eat and *desirable* to the eyes and that the tree was attractive . . . " (Genesis 3:5). Suddenly, it's all about outward appearance, about the desires of the senses, about feeding oneself. The focus has shifted. It's no longer what Adam can give but what Eve *desires*. It's no longer "Is Adam a good man?" but "Is he appealing to me?" But, of course, falling in love means that the focus has to be on the object of your love. Like making love, it's something that must be done with someone else. Making love with yourself is called masturbation.

But the selfishness was not entirely Eve's fault. According to the ancient rabbis, it had already been evinced through the poor and selfish conduct of Adam, when he engaged in the worst of all male sexual sins, namely, a selfish desire to climax well before his wife was ready to do so. When asked why the serpent speaks to Eve and not Adam, some of the ancient rabbis explain that Adam and Eve had just made love, and that Adam—typical selfish male!—was asleep. True to his linear masculine nature, he went straight for his own satisfaction. Of course, this also implies that Eve was not sexually satisfied; Adam had his own needs attended to and that was all he cared about. So unable to fall asleep, Eve wandered off and was met by the serpent. Even in Eden, the male inability to be selfless eventually led to a tragic end. In other words, selfishness begets selfishness.

Try a Little Selflessness

Once they understand the ramifications of their actions, Adam and Eve take steps to make up for their selfishness. After taking her famous bite, Eve immediately brings the fruit to share with Adam. Biblical scholars have suggested that Eve is panicking in this passage, that she runs to share the fruit with Adam because she fears she will die by herself, alone. Now, why does Adam eat it? He knows it's wrong. He eats it because he decides that if Eve is going to die, he wants to die with her. He can't live without her. So he is prepared to bite the fruit, and the bullet. As a demonstration of his love for her, he is willing to make the ultimate sacrifice. It is a phenomenal demonstration of his burgeoning capacity to love.

Adam makes another potent gesture of sacrifice on behalf of his wife later in the story, which shows that he was prepared even to risk his relationship with God for Eve's sake. Notice that God first commands Adam not to eat from the Tree of Knowledge, warning him that if he or Eve should partake of its fruit, they will die. But Adam is concerned that Eve might touch the tree, fall in love with the fruit, and eat it. So, to God's admonition that they must not taste the forbidden fruit, he has the presumption to add his own prohibition—against even *touching* it, lest Eve be tempted and fall prey to its allure. We know this because in Genesis 3:2 we hear Eve tell the serpent what Adam says God told him: "But of the fruit of the tree that is in the middle of the garden, God said, 'Do not eat it, and do not [even] touch it, or else you will die.'" And yet, when we heard directly what God had told Adam, it did not include the touching part.

Notwithstanding the role it played in the birth of this cataclysmic sin, though, Adam's gesture here is an inspirational lesson for lovers everywhere. Adam knows it's wrong to eat of the tree;

God made it more than clear that dire consequences would follow. But when Eve starts to cry, her pleading, desperate tone of voice makes her request irresistible. Aware that he is facing certain oblivion and divine disfavor, Adam nevertheless responds to Eve's entreaty, in one of the unforgettable moments in this greatest of all love stories and a true sign of selflessness.

Why Women Love Bad Boys and Men Chase Beauty

Once Eve got a look at the serpent, of course, Adam became the nice guy, and nice guys haven't had a fighting chance since. From then on, the curse of Adam and Eve dictated that as far as relationships were concerned, women would always fall for bad boys ("He's a challenge! It's exciting!") and men would always fall for looks. ("What a hottie.")

I see it all the time.

My friend Jessica is a smart, able, and grounded woman who came to me seeking a match. Her own lack of time and opportunity, and a small scope of potential mates, led her to ask me for help, and I was happy to lend a hand. I immediately thought of Alan, a kind and compassionate friend of mine, an obsessive reader who visited his bedridden mother almost nightly. I told Jessica about Alan. "Well, Shmuley." She yawned. "Let's see. Kind and giving and visits his mother. Hmmm. I'd really love to go out with him, but Wednesday I really need to exfoliate the soles of my feet, and Saturday night I'll be changing the kitty litter."

Cut to two weeks later. Having learned from experience, I tracked down a man with piercings in six extremities, a little black book that needs its own computerized cataloguing system, and knowledge of every dark bar in the East Village. I called Jessica and gave her the rundown. "Well, Shmuley," she said, "I was planning to redeem that all-expenses-paid trip I won to the Bahamas, but I can give that up. Can he meet me tonight?"

It's a time-honored tradition. Catherine could never give up Heathcliff; Rhett would invariably win out over Ashley; ER's Dr. Ross (George Clooney) is always fighting off his female patients' advances, while Dr. Green (Anthony Edwards) takes the train home to eat Chinese takeout on a Friday night. Women like bad boys. So many women, like Eve before them, are forever being seduced by snakes. Sure, they also enjoy the company of the good guys, that is, when they need to move a few boxes on a Sunday afternoon. (Next time Jessica's getting ready to move into a new apartment, remind me to warn poor, unsuspecting Alan.)

Meanwhile, whenever I tell a man about a woman I have in mind for him, his first question is, "What's she look like, Shmuley?" "Well, she has the heart of Mother Teresa and the mind of Marie Curie," I always respond. Then I snap my fingers in front of their face to recapture their attention.

So why do so many women fall only for bad boys? And why do so many men fall only for pretty faces (or figures)? Like so much else, I believe that this all started in Eden. God's curse to Adam was that he would have to perform backbreaking labor to redeem himself, so it's no coincidence that even today what men want in a relationship is peace and tranquillity, often in the form of a beautiful woman to gaze upon. God's curse to Eve was to make her the object of that gaze, a figure of whom only passive beauty would be expected. So women are attracted to men who can bring excitement and amusement to their lives.

This is a problem that's made worse by modern culture. Today most men act as if they came into the world a big zero. And instead of looking for affirmation in the arms of an understanding woman, they try to redeem themselves from the great abyss of anonymity through an athletic-style pursuit of success, convinced that they're only as great as the wallet they carry, or the LSAT scores they've racked up, or the golf handicap they can boast. For relief from this demoralizing power chase, men go looking for an end to the pain through dangerous behavior. Even the most famous masculine figures of our time seemed to harbor a death wish: Ernest Hemingway, facing down dangerous game in the jungles of Africa; Ted Turner, facing down monsoons in his racing yacht; Richard Branson, dropping from balloons into the middle of the Atlantic Ocean; even Bill Clinton, endangering his lofty position for a little taste of sexual danger. These men court death, literally or figuratively, because of the peace it promises. (And if it's "the little death" they're after—

la petite mort, as the French call orgasm—it can become a down-right addiction.)

When it comes to choosing women, these men show signs of a kind of addictive behavior. They look for the same kind of simple, overwhelming rush they get from snowboarding or wave-running or vodka tonics. They don't want to have to struggle to analyze the attraction. They want beauty that can give them an instant high. But like a heroin addict who seeks to escape the pain of life, not by getting his life in order but by taking another dose, these men numb themselves for a while with one hit of beauty, then go in search of a new high once they've developed a tolerance for—that is, grown bored with—what they have.

As for the womanly sin of seeking out bad boys, many will explain it as a woman's desire to be a savior to a man. *Here is a rough diamond I can cut and polish.* There's a certain truth to this, but I believe there's another, deeper force at work. In the same way men miss feeling they're special simply for who they are, women miss having the thrill and excitement that men seem to get out of life. They want to be rescued from the yoke of passivity. I can't tell you how many times I've asked a woman why she loves her man, and the first words out of her mouth have been "because he makes me laugh" or "we have such an exciting life." Saddled as they've been for centuries with the task of keeping the home fires burning, they want a man who knows how to light his own fire. A ride on the freeway on a Harley-Davidson, a thirty-six-hour date of dining and debauchery, a bar brawl with drunk Russians in the East Village—you're not going to get that kind of rush dating a bookkeeper, but a drummer in a seedy blues band is another story.

The only trouble is, sooner or later we all grow up. And when we do, we find that our old character-type fetishes suddenly don't serve us all that well. The bad boy doesn't clean up all that well; the glittery beauty turns out to be a bore. Instead, men must transform their need for mind-numbing beauty into an appreciation for inner beauty. And women must discover that the greatest thrills come not from bad-boy antics, which often as not lead to tears, but from the rush of having a man who makes them feel like a woman.

The Serpent as a Symbol of Desire

Before we move on, let's take another close look at that serpent. The serpent represents desire, especially for material things, and his story echoes the downfall of many relationships today. How did it happen? When we meet them, of course, Adam and Eve have all of Paradise, the most beautiful Garden, before them; they also have each other. In short, they have every reason to feel satisfied. This was the original case of "love is all you need." What more could they have asked for?

Came the serpent, though, and all bets were off. The serpent is the symbol of insatiable desire, of never feeling satisfied. As the ancient rabbis pointed out, God's words to the serpent—"on your belly you shall crawl, and dust you shall eat, all the days of your life" (Genesis 3:14)—doom the snake never to have a satisfying meal. You will permanently hunger. To us, the snake is an instructive symbol of the dangers of materialism, of the endless pursuit of sexual variety, indeed, of unchecked ambition in all things. The serpent says: *You've gotten it all wrong: Innocence will get you nowhere. But knowledge—in the form of experience, judgment, possessions, fulfilling your own desires—that's where it's at.*

We teach each other the same bad lessons all the time: You need experience. Find another man. Date another woman. More is better. Like a snake that eats a mouse whole—never tastes it, never grows fatter—we have countless sensual experiences but none that edify and enrich us. We shed relationships like so many layers of dried skin, untouched and unchanged. We greet a constant parade of members of the opposite sex but always feel cheated, always suspect that someone better is just around the corner. Those bitten by the serpent are doomed to live to work, not work to live. Their lives become endlessly lonely, as they slither through the cracks and crevices of their dry world.

Among singles today, there are two kinds of people who have been bitten by the serpent, two kinds of superficial daters who cannot fall in love. First, there are those who date only for pleasure. What they're looking for is sex without connection, sensual pleasure without real emotion. And whether they realize it or not, they're using people for their own satisfaction. Eve, who partook of the Tree of Knowledge because it appealed to her senses, is the prototype for this modern-day sensualist, but men and women alike share the title today.

The second kind of dater dates not for pleasure but to enhance his or her feelings of control. Driven by deep insecurity, such persons are so preoccupied with their own thirst for dominance that they make every relationship a matter of winning, whether through sexual conquest or by dating someone and suddenly breaking it off, as if to prove a capacity to do without love. This is the premature rejecter, the man or woman who dumps a new love just as things are starting to go well, as a (futile) way to remind everyone who's boss. Adam—he who lost his Paradise through a woman's wandering eye (not to mention his own failure of responsibility toward his wife)— was the actor this part was written for.

As we've seen, Adam and Eve received punishments that fit their crimes, punishments that go right to the heart, demonstrating God's sense of the ironic. Eve, who fell victim to sensual pleasure, finds that the joy of childbirth will forever be mixed with physical agony. "And to the woman He said, 'I will make the pain of your childbirth great, and also your longing will be for your husband' (Genesis 3:16). The second half of the sentence—and it is a *sentence,* isn't it?—notes that Eve's life will also be marked by longing for a man. In other words, the empty aesthetic life will eventually leave her hungering for intimacy. The lesson for us: Those who engage in relationships solely for the purpose of pleasure will, in the long term, find pain instead. They will date without commitment until the pain of loneliness overwhelms them.

And Adam, whose base desire is to be the *Übermensch,* the ruler of his domain, is sentenced to work the soil, giving him "anguish all the days of his life." All his attempts to subdue nature will be met with fierce resistance. Even when he plants wheat he will grow chaff, reminding him that he will always be subservient to God. *Try as you might to conquer and dominate others,* God is telling us, *you will always be frustrated in your quest.* You say, "I don't need anybody. I'm made of steel. And I will purposely date those who are subservient to me, so I can call the shots." But lo and behold, insecurity will dog your heels, and you will yearn to share your life with an equal who is your complement.

The Silver Lining

Within this dark cloud there is a silver lining, for Adam and Eve are exiled *together*. Once they're expelled from Paradise, all they have in their alien new world is each other. And as we're about to see, that adversity, their shared experience, brings them back together. They become each other's salvation.

The lesson here for the modern Adam and Eve is about sacrifice. *Sacrifice?* Singles of the Me Generation—the self-help generation, spoiled Gen Xers and Nexters—recoil at that word. But as we've seen, the very nature of romance, the pledging of oneself to *one* exclusive mate, involves a kind of sacrifice. We compromise with our lovers, creating a space between us in which to share our desires rather than trying to dominate the arena. Even the greatest lovers, the most passionate and compatible couples, demand some mutual sacrifice; there is no union without compromise. And the sacrifices we make on behalf of our lovers endear them to us. Their presence in our life is compensation for the things we surrender, which are of far less significance.

When we give ourselves over wholly to a new relationship, we honor the choice we make by closing the door to other options. Many contemporary singles try to string as many casual lovers or prospects along for as long as possible, trying vainly to avoid having to make a choice. But such selfish manipulation can lead only to unhappiness, for he who is pledged to too many is pledged to none at all. Did Adam and Eve try to cheat on each other? Had God intended trysts and affairs, he would probably have put two couples in the Garden. If you aren't prepared to give up the rest of the opposite sex for the sake of your beloved, then you have no hope of falling in love. And as long as you find yourself dwelling on better options, you have no hope of remaining in even the most promising relationship.

In ancient Israel, sacrificial rituals entailed the slaughter of an animal upon God's holy altar. Similarly, for all of us, committing to a relationship should involve killing our beastly selfishness, and our other lower desires, at the altar of love. We must slaughter our animal rage and anger, our insatiable lust for material possessions or sexual experiences, everything that feeds us only physically and not spiritually. In modern terms, this can be as simple as a husband being patient in bed until his wife enjoys the sexual experience, rather than charging ahead for his own pleasure. It can mean that when a husband loses his job, his wife's first thought is not "There goes our trip to Rome," but comforting her man. When you look at it this way, as Adam and Eve came to look at it after they had been forced out of Eden, love is no sacrifice at all.

7. Differentiation

Another aspect of the male-female dynamic established in the story of Adam and Eve is the importance of the difference between the sexes. When God saw Adam's loneliness, He could have provided him with what might logically have seemed like a more compatible human companion, another male. And they could have become great buds, giving each other high-fives and butting heads together; they could have turned the Garden into one big Iron John retreat. Instead, by creating a female, he bestowed on humankind an appreciation for the importance of difference in relationships.

God creates Eve as an *eizer kenegdo*, an opposite who is his helpmate, a complement who is different. She has to be his opposite, for if they were merely the same, there would be no grounds for attraction. If both had the same skills and qualities, neither would have made it. Eve has no interest in dirtying her hands in the Garden, toiling away like Adam. She desires not dominance, but pleasure. She has no interest in ruling the world. For his part, Adam lacks Eve's curiosity, her desire for sensual pleasure, her craving for forbidden fruit. He is stiffer, more goal-oriented. But as two different people, with two different interests, they are able together to be whole.

They also reflect the attributes of the line and the circle, and the need for both in a relationship. Adam is the doer; he deals with the nuts and bolts of their domestic life in Eden. He's the worker bee, the line focused on the forward march of their history. Adam is the strict disciplinarian who heeds God's call not to eat from the Tree of Knowledge. But there is something deeply Spartan in Adam's soul; he lacks a softer side. This, in turn, is supplied by Eve. She is the circle, the one who gives birth to new life. She is reflective and introspective. *What else is out there?* she muses, and next thing you know she's plucking a tree. Any good relationship today reflects both these divine energies: the historical and the creative, the immanent and the transcendent, the specific and the general, the spontaneous and the constant.

The tendency for people to look for lovers too much like themselves shows how much we overlook the positive effect difference can have on relationships. This is the problem with men and women whose lives are filled with friends of the opposite sex. In this new age of social and gender equality, of opposite-sex *indifference*, men and women have ceased to be the object of attraction for each other. When a young man looks to a female best friend as someone to comfort him in moments of pain, to share his hopes and aspirations with, *yet never sees her as a lover*, he's seeing her as a man in a woman's body. Erotic attraction can be maintained, ironically, only where there is a gap, a distance that must be traversed. This allows the couple to remain distinctive and provides for the possibility of constant pursuit. When we're always trying to lean in toward each other, we can never take each other for granted.

In the Orthodox Jewish tradition, men and women are separated from each other in synagogues. Many people believe that this is done to keep the sexes from being tempted or distracted during religious activity. In fact, exactly the opposite is true. We believe that to keep the attraction alive, men and women need distance, both figurative and literal. We don't want to be desensitized to the exciting differences between us. We want always to be leaning toward each other.

The Joy of Difference

Instead of celebrating sameness, which can lead only to monotony and boredom, the relationship of Adam and Eve is a testament to the joy of difference, not just the simple distinctions between man and woman, but the thousands of tiny differences between any two people that excite curiosity and inspire investigation.

Just as some people are drawn again and again to people with whom they're fundamentally incompatible, others allow their own personalities to be subsumed into those of their partners, leading to a weariness that can be deadening. Even in homosexual relationships, personality differences are usually crucial, and in most gay relationships masculine and feminine traits still play a distinct role. Gay or straight, most partnerships work because each partner finds himself or herself undyingly curious about the other. Without that curiosity, that awareness of the intriguing and mysterious otherness of one's partner, no relationship is likely to last.

Some of us get lazy nowadays about accentuating the difference, especially in the bedroom. When I arrived in Texas recently to deliver a lecture, I was picked up at the airport by a gentleman who'd volunteered for the job. It soon became apparent why. He was having marital problems, specifically sexual problems. "We're sexually incompatible," he said. "I had a lot of sex before I married. My wife was a virgin. So we make love, and I always satisfy her. And she admits that. But she doesn't satisfy me. She's too prudish. She can't let go. I need something more kinky. I need a woman who can talk dirty, dress up, get a little wild with me." His problem, as I tried to find a gentle way to tell him (me, gentle?), was that he wasn't taking the time to appreciate his wife's different approach to lovemaking—to understand it, work with it, blend it with his into a third way. After all, women generally have a stronger sex drive than men; they just work differently. A woman's sexuality is like that of a piece of coal, burning from within; it needs to be fanned into a flame. That should be the highly coveted role of the man, who ideally gets to corroborate his own masculinity—gets to "feel like a man"—by transforming his seemingly modest wife into a sexual tigress. Conversely, she gets to feel like a woman, corroborating her own desirability by having the undivided attention and focused endeavor of her man. But that can happen only if men and women alike start seeing their basic differences as a challenge, not a hindrance.

8. Shared Experience

The eighth component is the happy sum of all the rest: the importance of a life lived together. Love isn't something discovered and sealed in an instant; rather, it's something that develops, deepens, and strengthens through a couple's shared experiences. The more time you spend together, the more openness you share; the more conversations you have and events you experience as a couple, the deeper in love you'll fall.

In addition to becoming one flesh through lovemaking and one spirit through shared spiritual goals, you must also become one mind through shared memories and one hearth through shared joys and pain. Hence, a long life of shared experience is the very fabric of love, weaving its intertwined threads into a single brilliant pattern. Love may have a qualitative aspect, but it also has a quantitative dimension. Look at your time together as an investment: The more you deposit, the greater the returns. See it as an occasion for nurturing love from genesis to fruition and beyond.

Shared experience fosters the love. Adam and Eve didn't date for forty years before they fell in love and married. They didn't even date for forty days and forty nights. No, their commitment came first; their love followed. When first they met, they saw that all the fundamental components were there, as we've already seen. And because of that they committed to each other, *then* fell in love. This is counterintuitive, especially these days, but it's crucial. *It is commitment that makes us fall in love:* commitment to daily and mundane shared experiences, domestic chores, the breakfast drill, casually holding hands in the park, advising each other about problems at work, coming to depend on each other, building a life together, raising kids together, and jointly navigating the vicissitudes of life. Like the hooks and eyes of a woman's dress, it's the tiny, seemingly insignificant details of everyday life that serve to fasten a man and a woman together until they begin to feel inseparable.

This is what all the lonely singles today, who date and date searching for perfection, ultimately don't understand. Love can't precede commitment. Sure, you can be strongly attracted before commitment. You can be "in like." But you aren't yet in love. Think of it: If one of your friends told you, "I just love my job; I start next week," wouldn't you think it absurd? Rather, you fall in love with your job over time. As you and the job grow together and define your experience, you come to love what it has become. The same is true of sharing a life. You choose a person who seems worthy and likely, and then the two of you grow together, ever more deeply into love.

If you, as a single person, are merely biding your time, waiting to fall in love before you feel ready to commit, I'd counsel you that love won't happen until you commit. We're so cautious today, unprepared to take a leap of faith until we have certainty. Yet as we've seen, certainty—monotony, predictability, sameness—can often be a recipe for disaster. It's a husband's certainty that his wife would never leave him, that she's a mountain he's already conquered, that leads him to believe he can have an affair and get away with it. "Well, my wife is totally won over," he thinks. "My work is done here. But that stranger over there, gee, I wonder if I could get *her*." That constant gap of difference, that little bit of uncertainty, is what keeps us from taking each other for granted. It may seem like a paradox, but it's true: In the most successful relationships, uncertainty actually contributes to the security of the partners' commitment, by pushing each to strengthen the partnership.

The great secret of falling in love, I believe, is that it can be summoned. You can actually decide to fall in love with someone, and your heart will follow. We must learn to be active in governing our passions, rather than being governed by them. Husbands come to me all the time, complaining, "I fell out of love with my wife. I'm no longer interested in my wife. She doesn't turn me on. That's why I'm having an affair." I tell them, "With all due respect, sir, you're being lazy. You *can* fall back in love with your wife if you want to, if you direct your heart to do so. But you don't want to. What if an employee told you, 'I'm sorry, but I'm no longer interested in working today'? What would you tell your children if they came home from school, propped themselves up in front of the TV for six hours, and said, 'Homework just isn't turning me on tonight. I don't feel like it.' I presume you'd tell them, 'Well, make yourself feel like it.

Have some respect for yourself, and make yourself put a little effort into it. Nothing good comes easily.'"

We have it in our own power to nurture love in our hearts, if only we set our minds to it. Those who fail to see this, I believe, have lost faith in their own basic ability to grow as human beings, to change and improve. They take the easy way out, looking only for signs that their new lover echoes the old things they already know about themselves. But when the two find they're not interested in growing together, and the magic wears off, they end up parting and wondering why love always seems to fail them. The answer? Because they failed to build it together. This is why I always say I don't believe in love at first sight. Would you believe in the young person who, when presented with a flesh wound, decides to "become a doctor at first sight"?

Love is an amazing blessing, but it takes work. As M. Scott Peck wrote in *The Road Less Traveled*, "If an act is not one of work or courage, then it is not an act of love. There are no exceptions. The principal form that the work of love takes is attention. When we love another we give him or her our attention; we attend to that person's growth."

Love Is Like Olive Oil

In the Talmud, it is observed that an olive releases its oil only when pressed. In the same manner, lovers release their richest love after they've been pressed, once life's challenging times have put them through the wringer. It's a life lived together that nurtures the greatest love.

Adam and Eve, it's safe to say, had rather a life-changing experience together. When they fell from the Garden, it was as if their company were downsized, their house foreclosed, their furniture repossessed, their SUV stolen, all in the same fateful week. Talk about stress. And yet they survived and thrived. The adversity strengthened them. They went on to settle in another neighborhood, sire a bunch of kids, live rich and rewarding lives, leaving the mistakes of the Garden as far behind them as possible while never forgetting the hard lessons learned there. Adam and Eve lived to the ripe old age of 930. I would speculate that it was after being expelled from Eden that they truly fell in love.

What I find interesting about the story is that it's the second chance they get together that helps Adam and Eve reach a deeper place spiritually with one another. Couples today need to find ways to nurture their love, to ponder their own lives and the lessons they've learned together. Not just in retrospect, at their fiftieth anniversary celebration; not just at events like birthdays or children's graduations; but randomly, whenever the spirit moves them: flowers to celebrate the first harvest from their backyard garden or a homemade audiotape of their favorite songs to celebrate losing five pounds. Or just a long, slow, and meaningful kiss accompanied by those three immortal words, "What's for dinner?"

It's the little occasions that give our lives their texture, that bind us together ever more surely. Memories, reminiscing about special times together, reaching goals set together, penciling in your kids' heights each year on the same wall, seeing each other in your children—a husband and wife's love is a finely woven sweater, dozens of years and thousands of tiny strands in the making. The trick is to build more and more strands every single day. Some strands are stronger than others. A passionate sex life, for example, or making each other always feel desirable is much stronger than talking only about bills and other functional obligations. But every detail of life is important, and even the petty details can be seen as moments of connection instead of minor annoyances. Even the weakest threads in the sweater—moments of weakness, of distraction, even of infidelity—can be overcome if the fabric is strong enough to support itself.

In the end, it is the most intimate thing two people can do: to go through life together. When our simplest moments are consecrated by love, they can become an eternity. All of these lessons can be found in the biblical stories, and all of us have it in our power to live a biblical love.

10

Mental Virginity

An Idea Whose Time Should Come Back

Marriage has many pains, but celibacy has no pleasures.

—Samuel Johnson

It is an infantile superstition of the human spirit that virginity would be thought a virtue and not a barrier that separates ignorance from knowledge.

—Voltaire

You have kissed and nibbled and poked and prodded and worried me there so often that my virginity was lost in the shuffle.

—Vladimir Nabokov, *Ada*

An eighteen-year-old woman I'll call Serena, who lives in Southern California's San Fernando Valley, called *LoveLine,* a radio show that gives advice about relationships and sex, on a night when I was a panelist. Sometimes, in the middle of calls, the co-hosts Adam Carolla and Dr. Drew Pinsky, ask the panelists to guess what's troubling the caller, and afterward to offer guidance.

Serena said she had intimacy issues, that she found it difficult to enjoy sex with her boyfriend. In our *Sex and the City* culture, this made her feel like a freak of nature, as if she were deformed in some way, marred by her lack of pure sexual desire. She just couldn't get into the physical act of sex. The other panelists and I went through our catalog of plausible explanations: Was she in physical pain? "No." Was her boyfriend pushing for sex too early? "No, in fact, I was the one who initiated sex between us." Was she truly attracted to her boyfriend, or was she having to force those feelings? "No, I've always been attracted to him, and actually cared a great deal about him as a friend before we ever became intimate."

Something wasn't adding up. Finally, I asked about her sexual history, a question that not only cleared up the mystery but also released a torrent of long-repressed tears. As a child, it turned out, Serena had been sexually abused by her father. She had tried for years to block the memory out of her mind, convinced that she could "get over it" and be a normal, sexually healthy human being. But now the memory of the abuse was rearing its head. "I just want to be innocent again," she said, sobbing. "Why was I never allowed to simply be a child?"

Serena's experience was like that of too many others I've seen, a common response among women who have been sexually abused or molested as children. Studies show that girls typically respond in one of two ways. One is to close down their private space, literally and figuratively, closing their hearts along with their ability to be sexual. The other is to be quite free sexually but to compartmentalize the sexual experience and keep it quarantined from their emotional nerve center. Studies also show that women who have been sexually abused at an early age develop a characteristically male approach to sex, separating mind from body when dealing with sexual relationships. This is usually how they coped with the abuse at the time, locking their emotions into a box and in effect telling the offender, "I am powerless to stop you from using my body, but you will never have my heart." In adulthood, they carry the same psychological mechanism over into their romantic lives. The results can be tremendously painful, as they struggle to reconnect what has so long been severed so that they can enjoy an emotionally fulfilling adult relationship.

Though the experience is far less traumatic, I believe that having casual sex with people we don't love can make any of us lose track of the connection between our heart and our body. When sex becomes a random sensual experience instead of the passionate act of soul-fusion it's meant to be, we simply forget how to share intimacy. Later, when we want to use sex to enhance our intimacy, it doesn't work. Once we sever that connection, it can be difficult to reattach. We take intimacy for granted, as if it can be summoned at will. In truth, the sharing of intimacy is one of life's most noble, but most difficult, goals. It requires not only attraction and affection, but security, trust, and faith.

We got another call that night, from a sixteen-year-old—I'll call her Rebecca—who had already had sex with more than ten partners. When asked whether she actually *wanted* to have sex with these men, she got defensive: "Well, they wanted to have sex with me, and if I didn't, they could have easily found a girl who would! You think a guy would stay with a girl who won't sleep with him? Yeah, right!"

Rebecca was sixteen, and she was already more jaded and cynical about love and relationships than many of the forty-year-olds I counsel. She had altogether skipped that wonderful stage of first love. Her voice trembled as she defended the series of choices she had made, which were not, in reality, her choices at all. Rather, they were choices dictated by a society that whispers to young people, and young women in particular, "Grow up, grow up already; you'll be so much more desirable if you show that you can do what the adults do."

It was clear that all Rebecca really needed to hear was that it was okay for her not to have sex. When we told her that she would still be normal and appealing if she opted out of sex until she was ready, you could hear the relief in her voice. All she'd wanted was to be told that, no matter who tried to take it away from her, her innocence was *her own*. And the same is true of all of us.

Virginity Lost and Refound

As I've emphasized throughout this book, one of the reasons so many of us have trouble with love is that we're all too experienced. Too many relationships gone sour have penetrated our tender hearts, rendering them used and abused. Experience has given us too much knowledge; it's violated our private spaces and left our emotional nerve endings raw and exposed. We've all lost our virginity, emotionally. We feel frustrated and in despair, because we fear we can never recover it. And yet the truth is that we can.

"You've been scarred," I told Serena, "but it doesn't have to be permanent. You can restore your innocence—you can heal the wounds—by reclaiming your mental virginity."

Bodily virginity is something that was hallowed by nearly all ancient cultures. From ancient Rome to Mayan and Incan cultures, virgin sacrifices were a fixture of even the most advanced civilizations. And as the center beam of Christianity, virginity retains enormous significance in modern thought. Virginity is still very much hallowed to this day by the Catholic church, a fact that springs, I believe, from the dualistic nature of Christianity. In a belief system in which body and soul are poised in opposition, the carnal act of sex naturally becomes the pollutant of the soul's sanctuary. Jews, on the other hand, believe that virginity, not intercourse, is the sin. As part of a monist tradition that speaks of the union of opposites and the orchestration of halves, Judaism holds that sex is the supreme glue that causes a man and a woman to become one flesh. Judaism has never glorified bodily virginity. As I describe in greater detail in *Kosher Sex*, God's commandment not only to marry and have children, but for spouses to sexually pleasure each other, is a living part of our belief system.

But Judaism has always valued a different kind of virginity, not of the body but of the mind. This can be a meaningful message for anyone searching for love in our jaded age, regardless of religion: The loss of sexual virginity does not necessarily mean the loss of mental virginity. If you can shake off the corrupting touch of cynicism; if you can overcome the ghosts of lovers past; if you are pure of thought, intention, and spirit, then you can proceed through life in joyous possession of your emotional innocence, or mental virginity. I believe that, like the Jews who guarded gold coins in their breast pockets after melting most of their gold to build the Golden Calf, none of us ever completely lets go of this innocence, this private space that belongs only to us.

Learning to recapture our mental virginity, respect it, and draw upon it in all aspects of our lives, especially the romantic aspects, is the challenge.

The Joys of First Love

Think back to your first true love, the first boy or girl who stole your heart, with whom you shared precious intimacies (the least of them sexual). At lectures, when I ask, "What's so special about first love anyway?" I rarely get a tangible answer. More often than not, the question triggers a flood of memories that are visible on people's faces. They go off into a dream world of sorts, as if they have stepped back in time, reliving the ecstasy and the agony of first love. The gaze lasts a moment, and then—snap—reality returns, along with the hard shell of cynicism. Most of the time, people seem abashed about their moment of sentimentality. Certainly you remember. No one forgets his or her first love. That person is unforgettable, and not always because he was the star football player or she was the smartest kid in the class. Rather, first love is about you and your feelings, all so new and fresh. That's why first love is so memorable. And if we want to reclaim something of that innocent experience, we should take a closer look at the feelings that went along with it.

The Seven Lessons of First Love

1. *We experience an enlargement of the self for the first time.* When we are very young, the world revolves around us. When we are hungry or sleepy, we cry, and someone attends to us. As we get older and start to realize that we cannot live in our own sphere forever, our circle expands to include playmates, siblings, neighbors, teachers, and others, and suddenly we discover that we have to share. There follows a period of awkwardness, as we try to reconcile our childish selfishness with the demands of the greater world. And then, typically at the age of fifteen or sixteen, we find someone who—gasp!—makes us *want* to share. We see the chance to expand beyond our own immediate needs and consider someone else's, and actually choose to do so. For

the first time, we experience the joy of genuinely considering someone else's needs before our own.

First love, in short, has showed our ego how to expand beyond ourselves. This is a wonderful thing. Liberated from suffocating self-absorption, we enter adulthood with an exhilarating sense of discovery. *Something beyond me merits my love and attention.* What a powerful discovery!

2. *We experience insatiable knowledge and infinite curiosity about someone else.* Once we've discovered this whole new world, we set out like Lewis and Clark to explore its great undiscovered territories. Until this point in our lives, the pursuit of knowledge has always seemed like something of a burden, associated with tyrannical teachers and the pressures of homework. But when we fall in love, we experience the joy of knowledge. We want to learn everything we can about our new love. No detail is too trivial; the intellectual journey is never cumbersome. It becomes our new obsession, the one and only worthwhile way to spend every waking hour, and plenty of dream time, too.

   Soon, we move from the simple factual stuff—favorite flavors, musical taste, family history—into the more difficult areas: hopes and fears, dreams and doubts, insecurities and strengths, deepest secrets. There is nothing more thrilling or more satisfying than coming to know someone else so wholly, so honestly. *So this is what it's like to be another person,* we think, *and a magnificent, exhilarating other person at that.* It's as if we're being given a key to a room—a key that no one else has. It is an honor, a unique privilege, and we understand and respect that with complete sincerity.

3. *We are free to be vulnerable for the first time.* As children we vent our feelings freely and easily, and yet, as we reach our teen years, most of us have begun treating even our parents as people not to be fully trusted. With no one to share our deepest feelings with, we imprison ourselves emotionally. Then, suddenly, a creature comes along to whom we want to unburden ourselves. The ramparts come down, the archers are relieved of their posts, and the citadel is transformed into a bazaar. The act of sharing fulfills our natural human need for confession. We experience the emotional release that comes with divulging all

our fears. And when we're greeted not with judgment but with understanding, we're suffused with a sense of self-worth that somehow transcends our parents' unconditional embrace. *Someone is actually choosing me*, we think in disbelief and wonder, and it is one of life's most innocent and affirming moments.

4. *We discover the joys of physical pleasure.* No, I'm not talking about sex. I haven't changed my prudish stone-age stance that sex is to be saved for marriage. Rather, I'm talking about all the subtle pleasures of physical love: discovering our heart racing for the first time, our skin tingling, our palms getting sweaty. And the simple joy of looking forward to another day. The thrill is incomparable. We remember every touch, every caress, the first kiss and many more after that. We walk and talk differently; we look at the world through new lenses. The discovery of physical pleasure takes us another step closer to adulthood.

5. *We forget fear.* As we've discussed, fear is the most debilitating of emotions, and especially so in adolescence, when our innate awkwardness magnifies our fear of embarrassment and rejection tenfold. But love and fear, we now discover, are antithetical. When we fall in love, we are no longer trapped by anxiety, worries, and self-doubt. Suddenly, anything is possible. We feel like Superman or Wonder Woman: We can jump higher, run faster, sing more sweetly, think more brilliantly. We become sharp and witty and amazing. We feel invulnerable: Another couple of laps? No problem. Advanced calculus? Bring it on! For a moment, love gives us the courage to conquer the world. And all because another person believes in us.

6. *We experience the joy of feeling special and unique.* When your first true love is also truly in love with you, all the wonderful attention you enjoy lavishing on him shines back brightly at you through his eyes. All of a sudden, someone else is fascinated with what *you* think about, with *your* quirky little habits, with the sound of your voice, things you never thought would interest anyone but you. You feel magical, like the ruler of the world. Is someone beaming a spotlight on you from on high? That's what it feels like. You radiate joy and light. People come up to you and say, "There's something different about you." Could it

be that perpetual cat-who-ate-the-canary grin on your face? You say out loud to yourself in the shower: "No one has felt like this ever before. I'm the first one in the world to know this profound feeling." And you mean it.

7. *We realize life's higher purpose.* Every teenager experiences the feeling that life is meaningless. Our bodies change before our eyes. The smooth skin of our cherubic faces becomes blotched and blemished, or breaks out in hair. Our hormones run wild, tearing apart our inner peace. Our minds and hearts no longer act in concert. Life, so simple in the past, has now become immensely complicated. But with first love, a sense of peacefulness comes over us, and everything suddenly has meaning. It dawns on us that we are put here on earth not as autonomous beings, but as organisms meant to find mates. Now all the pieces fit together, and the whole world gains larger meaning. There is suddenly an order to nature, and we are a part of that order, not separate from it.

This deeply spiritual understanding makes us feel generous and benevolent. We help old ladies cross the street. We leave bigger tips. We decide, finally, to put on a new pair of socks. We want to share our love with all the world.

Beyond First Love: Business as Usual

The reality of modern romance is that, for too many of us, all that idealism of first love fades away quickly. Thereafter, we settle into a pattern of relationships that are the antithesis of those seven aspects of first love, as our innocence is slowly bullied aside by experience. Rather than expanding beyond the bounds of our self, we are made rigid and calcified by the endless cycle of dating. Suddenly we're picky and exclusive, and we develop a new, tougher shell to protect ourselves from the inevitable sting of rejection. Our curiosity gives way to boredom, and we become numbed to the magic of another human being. We trade vulnerability for manipulation and game-playing, trying to divert attention away from our insecurities. We conceal our inner selves with the smoke and mirrors of our latest accomplishments, our newest luxury acquisitions, our recent sexual conquests. Having discovered sex, we turn it into a performance or a competition, learning to fake orgasms or conceal our dissatisfaction. Physical nakedness becomes a substitute for emotional nakedness. And over dinner with the newest applicant, we stop ourselves midsentence and think, "Wait, did I tell *him* this, or the guy I was out with last night?"

In short, we're left flummoxed, convinced that none of it makes sense. Plunged right back into the touchy disaffection of our adolescence, we wallow in cynicism and despair. We look around at all our coupled-off friends and decide that not one of them is happy. Yet we are unhappier still.

Mental Virginity and How to Reclaim It

Oh, to recapture that blush of first love. But how to do it? The way back, as I suggested a moment ago, is through the lush green foliage of Garden of Eden. If you'll recall, in the previous chapter we looked at the eight essential qualities of love as exemplified in the story of Adam and Eve. Now I offer seven suggestions for reclaiming your mental virginity.

Reclaim Curiosity

1. Practice radical honesty. If you're already in a relationship, start revealing things to your lover that you've been afraid to talk about, everything from childhood nightmares to concerns about being fired. Share stories that have made you think about life and about yourself. Likewise, start asking your mate questions you've been afraid to ask. As long as you do so diplomatically, there's a lot to be gained by boldly going where you've never gone before. Instead of relying on chatter and merely functional conversation, delve deeper. Allow yourselves to plumb each other's souls.

2. Instead of the same old round of dinners and movies, try an activity you've both been interested in but never tried before. That way, you'll both enter into it with the same degree of experience (none) and the same degree of curiosity (a lot).

3. Stop having sex so soon! There's no need to reveal everything about your physical self all at once.
4. Take a sabbatical from gossip. Try to go a month without sharing or even reading celebrity gossip, or political gossip for that matter. Don't let yourself be dragged into the baser forms of curiosity, speculations about the sex lives or orientations of people you've never met. Spend a little time on your own romantic life instead; it's much more interesting.
5. Read, read, read. Expand the breadth and depth of your knowledge. Read the Bible and the great classics. Explore authors who expand your horizons and broaden your understanding of life, love, and the human condition. Learn to read to each other and to share what you've read with your lover. Like a circle that endlessly renews itself, this kind of sharing will foster further curiosity.

Rediscover Wonder

1. Learn to stand back and observe, rather than moving in for the kill. Keep your aggression—your need to conquer—in check. Stand back and behold. Drink in the beauty of your loving partner. Stare deeply until you behold her glory and experience her wonder. Open yourself up; allow her to impress you.
2. Nourish your respect of nature by indulging in activities that involve natural, beautiful settings. Go for walks in the woods or local parks. Visit beaches—on a regular basis, not just twice a year.
3. Don't try to change everything. Learn to accept some things the way they are. You don't have to be in control all the time.

Pursue Subjectivity

1. Stay away from pornography. Once you've seen it all, in airbrushed Technicolor perfection, what's left? No real people are going to live up to those illusory silicone fantasies, and you wouldn't want them if they did.
2. Don't date purely for recreation. Too much dating can leave you callous. Date to meet someone to fall in love with.

3. Lose the mental checklist. All your preexisting expectations should fall by the wayside as soon as there's a real person at hand.

4. Have sex only with people you love and with commitment, not merely for the fun of it. If you really want to make it special, save it for the person who commits to you in marriage. Once the complete trust of marriage has bonded you for life, you'll find you can let go and enjoy yourself as never before.

Manifest Mystery

1. Read romantic literature. Then discuss it with someone you love.

2. Keep your distance. Familiarity doesn't necessarily breed contempt, but it can certainly breed boredom. From time to time, make yourself scarce. If you're at a party with a date, don't cling to your partner all night long. Leave some distance, some sense of autonomy, so that something is left to discover later on. Give the other person the opportunity to pursue you, not through "rules" or cheap manipulative tricks, but by indulging your natural mystery. Open yourself up only to those who prove themselves worthy and who take your relationship seriously.

3. Maintain boundaries in same-sex friendships. Too much familiarity can cause you to lose the sense of discovery in the opposite sex, a failure that will carry over and hurt you in your romantic life.

Trust Your Own Innocence

1. Strive to assume the best in others. Develop a "good eye" that seeks to find virtue in everyone. Judge people favorably. Do not anticipate the worst. Act on the basis of pure motivation, and trust that others are doing the same to the best of their ability. Learn to bestow forgiveness freely and openly. Never bear a grudge. Purge yourself of confining emotions.

2. Take a dating hiatus. There's no shame in feeling a little jaded. Take a break, so that you can return fresh and unfettered. A few weeks off can provide much-needed rejuvenation.

3. Practice acts of charity. Soften the rigid heart by learning the pleasures of giving. Invite dates to join you at charity events and fund-raisers. Run a 10-K benefit with your date (a 3-K walk is okay, too).
4. Spend some time with kids, with a date or on your own. Go to the playground and watch them. They're not acting; that's unfeigned innocence. Better yet, offer to take your niece and nephew, or the children of a friend, out for the day. Watching children can be a refreshing, if sometimes exhausting, breath of air. Share their enthusiasm for life, their infinite curiosity, their unbridled playfulness, their creativity and forthrightness. Internalize and emulate their example.
5. Consciously tell yourself, "I refuse to be afraid."

Live a Life of Integrity

1. Avoid games and manipulation. Learn to rise above the slights of others. Don't resort to vengeance. Never use others for your own selfish agenda or pleasure. Don't date—or use—guys or gals on the rebound, even if you think their eyes are open. Always ask yourself *why* you're doing something, and make sure your motivations are loving and pure. It goes without saying that you shouldn't lie to or mislead others. But neither should you lie to or mislead yourself.
2. Maintain a sense of privacy. Keep some parts of yourself out of the public eye. Keep private things private—especially your bodily functions. It's none of his business if you're having your period. (And no, it isn't cute to tell her about your jock itch.)
3. Train yourself to catch yourself bragging about things you've bought or people you know and stop. Go into every date with the confidence that you, yourself, are enough. Trust in the simple virtues you have to offer.

Make Shyness Sexy Again

1. When you're out on a date, or just out on the town hoping to meet someone, try not to dominate the conversation. It's not a competition; step out of the ring. Give the others a little space.

Remember that sometimes standing back can be more alluring than jumping forward.

2. Be natural. Show people your outer person, and hint at what lies beneath, without revealing it all. Invite others to discover your inner light themselves.

3. Learn how to blush again. Okay, blushing is supposed to come naturally; it's not exactly something you can practice in front of a mirror. But if you make an effort to rid yourself of your more distrustful or cynical emotions, the moment someone gives you a compliment your cheeks will naturally light up in a most appealing way.

4. Less is more. Err on the side of conservative. You can always give more later, but you cannot retract what you've already said or done. Listen to others, and work on your sense of timing. Know when barriers can be a good thing. Avoid instant intimacy, so that when an opportunity for true revelation comes, you'll have something to offer.

These tips aren't just for those who feel they've lost the state of innocence and grace that Adam and Eve started with in the Garden. They're intended as a kind of jump-start checklist for anyone who wants to regain the ability to love. And that's what they are, just a start. In the next chapter we'll explore how the eight essentials described in chapter 8 can help you *fall* in love.

11

Living the Eight Ingredients

Exercises for Falling in Love

Do, or do not. There is no "try."

—Yoda, *The Empire Strikes Back*

Jump.

—Joseph Campbell

What would men be without women? Scarce, sir, mighty scarce.

—Mark Twain

If Adam and Eve could have seen into the future to today's singles scene, a cold and judgmental landscape strewn with shattered, disillusioned, and hardened hearts, I can't help wondering how they would have responded. "Honey, *really*, I beg you," Adam would plead even harder. "Whatever you do, please don't touch that fruit. It looks like a jungle out there. We've got it too good here in the Garden. Let's not mess with a good thing."

But if Adam and Eve had never made their mistake, we could never have learned from the lessons of the Garden. As it is, most of us still ignore those lessons, playing Russian roulette with our hearts. On the one hand, we believe we can find our love match the same way we found our job: through a dogged and focused search, aided by superficial insights garnered from magazines, self-help books, and this week's most popular relationship guru. That's the free will approach: "I *will* be married by the age of thirty-two, right after I make my first million." A second strategy is to throw up our hands (and all those misguided books and mags), say a prayer, and mumble our mantra: "If it's meant to be, it will be; if it's meant to be, it will be." I hear this some-enchanted-evening strategy all the time. "Look, Shmuley, of course I want to be in a relationship," one woman told me recently. "But you can't try too hard. I'm not going to degrade myself by asking my friends to introduce me to someone. It will find me." The only problem is that when people keep making the same bad choices they've always made, nothing ever changes.

The whole truth is, love doesn't "just happen." Furthermore, when it does, a fair amount of diligent work is required to keep it alive. You have to water it, fertilize it, and weed it if you want to nurture it into a full-blossoming healthy specimen. Love can strike at any time, of course, and more often than not it strikes when you least expect it. But the real problem with falling in love today has less to do with *when* the opportunity arises, or even *whom* the opportunity arises with, but rather what you've done *before* that magical moment and what you do about it when it finally comes. The fact is that thousands, maybe millions, of potentially rewarding love matches fall by the wayside each year because people fail to do what's needed to make them work. With all the pitfalls that have grown so common in our society—from impatience to self-involvement, from shyness to hypercritical overevaluation, as well as all the obstacles we've explored in the previous chapters—it's no wonder people miss the mark so often.

If you care enough to want to make it work, there are plenty of practical ways to improve your chances of falling in love. This is true whether you've recently met someone who could become special to you, or you're tired of lackluster blind dates and pallid three-month relationships that fade into extinction, or your long-term commitment is starting to feel more like a ball and chain than like a newfound Eden. Drawing on the eight essential ingredients those lovebirds in Eden taught us, we now turn to living according to those principles.

Now I'm no Simon Legree; I can't whip you into following these exercises. And, believe me, I've heard every excuse in the world by now, from "I'm still mourning my last breakup" to "All the single guys are gay" to "I've tried and failed so many times—I've taken it as a message from God that I will die single." But allow me to summon the voice of Yoda, the midget prophet of the Force, for my own purposes: I say unto you, *There is no try; just do these exercises.* Just reading them, even thinking really hard about them, is not the same as doing them, living them. It will take practice and patience. Neither Rome nor love was built in a day. Keep in mind the sage advice of Maimonides: Do something once, and you will be someone who did something once. Do it twice, and you will be someone who's done it twice. But do it three times, and you become the thing that you've done. What starts as a verb becomes a noun. So if you behave lovingly once or twice, you are a person who practiced love. But by the time you've done it a third time, you have *become* a loving person. Love is not something you do on the outside, but something you experience within. Once you've internalized love, as I hope these exercises will help you to do, it will become an integral part of your character.

1. Exercises to Overcome the Pain of Loneliness and Vulnerability

Admit It

Admitting loneliness was rule number one, way back in the beginning of this book. As we saw later, God's first observation about Adam was that he was lonely. So accept it: Loneliness is the primal human condition, and it's nothing to be embarrassed about. Pushing it away does nothing to remedy the problem. In fact, denial will only push you deeper into the existential abyss of isolation and alienation.

Also, remember your new aphorism: *Need is good.* It's the strong men and women who confess that they need someone in their lives. It's the weak ones who put up thick walls and facades to cover up that need.

If it's any solace, remember that throughout history moments of great vulnerability have brought people together. Just think of all the couples who met in the midst of wars, married, and stayed together forever. I also believe that many sincere office romances come about as a result of bonding by coping with the same stresses, pressures, and ridiculous bosses. There is nothing so deeply attractive as the selflessness of one person extending himself or herself to comfort another.

Meanwhile, here are several exercises to help you slowly break out of your lonely shell.

Visit a Homeless Shelter or a Retirement Home

Two reasons: One, to offer help. By throwing yourself into helping others, you will be surrounded by a small community of volunteers and recipients, which will help ease the suffering of one level of loneliness. And two, seeing how lonely the lives of homeless people and the elderly can be—and how gratefully they welcome your friendship—can't help making your pain feel less heavy and allowing you to appreciate the loving people who surround you.

Make a Little Gesture

Reach out across the divide from yourself to another. Extend yourself. If there's someone special you want to get to know better, a small gesture can go a long way—a quick note or a simple gift you know will come in handy, like new earmuffs for someone who has lost a pair, says that you're thinking about that person. Save the great big hearts-and-roses gifts for later. Once a friend of mine was on the fence about whether to commit to his girlfriend. When his beloved 1973 BMW 2002 died, she sent him a condolence card. That sealed it. He realized that only she had known how much the car meant to him. The next week he proposed to her.

Confess

No, not to your priest. And not that you did time in Sing Sing. Start with a small confession. Do you worry about whether people at work like you? Does it bother you that you don't like certain people in your yoga class? Or that you're such a klutz that you're always getting injured in your yoga class? "Tell her about it," as Billy Joel used to say; it'll help prime the pump. If the other person doesn't chime in with similar confessions, say, "Tell me a secret." You may be surprised at how well your partner rises to the challenge. It's these little secrets that make people feel lonely, as if they're the only ones in the world who feel this way, until they discover that we all do. (And along the way, you might find out that you both hate yoga.)

Get Over the Big Taboo

As we all learned in junior high school—and why didn't we get over it back then?—the hardest thing in the world is still to tell someone you like him, as in *like him very much*. There's a way to do this that can make it a little less treacherous than diving into a pool of sharks. Do it subtly and from the start. After the first date, simply say, "I had a really fun time. You're very nice." *Ta-da!* There, you did it. No sweat. You've broken the ice, put a plank on that bridge from one heart to another. During the second date or shortly thereafter, after your date has said or done something endearing, say something else complimentary and personal, such as "I really like you"; say it as though you're saying it to no one in particular, least of all to that person. It's just an observation, an empirical fact, not a major expression of affection. Each time you say something like that, you are making it easier for yourself, and for the other person, to up the ante, as it were. Soon you will be swooning in each other's arms, I promise you. If not, at least you've spread good feelings to someone else.

Sign the Declaration of Dependence

What's stopping you? Go directly to chapter 8, read the declaration, and slap down your John Hancock. Read it to a loved one, have him or her sign it, and pass it on. Together we might start a whole new revolution of our own, the love revolution.

Learn to Be Understanding. Understand?

It's important to understand the importance of understanding. Many people are so caught up in their own need to be understood, to find that perfect ear, that they forget that understanding needs to go both ways. Our culture of therapy encourages us to think of those close to us as one-way-street confidants rather than as truly equal partners. We unburden ourselves so relentlessly that it becomes easy to forget about our partners' own needs. This can be damaging on many levels and at many stages in a relationship, from first dates that go awry to established relationships that are teetering on the edge of long-term commitment.

Maria and Tom were dating for two years until eventually, as women often have to do, Maria issued an ultimatum: If Tom couldn't commit to her, she'd move on. When Tom brought his problem to me, his emotions were complex; he felt confused, threatened, and angry, but his feelings were entirely self-centered. When I made the simplest of suggestions—"Let's try to think about how *she* must feel"—it came like a bolt of lightning to him. I encouraged him to go home and think about Maria's words: to consider that, at twenty-nine, eager to marry a man she loved and who professed to love her, Maria might well be justified in her anxiety. The next time I saw him, Tom had done a lot of thinking. "I understood how painful that really was for Maria," he told me. "I felt her sense of rejection, and it made me feel so much closer to her."

What Tom learned is empathy: identification with and understanding of another's situation, feelings, and motives. Empathy can help ease the deep loneliness of not being understood. When a problem crops up in a relationship or potential relationship of yours, whether it's trying to agree on whether to get married or simply how to spend your first all-weekend date together, take the time to think through what your partner must be thinking and feeling. Put yourself in your partner's shoes. Not only will this draw you closer together; it's also a wonderful way to avoid arguments in relationships. In a sense, love is a unique kind of heightened empathy, and if you work on building that empathy from both sides, not just dumping all your problems on your partner's lap, you'll be opening the door to love.

Try these exercises to practice empathy:

- ♥ *Trade places.* Literally exchange lives for a day. If possible, follow your significant other around. Visit her office. Meet her coworkers and boss. Take the commute with her. As much as possible, see what it would feel like to walk a mile in her shoes.

I'll bet you'll have a much better understanding, and probably more empathy, when your mate starts complaining about the commute or the petty officemates.

💜 *Relive your partner's past.* Hearing stories from your partner's childhood is one thing, but seeing where they took place will bring them to life. Spend an evening looking through old family photo albums together. Pull out all the childhood home movies. Then plan a weekend devoted solely to a stroll down memory lane by visiting his or her hometown. Stop by the old neighborhood, see the house, the schools, the site of that first kiss. Now all that talk about the old days will suddenly make a little more sense, and you'll have a much richer understanding of your lover.

💜 *Trade positions.* When you've hit an impasse in an argument, try taking your mate's point of view as your own and argue it. Let your partner do the same. You'll be amazed at how much it softens your own position and how ludicrous the argument was in the first place.

💜 *Practice two-way communication.* I don't mean anything fancy, just two people talking *and listening*. It's worth giving explicit instructions, because conversation is becoming something of a lost art. So let's bring it back, step by step. Get a three-minute egg timer. First, let one person talk until the sand drains out, while the other just listens, with no interrupting. Before the second person talks about whatever he wants to talk about, he must first repeat back what he heard in his own words: "You said . . ." It's not easy, so give yourselves time to master the task. Once you do, you'll be amazed at what comes out of the mouth of your partner. Part of learning how to converse is to turn off the TV, the stereo, and the computer humming in the background. John Lennon, who had the TV in his Dakota apartment switched on permanently, once said that in our time the television has replaced the fireplace. With due respect to John, I advise you to turn the darned thing off and light a real fire instead.

💜 *Study faces.* Empathic persons can tell what others are feeling by more than what they say. They are experts at reading body language. Is the person stiff or relaxed? Are her arms crossed? Is he leaning forward or sitting way back in his seat? For real insight into people's feelings, look at their faces. Empathic people can look into people's eyes, examine the tension of their facial muscles or the ease of their smile, and tell whether a person is frustrated, hopeful, suspicious, or eager to know you better. Depending on your read, you can respond in kind. Or not. One way to practice picking up nonverbal messages is to watch television dramas with the sound turned off, especially soap operas. But even in good shows like *ER* or *The West Wing*, actors have to use their whole body to sell a line. Sometimes you may wish you could turn down the sound on your date, but that wouldn't be very empathic, would it?

2. Exercises in Nakedness

Work on Your Self-Confidence.

Emotional nakedness requires a leap of faith: the faith that when you do reveal your true self, it will not be trampled, ridiculed, laughed at, or otherwise judged poorly. Opening oneself up to another person is scary stuff. The best way to get to that place without fear is to build up your confidence, both with your partner (prospective or current) and with the world.

Did you ever crash a party, or even attend one alone, when you knew only the host? Or go along with a friend to an event you weren't invited to? Ever jump into a conversation with a bunch of strangers or ask a fellow bookstore browser about a book you're considering? Many of us have a hard time summoning enough confidence to take a chance in a social situation, and even those of us who do often have the hardest time asking people out or being candid about our feelings once we're in a relationship. Often we're afraid that if we reveal weaknesses on a first date, like anxieties, frustrations, and fears, we'll be rejected. And we all have different ways of coping with these fears. Many singles act overly confident on a first date, hiding behind a facade of self-assurance, while others go to the opposite extreme, agreeing too quickly with whatever their dates say, giving them free rein to monopolize the conversation. You can always spot these people in a crowded restaurant. Their heads looks as though they're planted on a spring, as they nod in incessant agreement with whatever their dates have to say. In any date like this, what's missing on both sides is confidence, the confidence to talk *and* to listen.

The same can hold true in established relationships: Partners who are afraid to rock the boat may put off their own concerns about problems in the relationship for too long, out of the nagging sense that they must be overreacting or that they're imagining things; in short, they act as though their feelings don't much matter. Of course, it's only a matter of time before one of two things happens: Either their resentment builds until they explode in a torrent of invective, or they atrophy from within, and their personality collapses altogether. Either way, losing faith in yourself is asking for trouble.

Lack of confidence often involves a feeling that we don't belong: at a social event, at a business meeting, or even on a date with someone we find attractive. It happens to all of us. Suddenly it's as if we're about seventeen, and everyone around us has a graduate degree in life. We sit there wondering, "How did they know that?" Or thinking, "Gee, they seem so comfortable." To compensate, we try too hard, press in a little too much, or laugh a little too hard at mediocre jokes, or else we clam up, perspire, fidget. But when we feel we belong, that our presence is not arbitrary but integral, we feel at ease, relaxed, in a positive frame of mind, sure of ourselves. And it shows. We are funny, compassionate, quick-thinking, free of stress.

If one of the keys to confidence is feeling that you are really needed, then *make yourself needed*. First, spend some time thinking about your own special gifts, the things people always notice about you, the things you love best and feel most confident about. It could be that you have a tremendous capacity to love, or to listen, or to empathize. Or it could be that you can make other people laugh. Or you're great at cheering people up. One way or another, you have gifts that no one else has in the same measure, with the same quality you bring to bear. Embrace these skills, even if you've always thought they were unimportant, and find occasions to use them. Make yourself indispensable. If you're a good baker, volunteer to help students put on a bake sale. If you're good with a hammer, offer your services to a senior citizens' center. Or if you just enjoy reading, offer to read to people who can't. Become a mentor: Coach the soccer team, join the Big Brothers/Big Sisters program, take on a young protégé at work. Passing down wisdom will remind you that you have wisdom to pass down, and it will enrich your own sense of well-being.

There's a story about a college student who once approached the Lubavitcher Rebbe and told him she lacked confidence. "Bring salt to the table at your dormitory," he said. What he meant was, Do something simple and essential. Make yourself belong. Do things for others. John F. Kennedy said much the same thing in his inaugural address: "Ask not what your country can do for you; ask what you can do for your country." Don't get carried away, of course. Take care not to let your altruism expand into arrogance or self-righteousness. The confidence of a pure heart says not "I am a somebody" but "I have something to give." Once you've mastered a few roles, take interest in some new undertakings, not to impress others but to enrich yourself. Take an adult ed class. Spend a day at a museum. Add to your knowledge constantly. Start learning a new language; nothing breaks the ice like a few tenderly whispered words of Urdu.

Though I'm not someone who glorifies the body at the expense of the personality, there's no getting around how our feelings about our own appearance affect our confidence. Do your best to look sharp and presentable at all times. Find a comfortable exercise regimen, and stick to it. Dress up, without overdoing it. If you believe in yourself, it will show itself in the way you carry yourself; a kind of grace will come over you, slowly but surely.

Make It Personal

Taking self-confidence to the dating scene, then, is a whole new challenge. Once you've gotten back in touch with what you like about yourself, you'll be ready to take greater risks in the world of dating, because your fear of rejection will have faded. If that guy doesn't like you, *it's his loss*. There are a lot of picky commitment-phobes out there, and they're the ones who are likely to end up lonely and tragic, not you. If rejection is the worst thing that can happen, put it in context: You still have your Urdu. Seriously, you still have your self-worth, and friends and family who value you.

So go ahead, open up. Even before you start thinking that this person might be "the one," reveal something about yourself that you ordinarily wouldn't. Trust engenders trust, so ask, and with luck, ye shall receive.

My friend Timothy once complained to me that he couldn't get to the next level with women he dated. At the time he was seeing a woman named Georgia, and the relationship didn't seem to be progressing. On the first two dates they passed the time discussing their favorite films and music, telling a few funny childhood stories, and catching up on friends they had in common, but it all felt rather by-the-numbers. So I suggested that if he opened up a bit, shared a more vulnerable side, he might be surprised by the outcome.

"What if she doesn't like what she sees?" he said. "Is it really a good idea to risk coming off like a weakling?"

"Enough with the *what ifs*," I said. "Just do it." (Like Yoda, I keep waiting for that big endorsement offer from Nike.)

On their next date, Timothy told Georgia about a situation at work that was making him angry and bitter. He'd started his own small legal firm; the following year he brought in a hotshot young friend with a talent for wooing big clients, and the firm started growing. But now his partner was practically holding him hostage for complete control of the business.

"I've put my heart and soul into that firm, and now I've lost control of it. It was my baby, and now I feel like a stranger in my own office," he told Georgia earnestly, watching carefully for her reaction. She held his glance. So he went on, describing how his concerns were all intertwined with his feelings about his deceased father, also a lawyer, whose respect he'd always hoped to earn. Georgia listened quietly, with him every step of the way. Then she looked down. "Here it comes," Timothy thought. "The big 'It's getting late . . .'"

Little did he expect what happened next. Timothy's moment of openness had touched Georgia and inspired her to return the compliment of his emotional intimacy. She began to tell him how she had lived with a man for four years who all along promised to marry her. Little did she know that in the last two years of the relationship he was cheating on her with someone else. Soon Timothy and Georgia were talking about things they had never shared with anyone else.

The ironic thing about vulnerability is that, time and time again, revealing your fears and faults to your partner has the effect of making you *more* desirable to your partner, not less. Human vulnerability makes people more beautiful rather than ugly. Did Timothy suddenly see Georgia as a woman scorned, rather than a potential wife? No. He began to see her as a whole person, someone with whom he could share a life. When Georgia trusted Tim enough to reveal the unfaithfulness she had suffered, "it made me start falling in love with her for the very first time," he told me later.

This can be tricky territory. I'm not suggesting that you plunge into every first date with a long speech about how lonely you feel or your trouble separating from dear old Mom. But if you're beginning to feel the urge to get to know someone a little better, after a date or two you might try posing one or two questions like these (and don't forget to listen to the answers!):

- How do you *feel* about your job?

- How do you balance your professional life with your personal life?

- What do you do to nurture your mind?

- Where do you see yourself in five years?

- Which of your parents do you think you're more like?

- If you could take a year off, what would you do?

Bring It Home to Mom and Dad

Our first teachers—in almost every subject, but especially in love—are our parents. Granted, too often we learn the wrong lessons from the examples our parents or grandparents set for us. Studies have shown that children of divorced parents, for instance, are often, and understandably, skeptical about their own potential for a successful romance. Those whose parents had happy marriages, on the other hand, can be intimidated by the example and may set themselves such high standards that they find it impossible to believe they can fall in love as surely as their parents did. Either way, we come to recognize through our parents that love is passed down from one generation to the next.

An important way to open yourself up to love is to come to terms with your parents' example, and the best way to do that is by talking with them one-on-one. This, of course, can be an enormous challenge for many people. *Isn't that why I've got my therapist?* you're saying. *So I don't have to talk to my parents?* Yes, but there's simply no substitute for having an honest, nonconfrontational talk with one or both of your folks about their experiences. (And think how much money you'll save in therapy bills!) Your parents are your flesh and blood, and believe it or not, they still understand things about you that no one else can. As long as you don't expect them to be perfect, and don't spend all your time looking for flaws in their arguments, it can be helpful and even cathartic to talk with them about love in their lives and your own.

How to broach the subject? If you don't think you can leap right in, you might consider proposing it as research into family roots. Let them know that what you're after is a sense of what brings people together and what pulls them apart and that you're asking them because you value their wisdom. Let them know it's not meant as an occasion to rehash old arguments or open old wounds, but as a research mission to help you move forward with your bigger project of finding and falling in love. I think if they see that as your goal, rather than putting their marriage under a microscope, you'll all feel more at ease.

If your parents' marriage ended unhappily, talk that over with them individually. See if they can shed any light on why things fell apart. You'll probably begin to discover a truth everyone should recognize: that love may be perfect but people are not. Taking time as an adult to revisit your parents' separation may be painful, but it will help you see that it was your parents themselves—their personalities, their desires and flaws—that led to their breakup, not the institution of marriage itself.

On the other hand, if your parents' marriage seems idyllic, encouraging them to talk about it with you openly, one-on-one, will almost certainly help you see that no one has a magic formula for happiness. Now that you're an adult, your parents may feel more able to open up to you about problems they've had along the way, helping you to recognize that even *they* had to work at it. Those who are still happily married will invariably send you away with one valuable lesson: that they couldn't have done it alone, that they couldn't have built such a contented life without the support of a loving spouse. Previous generations understood this in a way we don't: Happy marriages are built on a foundation of faith.

If they're still alive, ask your grandparents the same questions. Or book some time with friends of your family who've been married for thirty years or more. These are our elders; they know so much and yet are often a largely untapped source of wisdom on the subject of love. Ask them if they could have gotten through life's vicissitudes without the support of a loving spouse. Ask your grandmother to show you her wedding album (and try to stay awake).

Here are a few questions you might ask:

❤ How did you feel before you got married? Were you lonely?

❤ What was your original attraction to Mom (or Dad)?

❤ Did that quality change? If so, how?

❤ Can you remember an incident that dramatically affected your relationship, for better or worse?

❤ When were you happiest together? Saddest?

❤ To married parents: Are you as much in love today as you once were?

❤ To divorced parents: Was there any way you could have made it work?

❤ How do you make your marriage work?

❤ Are you satisfied with yourself as a spouse?

❤ What would you do to make the marriage better?

Get Naked

Take a chance on nakedness. This doesn't mean flash your partner on the first date; we don't want to get you arrested. But here are some icebreakers to ask your date:

❤ What does love mean to you?

❤ Do you think there's a difference between loving someone and being in love?

❤ What are your greatest fears, and how do you overcome them?

❤ Who are the people you most admire in life, and why?

❤ Do you believe that people are basically good? Do you have any doubts?

❤ What's the kindest thing anyone has ever done for you?

❤ Have you ever felt betrayed by someone close to you?

❤ After we're married, would you mind if we vacationed on Temptation Island?

If this kind of third degree doesn't send your date looking for the exit, it should help you cut through a lot of small talk, save a lot of time, and perhaps save you heartbreak later. Here's another idea: Using chapter 9 as a springboard, bring up your thoughts on one of the eight essentials we learned from Adam and Eve. If that works, move on to the seven lessons of first love in chapter 10. I can guarantee you that even if the relationship doesn't work out, you will not be forgotten.

The point is, as soon as you can, take off your body armor and talk to your partner about what you're truly feeling. Reveal what you know about yourself already and what you'd still like to find out. Demonstrate that you are a person of depth. Depth may not be what makes a person a hottie these days, but it's a quality that will never go out of style (unlike words like *hottie*). If depth doesn't register big numbers on the first-date Richter scale, down the road it will. And that's where you're looking, down the road to your goal—love.

3. Exercises in Innocence

Don't Compare

We live in a world of comparison shopping, a world that turns human beings into commodities, that micromanages our every interaction. So it's only natural that we all spend time stacking our current partner up against past lovers or against the other candidates who sidle past our table at a restaurant. That kind of behavior may make great bargain hunters, but it makes terrible lovers. Now's the time to turn over a new leaf. Don't waste time wondering whether you could be getting a better deal. Work with the person in front of you. Because this much is true: If you're constantly looking over your partner's shoulder at every new woman who comes along, or comparing today's blind date with yesterday's boyfriend, you'll never fall in love. Staring at others while out on a date isn't only rude and inconsiderate; it's also self-sabotage.

Stop waiting for the person you're dating to prove deserving of your love. That's what I call Mafia love, waiting for someone who's so special he makes you an offer you can't refuse. The real question here is: Are *you* capable of loving? Is love something that you can offer freely? Because if you can't, there's no way you can be in a relationship.

As we learned from Adam and Eve, we should approach a new potential partner as if he or she were the only man or woman in the world. Wean yourself off your old bad habits by practicing these exercises:

Call a Moratorium on Dating

That's right, stop dating. Like an addict who can't control his need for one more fix, you have to go cold turkey. Not that dating is bad, but your attitude toward it is. When dating is no longer a matter of highs or lows, just a constant stream of forgettable (and soon forgotten) faces parading across your horizon, you need to retreat and regroup before you can regain your sense of wonder. Serial dating can be a profoundly disillusioning experience. It fosters many of the bad habits we've discussed, from judging too harshly to behaving badly on the dates themselves. Ultimately, it can also breed a kind of superiority complex, as you become distanced from the process, flitting from rendezvous to rendezvous like a millionaire gambler cruising the floor of a casino, never risking more than a few dollars along the way.

Going cold turkey can be a way of renewing your interest in the process and getting back in touch with your true priorities. It can counter the layer of cynicism that has kept you from being open with the opposite sex. How much time you take off depends on how severe your addiction is. For some people, four to six weeks is plenty, enough time to lose four or five pounds, get a new look, and catch up on some long-overdue correspondence. For heavy abusers we might be talking three to six months, enough time to miss dating so much that your first date afterward will seem like your first ever.

For ideas on what to do with all your free time while on hiatus, see the section "Exercises in Desire and Wonder."

Reevaluate Your Evaluation Process

While you're on your dating sabbatical, put some thought into whom you date, and why. Look for your patterns. Where do you meet people? Who sets you up? How long do you usually date? Who usually loses faith first? Write down the names of all the people you've dated, from one-time meetings to long-term love affairs, and review what went right and what went wrong. Take responsibility where you should, for both the good and the bad. Now write down three things you think currently prevent you from falling in love. Be honest. Would you simply *like* to have a man (or woman) around, or do you really believe you *need* one? Are you prepared to admit you're lonely? And if you never really feel lonely, ask yourself how you've become alienated from your most vital needs. Drawing on the ideas in this book, jot down three things that might help reverse your patterns. Keep in mind that dating is supposed to be about meeting someone to fall in love with. Sport dating is for jocks and other knuckleheads. If you're going to evaluate a date, do it before you go out. Rather than dating and breaking up impulsively, use more discretion up front.

Consider a Matchmaker

Ever given it a thought? *I'm not that desperate*, you might be thinking. (Or *I never liked* Fiddler on the Roof.) I'm a strong advocate of the grand old and rather reliable tradition of matchmaking, and not just because I've been a matchmaker myself. The role of the matchmaker is as old as creation: How did Eve meet Adam, after all, but through God's matchmaking? (It might also be noted that my wife, Debbie, and I were introduced by a matchmaker, although, truth be told, Debbie's parents are thinking of suing him for malpractice.) You can find fairly hip matchmaking services advertised in many big-city newspapers and magazines, and even Internet dating services are proving useful for web-minded types.

Like it or not, many of the people who get dates without much help are those with easily spotted external virtues: obvious beauty, ostentatious wealth, easy charisma. Even though she may prove to be a lousy date time after time, the woman who is beautiful will always be asked out on a date before the one who is kind or has a great personality. Matchmakers can help to even the playing field, giving people with subtler and more meaningful qualities a fighting chance.

Another thing matchmakers can do is get all the evaluating out of the way, saving you a lot of wasted energy. As your PR person, any good matchmaker will talk you up so you don't have to sell yourself; you can settle in comfortably, knowing that the matchmaker has already explained that you sold your dot-com before they all tanked and you're worth fifty-eight million dollars. You get to focus on falling in love, not hyping yourself.

Matchmakers also serve as professional middlemen, saving one or both parties a dose of rejection on the back end. After the date the matchmaker calls each party and, often in an accent that sounds like Yenta the Matchmaker, asks, "So how did it go?" Then she gets back to each of you. If your date tells her, "I wouldn't go out with her again if we were stranded on a desert island," she'll tell you, "He liked you very much, but he's just been transferred to the Galápagos." This saves everybody heartache and guilt.

If you don't want to go to a pro, don't be afraid to give your family and friends a chance. We all want to be matchmakers; even more than feeding the hungry, alleviating people's loneliness is the highest form of charity. Traditionally, people dated and then married within their own community, and therefore the community participated in the matchmaking. While there is a lot to be said for personal autonomy and the freedom to choose anyone your heart desires, you shouldn't discount your friends and family as sources of potential mates. They know you better than most people do, and the last thing they want is to cause you heartache.

Evaluate Your Friendships

I don't mean to get too personal, but have you spent much time thinking about the company you keep: your friends, who have more influence in your lives than your parents; your spiritual counselor; your therapist (and even me)? Peer pressure may be subtler in adulthood than it was when we were teenagers, but it's just as powerful, and if you don't watch out, you may find yourself taking on your friends' bad attitudes as your own. If you and your friends spend most of your time sitting around trashing the opposite sex, playing manipulative games—talking about dating and sex the way guys talk about the playoffs—then it might be time to think about hanging with a different crowd or simply spending a little more time alone.

Here are some other ideas: Limit the time you spend with friends of the same or opposite sex to a maximum of three nights a week. That leaves two for dating and two for you to spend alone regrouping. When friends start degrading members of the opposite sex, take a pass. Examine your phone bills to see how much time you spend talking to friends about dating, instead of actually dating or pursuing other interests. Limit these conversations to a maximum of two hours per week.

If in the middle of a date you find yourself thinking "I can't wait to tell my friend Alex what this person sitting across from me just said," an alarm bell should go off. Get focused back on your date, and when you get home, make sure you *don't* call Alex. The purpose of dating isn't to provide a supply of interesting stories for your friends. Eventually, you should be able to talk *to your date* about your date.

Try counting the number of opposite-sex and same-sex friends you have. If the former outnumber the latter, that may be why you haven't felt a stronger need to find a compatible love partner. You're so surrounded by the energy of the opposite sex that you rarely miss it in any deep way. Reverse the trend now. If you're the kind of woman whose male friends bring you their relationship problems for advice (you're everyone's best friend and no one's girlfriend), break out of that mode now. You're a woman in your own right, not someone else's relationship counselor.

Focus, Focus, Focus

Wandering eye is a disease that's reaching epidemic proportions among both sexes, among singles and married couples alike. It's that selfish serpent of insatiability nipping at our heels again, that old shopaholic twinge. I've seen it destroy many a relationship. Men I know who are in committed relationships have come to my office and asked, "Who is that?" when an attractive woman walked down the hall. "What do you mean, 'Who is that?'" I ask back. "Oh, just wondering," they reply nonchalantly. I may have spent years in a seminary, but I know this much: No one's ever "just wondering." There's no such thing.

Every time your thoughts stray to another man or woman, slowly redirect your mind away from him or her and back to the one you love or are interested in loving. Every time your eye roams, do the same. We all know the difference between looking and staring. And between staring and leering. Remember Maimonides' tip: Do this three times (or sixty, if necessary) and you will succeed.

When you come back from a date, call a friend and talk about the date *without comparing that person with the last seventeen people you've dated.* And for goodness' sake, don't even mention the one who broke your heart, the one no one will ever come close to (you know the one I mean).

It might even help to learn to meditate. Simple meditation practice (mantras and incense and flickering flames are not necessary) involves training your mind to focus on your breath going in and going out. Mindfulness meditation, based on a Buddhist tradition, is taught at meditation centers in most cities throughout the world. The practice forces the mind to be patient with its own wanderings; eventually you get so bored with the practice that you succumb, and suddenly you realize you've gone three breaths without thinking of Richard, who never called you back; or that pending deal; or cleaning your oven. So sit down and take a load off your mind.

Stop Flirting

That means even when your partner or date *isn't* around. Stay chaste and pure. Turn off your sexual antenna, except for the object of your emotional attention. That includes waitresses, FedEx delivery guys, and any postman who rings twice.

Cancel Your Subscriptions

This may seem trivial, but its importance can't be overestimated. Women should give up those monthly magazines that serve up endless helpings of advice on *how to judge whether your man is right for you.* And men, visual creatures that we are, need to give up *Playboy* and *Maxim,* with their invitations to ogle pneumatic bodies and perform mental comparisons between Carmen Electra's assets and those of the actual, unenhanced women in our own lives (the same goes for porn websites and videos). While a species of subtle porn has grown omnipresent in our cultural mainstream—from billboards in Times Square, to booty-bumpin' music videos, to the sophisticated entertainment of the *Wild On . . .* series on the *E!* network—we still have the power to change the channel or walk on by. You're under no obligation to memorize each new sexy image you see for further contemplation. Here's an experiment: For one week, try averting your eyes every time you see a sexy image in the media. I'm advocating not that you regress to the level of a Victorian prude, but only that you recognize that the cumulative effect of these influences could spell trouble. They make it difficult not to compare, and they can create distance between you and your spouse as you embrace. Think of the influences that infiltrate your mind, through your eyes and ears, as toxic chemicals forever poisoning your psyche. And that includes the Victoria's Secret mannequins!

4. Exercises in Desire and Wonder

The Emotional Striptease

We live in an age of instant intimacy but little real closeness. There are too many river and kettle relationships, too few bird relationships. Meanwhile, attraction between the sexes has been all but nullified. The slow-boil seduction has been condensed, the way film previews these days show you the whole plot in a minute's worth of fast-cut action and a few catchphrase sound bites. With so much teaser, who needs the whole movie? I propose that we return to "slo-mo," putting the brakes on as much as possible and allowing the mystery and intrigue of the opposite sex to return to center stage. Here's how:

Come Under Better Influences

Earlier, in the section on innocence, I recommended taking a break from the dating habit. What you do with those free evenings can be critical. This is not a time to pout, call all your friends and bemoan your self-imposed retreat, or take out a subscription to the Playboy Channel. It's a time to fill your world with positive influences, influences that will inspire you and remind you of the real reasons you're dating. Read great romantic literature, not dime-store romance novels but classics like Solomon's *Song of Songs* or Hemingway's *The Sun Also Rises*. There are also wonderful films to rent, ranging from *Casablanca* to *As Good as It Gets*. Let yourself cry watching *Terms of Endearment*. You might even want to take notes, as though you were auditing a seminar on love. Perhaps it's a good time to find some of those self-indulgent romantic poems you scrawled in college and revise them or write a few more.

Do romantic things alone, like sitting by a fireplace or taking a walk on a fogged-in beach. And *miss* doing it with another person. Or if you really want to torture yourself, go to a movie alone where you'll see lots of couples, and remind yourself how much fun it is to sit in the dark with someone.

Taking a sabbatical from dating is not deprivation therapy. You're not giving up anything. You're gaining perspective, clearing your head and filling it with positive influences. It's a time of renewal, not necessarily a time to do anything but a time to *be*, to get back in touch with your true nature. It's a time to become ready for love.

Limit Your Time Spent with Friends of the Opposite Sex

Of course those friendships are platonic; I understand that, and I trust you. But that's the whole point. If you can get all the emotional comfort you need from a platonic, opposite-sex relationship, the only convincing reason you're going to have for missing a romantic relationship is sex. And that's not enough of a reason to compel you to be on the lookout for love. You can also get sex without love.

So what to do when friends of the opposite sex ask you to go to dinner or a movie, or suggest a cup of coffee to talk about their problems with people they're dating? It's a dilemma, I know. On the one hand, you appreciate being invited out, and it sure would be nice to be in the company of someone of the opposite sex. We convince ourselves, even when we think of the person in question as just a friend and not a datable prospect, that hanging out with the opposite sex is good "practice." But it's the wrong kind of practice: If practiced regularly, it conditions you to turn off to the opposite sex, not on. All the single thirty-something people I see in Manhattan who never feel lonely have one thing in common: They have extremely close opposite-sex platonic relationships. And the honest ones always admit to me that this has much to do with why they're not in a romantic relationship. But it's cozy and uncomplicated, so why change it?

When such friends ask you out, politely decline, saying you're too busy or otherwise engaged. If you keep saying it, after a while they will get the message. In a pinch, you can tell them I put you up to it. It may be harsh, but keep in mind that falling in love is your goal, not collecting a lot of opposite-sex friends. After you meet the love of your life, you can invite them all to your engagement party!

Alternatively, suggest that you go out as a group with some other people. That way you can see a bunch of your friends, male and female alike, but avoid all that intense one-on-one time that's so distracting.

Take It Slowly

Overexposure to one prospective partner can be just as misguided as too many dates with too many different people. Even if you feel you might fall for a person right away, don't make the mistake of spending every waking (and sleeping!) moment with him or her too soon. The best first dates often succeed because an air of mystery is created between two individuals; each partner is left feeling curious, wanting more. Make sure your relationship unfolds as a journey, rather than quickly hitting a dead end. The trick is not to let curiosity run away with you, or from you. Realize that there's a difference between unavailability, the product of manipulation, and unknowability, the product of unfeigned mystery. Let the attraction build over a series of well-spaced dates, leaving perhaps a week between meetings in the beginning. It's fine to stay in touch via phone and E-mail. Even good old-fashioned snail mail adds a genteel touch these days. Sending a note, or taking the time to make a phone call, can reveal another side of you, without the physical distractions.

Make sure not to rush into bed. Having sex too early in a relationship can have the effect of weakening desire (just look at how men behave right after orgasm), of short-circuiting the dynamics of an unfolding relationship by serving up physical intimacy before the emotional groundwork has been laid. As you'd expect, I suggest delaying sexual intercourse until your wedding night. But I'm also a realist. At the very least give the relationship a few months, so that getting physically naked has been preceded by getting emotionally naked. Otherwise, you won't be making love; you'll just be having sex, and it will feel that way in the morning. If you learn to appreciate your partner's personality before you make love, you'll be giving yourself the chance to invest the eventual lovemaking with a far greater sense of intimacy and meaning.

Be Discreet

Our tell-all culture encourages us to show people everything, from cleavage to hernia scars, on a first date. Nothing can ruin people's appetite—their appetite to see you again—faster. The process of revealing aspects of yourself should be like a slow striptease. Show a little, conceal a little. Tantalize, invite, let your audience know there's more to come, even where they'll find it, but hold back. You can make a climax (no, not *that* kind of climax) last a very long time. A lifetime! And remember: Save the stripping for someone you feel is worthy of the show, someone you want to know your depths.

The same holds true with how you dress. Low-cut blouses that reveal too much cleavage are like movie promos. Tight jeans that reveal your manly bulge give away the family jewels, so to speak, before they're even ready to be shown. Give it all away in the promo, and you take all the zing out of the full-length feature.

This slow-burn revealing of oneself can apply even after you're married. So ban the TV from the bedroom—not just for a while but permanently, if you can. Limit reading in bed to novels or good non-fiction, and call a moratorium on *Wall Street Journal* pillow talk. Make bedroom time a sacred time between you and your spouse, with no plan whatsoever. Once the kids are asleep, the bills are paid, the garbage has been taken out, and the TV is off, what else is there to do?

Abstain

If all else fails, stop having sex altogether, even if you're in an established relationship. Periodic abstinence was one of the most popular ideas I presented in *Kosher Sex*. In Orthodox Judaism, intercourse is supposed to revolve around a woman's menstrual cycle. This turns out to be an excellent way to delay gratification, which is the essence of maintaining lust, and there is far too little lust in long-term relationships these days.

In *Kosher Sex*, by the way, I also advocated all kinds of exotic marital sex (with the advisory to make sure the chandeliers are bolted in nice and solid). The one exception was, and still is, sado-masochism. Why bring it up here? Because S&M suggests to me that normal sex has become so boring that the only way to spice it up is to add physical pain to it, which seems to defeat the purpose. Having to use a staple gun on your genitals to get an erotic thrill strikes me as pretty darn desperate. It's a bit like Bruce Willis's *Die Hard* movies. In the first one, only about ten bad guys die. In the second one, about three hundred people die. And in the third, the whole city of New York is about to blow sky-high. The more you become immune to the ordinary pleasures of life, the more you have to push the envelope to the bizarre and downright nasty.

The need for violent sex is just another indicator to me of how inured we've become to the natural and simple attraction between men and women. As far as I'm concerned, taking those whips and chains to the pawn shop and trading them in for a nice Japanese fan and an exotic mask would be highly acceptable.

5. Exercises in Compatibility

Go for the Core

In the rush to find someone right, we often unknowingly settle for someone right now. I say unknowingly because we believe that the person is the right choice, usually on the basis of the old surface checklist: right look, right career, right recreational activities, right family background, right sense of style, right domestic habits. Checklist relationships often don't pan out in the long run. Why? Because they're based on a superficial understanding of compatibility. Here are some exercises to help you determine the true chances of compatibility with a potential mate and to help you become more versatile yourself.

Cultivate Your Own Interests

All work and no play make Jack and Jill a pretty dull couple, and chances are their relationship won't get anywhere if they don't learn to spend time doing more than pushing paper and collecting paychecks. People who lead such one-track lives have a hard time seeing beyond their own noses; as we've noted, it's difficult to extend empathy to another if you're caught up in your own world. And it's also true that cultivating a richer, fuller life will exponentially increase your chances of developing a lasting relationship. So once again: Go to church, pray, take classes, read, volunteer, pursue a hobby, travel, immerse yourself in spiritual pursuits. It'll make you a more attractive person, for one thing; for another, it'll give you more to share with a prospective partner.

Ask the Right Questions

Since compatibility is about deeper concerns, after you've run through the usual opening round of questions—Beatles or Stones? Sushi or Italian? Jogging or tennis? Matzo balls or noodles?—probe further, looking for core values. Is this person altruistic? Is he or she passionate about something other than making money or having buns of steel? Does this person want to have children? Are there social or environmental issues, cultural interests, intellectual pursuits that are of prime importance to him or her? And then drop the bomb: Do you see yourself married in the future? Do the responses match yours? Now you can assess your compatibility.

Look for a Complementary, Not a Duplicate, Partner

Don't look for yourself with different plumbing. Find a "helpmate who is your opposite," as God found Eve for Adam. To do so, you'll first need to identify your deepest needs and your greatest deficiencies. If you are an ambitious, life-in-the-fast-lane type, the last thing you need is someone just like you. That kind of disposition is almost always born of insecurity. Find a member of the opposite sex who has much less to prove. His or her confidence will offer you limitless comfort, and confident people have a greater capacity to love. Conversely, if you're the shy, reflective type, look for someone whose strength is the ability to light up a room with her personality; you can bring intimacy and closeness to the relationship, and she can bring the passion and intensity.

Stay mindful of your greatest vulnerabilities as well as your strongest gifts. It'll help you understand what qualities you're attracted to and why. Have realistic expectations. Those who are searching for "the best" person value perfection more than love, faultlessness more than tenderness, solitude more than companionship, and they often remain lonely too long, even throughout their misguided marriages.

Let Go of Losing Propositions

No commitment-phobes, no severe emotional cripples (unless they show a commitment to change), and no married people. Stay away from them, got it? These days, it's not just men who are afraid of commitment; there are plenty of women who fear the altar as well. Since they come in all sizes and shapes, here are some screening questions you can ask to determine who they are:

- ♥ Have you ever been engaged and broken it off?

- ♥ Do you have trouble saying words like *marriage, commitment,* or *couple?*

- ♥ Do you find yourself stuttering over *any* word that begins with the letter "m"?

- ♥ Do you have any friends who are married?

- ♥ If so, did you break out in a cold sweat when you went to their weddings?

- ♥ Are your parents married or divorced?

- ♥ Do you prefer talking to your plants over talking to your dates?

- ♥ Would you still want to date me if I told you we couldn't make love until our wedding night?

If interviewees avert their glance, hem and haw, or jump out the window, you have your answer. Don't date 'em, don't even hate 'em, just move on.

No Movie Dates at First

As wonderful as movies are, going to the movies tells you little about other people except whether they like popcorn and can sit quietly without fidgeting and kibitzing over the best lines. You're in the dark, facing forward, fixed on someone else's life. Is watching Arnold Schwarzenegger trying to fake a cowboy accent going to do much for your love life? And is staring at Demi Moore's enhanced mammary glands going to endear you to a woman whom you've just met? Save the dinner-and-movie dates until after you get to know each other. By then, you'll have an easier time agreeing on which movies and restaurants to go to.

Date Creatively

Instead of going to the movies, attend events and go to places that will give you something to talk about: lectures, readings, museums, religious celebrations. Try to spend time with nature, like taking long walks near the river or leisurely hikes through majestic vistas. Watch the sun go down together (if you're watching it come up together, you've probably already broken one of my rules). If you're both great at tennis, go bowling, or do something neither of you has done since junior high school. Go record shopping, and take your CDs and tapes home and listen to them together. Take a day trip to someplace neither of you has been to. Have fun surfing the Internet together, looking for travel destinations. Or take a long afternoon walk through your neighborhood, challenging yourselves to find something you've never seen before. How about that all-you-can-eat pancake breakfast at the VFW next Sunday morning? Remember to be open to your partner's ideas: VFW meals aren't that bad.

Avoid Meaningless Sex

Why? It stiffens the heart and dulls the body. Great sex is about being natural. Sex with a stranger, anyone who hasn't gotten naked on all levels, makes it impossible to let go and lose control. Afraid of submitting to instinct, because you might end up in an uncomfortable destination, you can end up with a lousy night of copulation and a sorry foundation for love.

While we know that men and women relate differently to sex, it's worth adding here that women sometimes try to emulate men on this score. This is largely because women have healthy sexual appetites, in many cases stronger than men's. Every women's magazine cover has headlines like "Seven Thousand Ways to Have Him Begging in the Bedroom," while men's magazines are just as likely to be dwelling on "New Generation Electric Drills." Women usually manage to integrate love and lust naturally, but when they try instead to act like men and compartmentalize, they find it difficult to reunite the two later on. That which is undone can be difficult to redo.

Use Your Newly Acquired Empathic Skills

If you have followed my preceding advice, you now can tell what people are truly feeling. If you see your date light up when a certain subject comes up, pursue it. Stay with that subject, and watch your partner blossom like a hibiscus. Watch how your interest in the subject increases his or hers.

Stay Compatible

When I see obviously married couples at restaurants, eating in silence, I want to go over and shake them up. "Wake up," I want to say. "This is your best friend. You can't have run out of things to talk about, experiences to share." They may be talked out on the mundane aspects of their lives: the house, the kids, the car, the bills, even juicy gossip about the neighbors. That doesn't mean there's nothing left to talk about. There's an entire universe of depth that we all harbor in our hearts—no matter how well we know each other.

We all get a little crusty over the years, even with best friends, and allow a part of ourselves to die. But we can be reborn; we can renew. If you feel you're reaching this kind of impasse in a relationship, try to take on something completely new and different together, something neither of you has done before. Take a ballroom dancing class or drive to the shore and watch the moon come up. Break out (but don't break a limb). Quit your jobs and volunteer to go to Africa with the Peace Corps; that ought to trigger some interesting dinner conversation.

6. Exercises in Selflessness

It's Why We Want to Fall in Love

Selflessness is the essence of love. It liberates us from our familiar little lives and reveals the refreshing joy of another person's story. We can pour all that suppressed desire to give of ourselves into a worthy vessel. Yet single people—and married people who are entrenched in their own workaday worlds—often become accustomed to tending to their own needs, to the exclusion of others'. We become selfish. We need to retrain ourselves to focus outward.

The following exercises will help you fall in love in any number of little ways. Making generosity a habit will spill over into your love life, as you find the impulse to give becoming your first instinct. After a while you'll discover that there's more joy to be found in the world by acting honestly and openly than by maneuvering craftily through life, a revelation that's crucial to falling in love. You'll soon stop seeing prospective mates as people to be manipulated and start seeing them as precious parts of your life. On a profound level, you'll be taking steps to reclaim your innocence: your sense of faith, your belief in a world filled with goodness.

The following set of exercises is directed at becoming selfless generally; the next is specifically aimed at relationships.

Being a Selfless Person

💜 *Keep your work in perspective.* Too many people are already married—to their jobs. Whether we know it or not, our jobs drain us of the ability to be selfless. What with downsizing and corporate cloak-and-dagger maneuvering for the corner office, or your office, our jobs force us to look out for number one. I can't change your work environment, but you can change your attitude toward it. It is not the be-all and end-all of who you are. You do not have to define yourself through your career.

Bring personal things to your desk—photos of family, friends, your dog, and your trip to Tahoe; inspirational quotations—and spread them around so the really important things in your life are not forgotten. The people who matter most to you are who you are.

Put some distance between you and your job by taking healthy breaks during the day. Walk around the block instead of sitting in the staff kitchen and griping about deadlines. After work, before you go home, swim a couple of laps in the local pool or sit in a sauna. Sweat out that work energy. All this will separate you from that thing that occupies so much of your identity: your occupation.

As "the man" said (so many have said it, I've forgotten who said it first), "On my deathbed I will not wish I had spent another hour late at the office. I'll wish I had spent another hour with my wife and children."

❤ *Temper your insatiable desires.* If selfishness is defined as catering to your cravings, reduce the temptations. Buy less, eat less, see fewer movies and other distracting entertainment. Focus on enriching your life with things that aren't ephemeral. Replace consumption with compassion, consumerism with caring. If you can't give up the weekend at the spa or the new leather jacket, at least see them for what they are: indulgences that feed your self-absorption. That realization should help make each new acquisition, each new sacrifice to the god of your senses, seem that much more hollow. Soon it'll dawn on you: "Who needs this Lexus SUV when I have no one to take romantic drives with anyway?"

❤ *Donate your time, not just your money.* You've noticed that sophisticated nonprofit fund-raising organizations first ask you to join a committee or volunteer for a telethon; then they hit you up for the bucks. They're no fools. Everyone knows that the cash follows the commitment. Political fund-raisers do the same thing. Even small donations carry the larger implication of involvement. Rather than writing a check to Save the Children Foundation, call and see if there's something you can do to help in person. Later, of course, you should write the check.

❤ *Talk to your cabdriver.* Or your waiter. Or the bellman at your apartment building. Too often we look at these people as our personal servants: nameless, faceless, lifeless. This is abhorrent behavior. It means that we have lost perspective on the infinite value of every human life; these people have become a means rather than an end, possessing no intrinsic value save to satisfy our needs. From there it's a short step to seeing someone we're dating in the same light. The woman sitting across from us may not be the waitress, but in our mind she may be merely the sex goddess, provided to satisfy our needs. It suggests that we think we are better, more important, and that the world revolves around us. Seek to impart dignity to all your acquaintances. Ask about their family, their personal life, what they do when they're not serving you hand and foot, and listen to their answers. (In case you were wondering, a big tip will not substitute for this exercise.)

❤ *Give it away*. This is so simple. Go through your closet, put everything you haven't worn in a year in cardboard boxes, and take it all down to the Salvation Army. Do it without great fanfare. Drop the stuff off, imagine someone in need wearing your Jim Morrison leather bell-bottoms, and smile.

Being a Selfless Lover

❤ *Visit your grandmother*. This may sound like an odd exercise. Years ago, when Debbie and I were dating, I was surprised to discover that whenever we went out shortly after I'd visited my beloved elderly grandmother, I was more attentive, more caring, and more genuine than I was at other times. After spending time with someone who meant so much to me, and to whom I meant so much, I found that my pretensions and manipulative strategies dropped away slightly, and for some time thereafter my selfish urges diminished greatly. The visits brought out feelings of compassion in me that would otherwise have remained repressed. All of us have goodness and caring on the inside; the trick is to bring these qualities to the outside.

Not all of us have aging grandparents to visit, but there's a lesson for everyone in this. It's much easier to open yourself up to love if you're already in a selfless, caring frame of mind. Aging people need a lot of attention. So if Grandma is long gone, offer your assistance to an old man who looks lost, or help a woman lift a baby stroller up a flight of stairs. Or find out how you can help at a senior citizens' center.

♥ *Apologize to someone you've hurt.* Right a wrong; rebuild a relationship with a friend with whom you've had a falling out. Learn to say you're sorry. Say it often so that it becomes second nature and effortless.

♥ *Be a nice guy (or gal).* If you've been dubbed the "bad boy" or the "icy woman," take a different tack. It's my guess that this is simply a facade, a mask of self-defense, constructed to keep the focus on you in the world of dating. Drop the mask and direct attention away from you and onto the other person.

♥ *Give a gift.* Bring a gift to a man or woman you're dating, but make it a gift that has no utilitarian value. Women particularly like such gifts, because all they say is "I am thinking of you." That's what flowers are all about. Men who send flowers by rote, however, are missing the point. A woman who gives a man a gift might be worried that the man will interpret it as having Great Meaning. So what? Let him. That's why you're doing it. It's about him; it's not about what you get back in return.

♥ *Lend an ear.* Attention is a gift that brings many rewards. Ask "How are you?" and mean it. Follow up the answer with another question. Even if someone says, "Fine, how are you?" make sure you return to the other person with further questions. This might be hard for some people, who consider listening passive, but listening can be active. It demands that you turn down your own inner monologue and direct your thoughts toward someone else. That can be hard work, especially for men whose attention spans have never matched their lovers'.

7. Exercises to Accent Differentiation

The powerful propulsion of the bird relationship is drawn from the strength of two wings flapping separately but equally, a man and a woman demonstrating their two distinct energies in a complementary manner. These days it's easy to forget the difference between men and women, and it can be easy to lose yourself in a new relationship. The paradox of love is that if you desire your mate too much, so much that you sublimate your own will to his or hers, you'll both tire quickly of the relationship. Love is about *interde-pendency* between two equals, not about one partner's giving himself or herself over entirely to the other. While closeness is the goal, keeping your distance can help to foster that closeness. The exercises that follow provide ways to ensure that men and women do not lose their innately male and female qualities.

Develop Your Own Gender Identity

Indulging in classically male or female activities—thoughtfully, of course—will put you in touch with the core meaning of your own gender identity. If you don't sew because you think feminists don't sew, make a radical statement and be a feminist who *does*. By the same token, realize that you can be a sensitive man and still love watching two brutal football teams knock the hell out of each other.

Men, pick a weekend and do typical guy things: fixing the car, chopping half a cord of wood, rewiring your sound system, ogling all the pictures in the latest issue of the Home Depot catalog (tricked you there). Revel in your maleness. Burp. Leave the dishes in the sink. Order in pizza and beer. Leave the toilet seat up. Scratch your-self (yes, *there*). And then clean up the place before your girlfriend or wife or a date shows up! When your woman comes back, you'll appreciate anew the civilizing influence she brings to your life.

Women, do likewise. Be totally feminine. Talk on the phone for hours. Do your toenails. Bake bread. Shop for beautiful pictures for your walls. Reread Betty and Anaïs (that would be Friedan and Nin). Ogle all the pictures in the latest issue of *Vogue*. Then mess up the place so your guy doesn't feel too alienated.

Don't Drop the Rest of Your Life

Once you start dating someone seriously, it's easy to leave your friends, family, job, cat, hobbies, and plants high and dry. Always remember that having a relationship may be important to you, but it shouldn't be so important that you're willing to repress your own needs and desires to preserve it. After all, if there is no you, there is no one for your partner to fall in love with. Encourage your partner not to drop his own hobbies, and don't always invite yourself along on his activities. Instead, suggest that he come back and tell you all about it, if he wants to. The message should be: *I value what you value for yourself*.

Don't Lose Yourself in a New Relationship

If you feel yourself at risk of being dominated, especially early in a relationship, take a step back and remind yourself of what *you* want. Contemporary women, reacting to today's commitment-phobic men, are especially prone to this problem, pursuing men too aggressively and swearing their fealty in overwhelming waves of devotion. *Big* mistake. Even the most egomaniacal man rarely falls in love with a woman who claims she can't live without him.

In fact, the ones they *do* fall in love with are the very ones who seem to be able to live without them just fine. My friend Ron had a habit of dating a woman for about a month, deciding that he wasn't falling in love, and then quickly discarding her. Each woman in turn professed her devastation to him: "You can't do this to me, Ron. I thought we really had something." Then he met Camilla and broke up with her. When Ron gave her his pat "Let's just be friends" rap, she had enough self-respect to tell him that she completely understood and that she agreed it was for the best. Of course, of all the women he'd ever dated, Camilla was the one woman he returned to.

Keep Your Power

There's compromise, and then there's buckling under pressure. To keep those wings balanced, both parties need equal access to that strong gust of wind. It's hard to know when to acquiesce and when to hold your ground for what you want. There are small skirmishes that are easily resolved. *Chinese or Thai?* That's easy: Tonight Chinese, next week Thai. *Children or no children?* That might be a little more difficult.

Here's where you need to practice the art of negotiation, of not giving up too much of yourself. The exercise is to make a list of negotiables and nonnegotiables. Then sit down with your partner and talk it through. Better to do this long before the actual decision has to be made, so that the discussion can be mature and not too emotionally charged. And remember that technique we discussed earlier: In the midst of a debate, try practicing empathy by switching positions for a while.

8. Exercises in Shared Experience

Give Romance a Chance

Love is a cumulative process. It may hit you on the head like a hammer, or it may creep up on you slowly, but in either case that's just the beginning. Real love builds on that beginning and stretches for a lifetime.

The reason for so much of our contemporary discontent is that we expect love to be handed to us on a platter, and that's not the way it works. There are opportunities for love all around us if we only take the time to nurture them. Love isn't a thing waiting to be found; it's a process we can begin at any time. Those who wait for love to sweep them off their feet usually end up with a lifetime of aching feet.

Start Simple

Shared experiences begin with the very first experience. After a promising first date, call or drop a note or send an E-mail saying "I'm really glad we got together. I had a nice time." What that says is that you're honoring the time you spent together. If you want to make a bridge to the next encounter, add "I hope we can do it again."

Make Time

Romance does not happen by itself. It requires a conscious choice, a clearing of space on your calendar to give yourself time to nurture the relationship. Whether you choose a fixed time every week or a more flexible schedule, you have to see each other consistently or love will die, like a plant without water. Just as you have to water a plant every day, even if you don't see your potential mate every day, do something thoughtful each day to send the message: *You haven't gone out of my thoughts*.

Take Your Time

When you find someone with whom you believe you can fall in love, give yourself, and that person, a chance. You don't want to force it. In the fullness of time, love will grow. Many of us make the mistake of giving up too early, deciding that things aren't working out, and moving on. In our disposable society, where instant gratification is our mantra, it's all too easy to discard a promising relationship that doesn't produce fireworks in the first few encounters. But love cannot thrive without time to grow. This is why people who spend a great deal of time together—in the past as neighbors, more often today as co-workers—often begin falling in love without expecting it. The joy of shared experience creates the foundation for a lasting union.

Don't Bide Your Time

At the same time, be careful not to overdo the evaluation period. You don't want to be too picky, because people end up settling for loneliness. Don't let pettier concerns—*Are we too young? Is this the right time?*—overwhelm your decision to pursue a commitment. It's far better to marry the right person at the wrong time than the wrong person at the right time. Similarly, don't let unimportant issues of geography scuttle an otherwise good relationship. It's better to be blissfully married and living in the wrong place than to be unhappily lonely in the most wonderful place. Remember, when Adam inhabited Eden, it wasn't Paradise until Eve came along.

Create Rituals

Go back to places you've gone to before. As your relationship progresses, try returning to old familiar places, like that little French restaurant where you first professed your deep feelings for each other. Or try something a little more creative, like singing that old

Temptations song every time you feel amorous. These rituals can also be more serious, like celebrating the Sabbath together and having a steaming bowl of chicken soup. Or you can simply claim Sunday as "your day," when nothing goes on the Day Planner but things to do together.

Make History

Keep a scrapbook together. Collect photos you've taken on trips or special occasions or no occasion at all, and together put them into the book. Make sure this is a joint project. Add notes to each other and newspaper clippings that remind you of experiences or conversations you've shared. When you take an exercise like this seriously, you're taking your relationship seriously, preserving it for yourselves and the family you'll have together.

Disappear on Your Own Island

If you can't afford to disappear on an island literally, do it figuratively. Isolate yourselves. Remember the idea that all men and women are fundamentally compatible? It follows that any couple cast away together in isolation will be likely to fall in love. So get in the car together with no itinerary, leave the cell phone at home, and drive and talk. Or take a retreat at home, telling your friends you're leaving for the weekend, pulling out the phone, and reveling in your apartment paradise. You can, and should, do this on a weekly basis. By setting certain times as exclusive times with your lover, you're giving yourself an excuse to spend time with him or her alone.

Embrace Commitment

Remember, love is like oil pressed from an olive. Commitment is what brings on love, not vice versa. Don't be afraid to get married. Look forward to it. Remember how excited you were in kindergarten, when you enacted mock marriages with every little girl in the class, or while you were dating your first love, when you just knew it would last forever. Be bold and hopeful. Envision yourself in a sharp tuxedo, radiant with anticipation, watching your beautiful bride walk toward you down the aisle in a flowing white gown. Feel fortunate that in embracing the commitment to marry, you are guaranteed to be one of those lucky individuals who will always have someone at their side to glory in the triumphs of life and to give comfort through its inevitable struggles. For what blessing is there in climbing life's highest peaks if, after all the struggle to get to the top, you discover that you are trapped there all alone?

12

Why Can't I Stay in Love?

Toward a Lifetime of Fulfillment

Marriage is like a violin. After the beautiful music is over, the strings are still attached.

—Jacob Braude

You may marry the man of your dreams, ladies, but fourteen years later you are married to a couch that burps.

—Roseanne Barr

Marriage is whereby a woman exchanges the attention of many men for the intention of one.

—Helen Rowland

The Death of Marriage

We began this enterprise with the question "Why can't I fall in love?" Yet many of us who have found partners but still yearn for happiness are struggling with a different, and somehow more poignant, question: "Why can't I *stay* in love?" With love and marriage, singlehood is cured. But what happens when you're five, ten, twenty-five years down the road, and you gradually realize that being single was the easy part?

In marriage, a whole new set of difficulties presents itself: keeping passion and intimacy. Over the years, conversations dwindle to a couple of words exchanged daily about functional problems and household chores. Sex becomes a perfunctory, predictable, and passionless experience, more burden than blessing. For too many couples, monogamy gives way to monotony, tenderness to tediousness, devotion to dullness, and liveliness to lifelessness. The confidences I have heard from some of my married friends are heartbreaking: *He's like a piece of familiar old furniture, unexciting but comfortable. She feels more like my sister, or my mother. We don't look at each other anymore; we look through each other. We have nothing in common anymore. I've outgrown him. Our marriage is just sort of dried up. If not for the kids, I doubt we'd still be together today.* Why? Because keeping the embers of passion burning is at least as great a challenge as lighting them in the first place.

Can This Marriage Be Saved?

Is your marriage less than what you hoped it would be? Or is this just the state of union, the natural result of years of mundane cohabitation? To test the strength of your long-term relationship, answer these questions:

- ❤ When you go out to restaurants together, are day-to-day activities your only topic of conversation?

- ❤ When you sit together in a room, are there long periods of silence?

- ❤ If your spouse interrupts your time alone, do you feel cheated?

- ❤ Do you know your wife or husband on a deeper level than you did when you married?

- ❤ Does the thought of spending time with your spouse excite you?

- ❤ If there were no fear of getting caught, would you have an affair?

- ❤ Are you currently carrying on a flirtation?

- ❤ If you could do everything differently, would you still choose to marry your spouse?

♥ When you talk about your spouse with strangers, do you find yourself feeling animated or listless?

♥ Are you still attracted to your spouse sexually? Intellectually? Emotionally? Spiritually?

The "right" and "wrong" answers should be obvious. The real question is: What to do about this?

A System for Staying in Love

First of all, we must invoke that word that used to scare the day-lights out of you: *commitment*. Commitment isn't a one-time ges-ture, a fait accompli that takes care of itself after the wedding vows. Commitment requires daily renewal. Don't worry, you don't have to call back the clergy and the caterer. But you do have to stay mindful of your relationship, every day. You have to believe you made the right decision in choosing your spouse, that you were preordained for each other, and that you're in this marriage because you're *meant* to be. Saying "I love you," and meaning it, should come naturally. But it's only a start: We all, at some point, if not constantly, have to *work* on our marriage.

If this kind of thing hasn't been coming easily to you lately, what you need to do is go back to the beginning and steal a page from your own book of love, the book you wrote when you were dating and preparing for the beginning of this commitment. If you're going to stay in love, you must remember—and repeat—what it was you did and thought and said that enabled you two to fall in love in the first place. Remember? You felt romantic, attractive, and attracted to the other person. Your lives took on new meaning; you talked for hours; you wanted to explore each other in every way—all of which aroused you even more and gave you greater respect for each other. Not coincidentally, the experience gave you a great belief in love and its potential for longevity, and that belief is crucial. Believing in something, psychiatrists say, actually gives it a better chance of happening. (Social scientists call it the *efficacy syndrome*.) It's the same thing we've discussed elsewhere in the book under the term *faith*. If you were able to take those vows in the first place without crossing your fingers behind your back or running out of the room, this is a belief you once held and probably held passionately. What you need now is to get it back.

One way to help recapture that faith is to make your relationship a little RACIER. (No, this doesn't involve latex rubber outfits—well, not *necessarily*.) What you need to do is to recapture the following qualities in your relationship:

1. Romance

2. Attraction

3. Communication

4. Inquisitiveness

5. Eroticism

6. Respect

Once we have incorporated these qualities into our relationship, staying in love becomes an enjoyable and rewarding experience. Let me break it down for you.

1. Romance

What is romance? I can't pretend to nail it all down for you—philosophers have been defining it since Sophocles—but here's a part of the definition that I think is too often lost: Romance involves doing something *completely nonutilitarian* for someone, extending a gesture whose entire purpose is to make someone else feel cherished.

That's why dishwashers are no good as anniversary gifts, nor, for that matter, are lawn mowers. Many men see flowers as a complete waste—two days later they're nothing but a pile of petals on the floor—but that's the whole point: They serve no other purpose than to express love. The same goes for jewelry. When a man marries a woman, he gives her a ring. Surely it would be more practical—even, in some way, a more powerful symbol of their union—if he were to make her a gift of the house they will share. But a ring is different. It says, This is about more than just where we live or what we do; this is about how special you are. It is about an ideal.

Romance fades when we get mired in the practical and lose track of the ideal. After the initial challenge of courtship has been met and we've sealed the union, it's easy to forget about the need to woo our spouses, and we become lazy about their affections.

But we need to keep wooing. This is why the Bible uses no Hebrew word for *wife* or *husband*; the word *isha*, which means "woman," is used for wives, and *baal*, or "proprietor of a household," is used for husbands. The implication, I believe, is that marriage is never a fully realized state; it is a process. The woman you're married to should never become just "your wife." She must always remain a woman, treated romantically, focused on, and lavished with love and attention. The man you chose should be made to feel similarly appreciated and cherished. And each of you should remember the importance of doing so on a daily basis.

Surprise!

Romantic gestures that come out of the blue are invested with far more meaning than holiday gifts, because they're free of the strings of obligation—and because they help break the routine of marriage and life. So surprise is an important ingredient of the romantic gesture. Marriages flourish when there's always something to look forward to. Romance is about breaking patterns, abolishing routine within a marriage. Of course, life cycle events will always be a big deal. But much more affecting is that call you get from your spouse in the middle of a lousy afternoon, reminding you of how much he or she loves you.

To keep your marriage from devolving into a mundane series of parental meetings and Sunday chores, it's important to remind your partner that you value him or her on the basis of human qualities, not for prowess at cooking or cleaning or for signing the checks. Every day, you should undertake a gesture whose entire purpose is to surprise your mate, interrupt a humdrum day, and shock him or her with your love.

- ❤ While your husband is doing the dishes, sneak up behind him and give him a peck on the cheek.

- ❤ Mail him a card with matches you took while on that weekend at the B&B.

- ❤ However corny it may sound, write your spouse a poem about his or her special qualities—then leave it in some easily discovered place.

- ❤ Without alerting him beforehand, arrange for a grandparent to take the kids for the weekend, and book a quickie holiday.

- ❤ Send flowers to her office because she made the commute safely.

- ❤ Call up your spouse and ask to meet in the lobby of a local hotel for a drink, and then proffer the keys to room 762.

Whenever I suggest these kinds of things to husbands, they look at me as if I'm insane. Of course, if they were having an affair these gestures would be par for the course. My advice to men and women alike is to think of your spouse a little less as a household comanager and a little more as your coconspirator in a wonderful, private affair.

Break the Mold

We all get a little stagnant as individuals from time to time, and the same thing is true within relationships. The way to conquer this is by remembering the importance of reinventing and re-creating yourself so that your lover keeps looking at you through new eyes. Break the patterns of your life by undertaking spontaneous getaways, and I don't mean the annual family vacation. Farm the kids out to relatives and friends, and let yourself go—psychologically, spiritually, emotionally, and physically. Make sure that when you go away you behave like lovers. Indulge in long foreplay sessions, and have as much sex as you want. Stay in and eat breakfast in bed. Give each other massages. Treat the time and money you spend as an investment; you're buying shares in your future happiness (not to mention insurance against expensive marriage counselors).

Whenever people tell me they can't get away because of the kids, I always answer that you *have* to get away because of the kids. Children learn so much about relationships and what to expect from them from their parents. If you as parents seem to bore each other, your children may well conclude that life is capricious, accidental, even basically unhappy. If, on the other hand, they see you as people who value each other, who love each other's company, who light up in each other's presence, they will have the best kind of future to look forward to.

Compliments: The Real Oral Sex

Another weapon in the romantic armory is the compliment. Compliments are to passion what oil is to a fire. Don't underestimate the power of a good word. We give compliments to each other for two reasons. The first is that the other person deserves praise, and the second is that we want the other person to like us. When you offer an admiring comment or flattering praise to your spouse, you're also subtly reminding her that her affection is important to you. So tell your wife she looks great in that color. Tell your husband you love the way his hair looks today. Compliment each other for things you know you want to be admired for, as well as for other things. Like everything else good, compliments can be enhanced by surprise, so let them drop when they're least expected.

Don't forget to let each compliment shine attention onto another side of your mate. Think of it as a portrait you're painting of him or her: Witty, wise, great gardener, handsome man, sexy lady, brilliant computer whiz, smart shopper, wonderful chef—keep the list going. Your attention to detail will be gratefully noticed.

And don't forget the compliments that show your spouse that you simply want to *be* with him or her. Create surprising ways to be in each other's company in wonderful settings. Take a trip to the beach on a Sunday evening and walk along the pier. Visit a new gallery exhibition you read about in the paper. Buy an interesting new cookbook, and spend some weekend time in the kitchen cooking together and trying out new recipes. Plant a vegetable garden together. Instead of watching television, during which you are totally passive, try reading to each other. Few actions are as deliciously romantic as reading to your spouse from a romantic novel, and if you feel like it, you can skip the dirty bits and act them out instead!

The old saying goes that men fall in love with their eyes and women with their ears. So, all you men who are reading this, listen up—and start talking!

2. Attraction

Falling in love, as we've seen, is and should be all about subjectivity, about dropping the urge to judge objectively, to rate or compare, and simply embracing subjectively. To love is to be rendered incapable of rational evaluation. And in a long-term relationship like marriage, there's nothing more important than remembering to look at our spouse using our heart, rather than our head. Love is lost in a marriage when a husband looks at his wife and compares her with his secretary, or when a wife looks at her husband and compares him with her best friend's husband, who always takes the garbage out and sends his wife flowers unexpectedly. Comparison is one of the great enemies of love.

As we've discussed, it's pretty darn difficult today to avoid the millions of temptations to compare ourself and our loved one with images the media casts our way every day. This visual age has taught us to accept perfection as the norm, and we're uncomfortable with anything less. We've seen too many naked bodies in person or in films and elsewhere. Today, 72 percent of American wives don't undress in front of their husbands because they feel ashamed of their bodies. This is an astounding statistic, because it means that a large majority of women feel uncomfortable in their most intimate relationship.

Another, deeper reason for the loss of attraction has psychological implications. Remember what Groucho said: "I wouldn't belong to any club that would have me as a member." This is the romantic version: "I'm not that special. If Adele married me, how special can she be?" This is an insidious kind of insecurity, and I've seen it damage too many relationships.

Re-creating the attraction that brought you two together, therefore, will take some self-discipline. But the steps are clear: Limit your exposure to things that will distract your attention from your spouse. In practical terms, this means turning off the television when *Baywatch* comes on. Instead of going to see *Summer Murder Among the Teenage Sex Goddesses*, try *The Goats of the Himalayan Mountains*. Subscribe to *Organic Gardener* instead of *Playboy*, *Playgirl*, or any of their less explicit (but still too tempting) stand-ins. Make sure you're always in the middle of a good paperback book, so that you can pull it out of your bag and get back into it whenever you're distracted by a sexy swimwear ad or TV show. Get indignant, not excited, at the media's crass attempts to manipulate you, and let your self-respect turn you back toward the excitement that's there to be explored in your love life.

Body Work

That said, there's no denying that looks count. Most of us put plenty of effort into our appearance before we're married, because we want people to look at us and like what they see. That's true for job interviews, church or synagogue functions, family weddings, and of course dating. Once married, though, too many of us lose that impulse. We wallow around the house in jogging pants and unwashed hair, not caring about the way we look. A recent survey showed that two-thirds of husbands don't shower before they make love to their wives. This wouldn't be a big deal, except for the fact that they would never consider not showering if they were making love to a mistress. We should never lose sight of the fact that our spouse also has a libido that needs stoking.

If you're afraid that the physical spark between you and your spouse seems to be dwindling, remind yourself of what you once liked about this person. If this means that you have to draw up a list, written or in your mind, then do that. Think about what makes this person attractive to you. Furthermore, think about what made you attractive to him or her, and work on preserving or reinvigorating those qualities. Your husband may have found you carefree and bubbly but now may be disconcerted at how you get bogged down with everyday chores. Your wife may have loved your energetic, outdoorsy nature, which won't be so apparent if you're happy now just lazing away on the couch. Working on these issues is among the responsibilities of a marriage, and it can lead to some pretty good rewards if you'll only put a little time into it.

Jealousy and Covetousness: Attraction Essentials

How can we combat the tendency to take marriage for granted? Here's a controversial suggestion: Make sure you're not always available to your spouse.

Let us briefly consider the subject of jealousy. With the possible exception of hatred, jealousy is the most intense emotion of the human heart. While it's generally thought of as purely negative and unwelcome, I would argue that the power of jealousy can be harnessed and used for good, by combating the complacency of marriage.

The key is the unique power of jealousy to help us see ourselves, and each other, through the eyes of a third party. When complacency has settled into a marriage, we need to be reminded of the beauty of our spouse, and the most direct way of doing so is by seeing him or her through other people's eyes. A husband can grow bored with his wife, but if he sees someone else checking her out— if a stranger can find the woman in his wife—the husband will be prompted to think about that woman, too. His insecurity about her will grow, just slightly, and he will decide he isn't bored with her after all. Better yet, the mere possibility that his wife could return the attention will jolt the husband awake and ensure that he no longer takes her affections lightly. The moment she expresses interest in someone else, even a passing, playful interest, she has reestablished her allure and annihilated his complacency.

One way or another, jealousy will make an appearance in almost every marriage. It's your choice to decide how to use it. Here's the positive way: Use jealousy to keep your love alive—in moderation. The tenth commandment is "Thou shalt not covet your neighbor's spouse," which means also that we *should* covet our *own* spouse. Do you hear that? *Lust after your wife*, the Bible says. Too many marriages today suffer from a dearth of lust. I suggest you use a healthy sprinkling of jealousy as the tool to encourage the rebirth of lust between you and your spouse. This doesn't mean that if you attend a cocktail party with your husband you should flirt outrageously with other men. But neither should you hang onto the arm of your husband. It may be giving him too strong a sense of security and subconsciously reinforcing the idea that, with you completely won over, he can let his eye wander wherever it might. Instead, even if you're shy (and shyness can be very sexy), there's nothing wrong with innocent conversation with both men and women. There's nothing wrong with encouraging him to think, "Hey, who's my wife speaking to? Where'd she go?" Your ability to circulate independently, and the spectacle of others enjoying your company, will make you more attractive.

3. Communication

David and Joanne came to see me a number of years ago for marriage counseling. Joanne said, "Look, Shmuley, my husband just doesn't talk to me anymore. I ask him how his day was, and the answer is always 'fine.' I ask him how work is going, his answer is the same. But then a letter from the company gets sent by Express Mail to our house, and I see a copy of it, and I realize that things are *not* going fine, that David might get laid off soon, and still he doesn't tell me what's going on. This makes me feel inadequate. I want to be there to help him, but he doesn't let me. Instead of being helpful, I'm becoming hopeless."

David didn't say much in his defense. He couldn't articulate why he felt unable to talk to Joanne, though he mentioned being worried that she would repeat everything to her mother, with whom she had a close relationship.

David and Joanne's lack of communication is typical of the way many couples operate. They don't trust each other with information. Instead of working out ways to build trust, they clam up and protect themselves from possible future disappointment. In the process, they hurt themselves more, because they deny each other the chance to bond. In any marriage or relationship, physical intimacy without verbal intimacy is like a body without a soul, a living corpse. A relationship where there is insufficient communication is lifeless and dull; worst of all, it robs both partners of one of the most beautiful aspects of a relationship: the ability to unburden yourself to someone you love, to be comforted over life's daily vicissitudes. The loneliest people I've ever met are married couples who feel they can't talk to each other.

Why is it that husbands and wives sometimes find it so difficult to communicate? Why do we find it so challenging to bring each other into our circle of trust? Why do so many married men and women continue to live enshrouded by silence?

The Four Barriers to Communication and How to Overcome Them

Following is a discussion of the four most common reasons for communication failures within a relationship:

Embarrassment

The potential for personal shame or embarrassment doesn't always disappear as fully as we'd like when a ring is placed on the finger. Couples who don't grow closer together, who keep their distance and remain strangers to each other, can harbor serious fears of rejection. In a way it makes sense, because whose good opinion do we covet most? Despite the comfort that marriage provides, we still want to make a favorable impression on our spouse. We want him or her to have only the highest opinion of us. And any married man or woman can feel tremendous pressure as a result. David, like many husbands, was convinced that his wife had married him because he was a success, and he was afraid to destroy the illusion. In the process, he almost destroyed the marriage.

Partners can also sabotage their chances for complete communication by ridiculing their spouse's overtures. Many men are afraid to say something romantic to their spouse, or to reveal some formative experience of their childhood, out of fear that their partner will dismiss it out of hand. Like serial daters who dump their potential mates so they don't get dumped first, they choose to hold back, to reject the opportunity to share, out of fear that they'll be rejected themselves. Recently, I had a friend call and tell me, "I think my husband is having an affair." When I asked her why, she said, "He called me from work today to apologize for what he said while we were arguing last night. He has never done that before. He must feel guilty about something."

If we close ourselves off to each other's overtures—if we make our spouses feel embarrassed when they try to disclose their emotions—we'll always be closed to each other, and the relationship will never blossom. So next time your spouse makes a nice gesture, try not to react the way Israeli bomb squads do to unclaimed packages at the Tel Aviv airport. People can and genuinely do change; indeed, they often want to change and better themselves. And it's our responsibility to open the door for change. In every aspect of your relationship, display an openness that will invite such gestures. And if you're feeling the need to open up, don't let fear get in the way.

In the final analysis, it's simple: Love cannot exist without trust. Trust cannot be built without communication. Communication cannot take place if there is fear of rejection or embarrassment. And the best way to build trust is to practice, practice, practice. Tonight, as soon as you put this book down, throw caution to the wind, and tell your spouse something extremely personal, something you might consider embarrassing. Chances are that after your spouse stops chuckling, rather than looking down at you he or she will return the favor, revealing something equally personal, and the process will draw you closer together.

Many couples have difficulty discussing the intimate details of their sex life together. It's too embarrassing. One solution is to try discussing it over the phone when you're away from each other: Absence makes the heart grow fonder, after all, and when two separated spouses are missing each other (and lusting after each other from afar), it can be much easier to discuss feelings about lovemaking. For that matter, discussing a very personal subject without having to look at (or away from) each other can help the words flow more easily. And having a romantic conversation over the phone can remind spouses that they're never far from their partner's thoughts.

Perceived Lack of Understanding

The second impediment to communication is the fear that your partner will never understand your feelings. *Why bother talking about it in the first place?* Time and again, when friends tell me they're going through difficulties at work or with their families, and I ask what their spouse says about it, they respond, "I haven't really said anything. She (or he) will probably just criticize me for doing something wrong. I'd rather work this out by myself."

Sometimes, there seems to be no reason to open up, because opening up won't help the situation anyway. Too often, when something about work has been troubling me, Debbie has seen the anxiety in my face and asked me what's the matter, and I've politely dismissed her concern, thinking *Why trouble her with this? Nothing she can do.* This attitude is, of course, a grave mistake, first, because it involves willfully depriving ourselves of the chance to be comforted, and second, because it makes our spouse feel useless and extraneous. The truth is that even if your spouse can't actually solve the issues at hand, he or she can soothe the pain the problem causes, lending the strength (and sometimes the insightful advice) you need to make the situation better. Couples need to draw closer together in moments of stress; in a healthy relationship, every seeming setback is an opportunity to love each other more and grow together, not to hide from each other. If the world knocks you down, who else but your partner is going to help you get back up?

The solution is simple; you must force yourself to talk. The more you feel yourself sinking into the abyss of your own inner blackness, the more you have to struggle to open up. Holler for help, so that your spouse can come to the rescue. There's no way around this other than practicing communicating when you least feel like it. After a while, it becomes like waking up early enough to get to work on time. First it's hard, but after a few times it becomes second nature.

What's the worst that can happen? Maybe you'll talk through the problem, but your spouse won't understand. Still, if your relationship is healthy at all, he or she should support you. It's much more likely that your spouse will understand what you're suffering through and be able to help. You'd be surprised how much we humans have in common, and there's every possibility that your spouse has gone through something similar. If you feel able to count on each other to make the effort to understand each other, in good times and bad, your relationship will be immeasurably strengthened.

Boredom

The third impediment to communication is feeling that everything has already been said. More than anything else, boredom is the bane of communication in marriage. Couples stop talking because they have nothing to talk about. In their minds, they already *know* each other. So what use is conversation when it's bound to be more of the same?

When we become caught up in the peripheral, we forget about what is central to a relationship, which is establishing high levels of verbal intimacy. We allow ourselves to be lulled into thinking that the routine ordinariness of life is enough for us, and we can't even think that there could be a deeper level to connect on.

They say that most of us use only about 20 percent of our brain. I have a feeling that we use even less of our heart. Rarely do we maximize anything more than a small percentage of our relationships. Watching television together in silence becomes a substitute for strolling down the street together in animated conversation. Going to see a movie replaces watching sunsets while holding hands. Working long hours to acquire larger homes that will only cause more hassles supplants coming home earlier so that we can spend more time together. We stop connecting. And after a while the boredom becomes pervasive; we lose the ability to be stimulated by our marriage.

To sustain novelty in a relationship, we must cultivate new parts of our persona and introduce them to our spouse on a regular basis. If life is a routine, we must find new insights into those routines and into our own relationship to them. Say, "I saw a homeless person on the street today and it made me feel . . ." Or "I discovered something interesting about myself today while taking out the garbage." Draw on your childhood experiences, your college days—you may well surprise your mate with stories of your past.

If you don't have new insights into yourself as you grow through the everyday routine of life, you'll have nothing to share with your spouse at night, and you'll run to turn on the TV. Or you'll resort to gossip, and talking about someone else can't do all that much to enhance your relationship. Instead, try finding some interesting item in the newspaper to discuss with your spouse. When asked, "How are you?" don't just say "Fine." That's a conversation stopper, not a starter. Instead, say something like "I'm feeling pretty good—do you know what happened today?" Or even "Did you hear that the Middle East is on the verge of peace?" Think of new subjects to discuss: politics, work, your childhood, something fascinating from history, a new theory you heard on the radio, even a new recipe. As you reach for new ideas to exchange, you'll find that a much more important exchange is going on: the exchange of energy between the two of you.

For the times when you do have to talk about everyday affairs, try to develop a passion for them. Strive to make the everyday unique and the natural miraculous. With the right attitude, you can find magic even in the mundane.

Unresponsive Partner

This is probably one of the most hurtful things that can happen in a marriage: when the dialogue becomes a monologue. You try to share all your pain and joy with your partner, and he or she just flips through the TV channels and moans, "Honey, I'm so tired I can't concentrate. Can't we talk later?" But later never comes. No one has ever had a meaningful conversation during a commercial break.

Television, which requires virtually no effort, has become one of the forces most destructive to human relationships. Not only does it fill our living room with sexy distractions, but the very nature of television instills a laziness in us that's hard to shake. We think of sitting in front of the box as the only way to relax, forgetting that just holding each other and stroking each other's hair is a far healthier way to relax.

Therefore, as banal as it may seem, I cannot emphasize the next point enough: *Get the television out of your bedroom.* Why allow late-night comedians to entertain you when it could be your spouse who is trying to make you laugh or make love to you? A TV in the bedroom ends up doing all the talking and loving for a couple. It takes the focus off the two of you and intrudes on your closeness.

But we love just holding each other at night and watching a movie, you say. Okay, I admit that this can be relaxing and romantic. But do it in the living room. Keep the bedroom sacred, or soon it'll be nothing more than a TV room where you can have an occasional quickie. Once it's gone, turn to your spouse and say, "This is important to me. I need you to listen to me." Turn off the cell phone, turn off the ringer on the regular phone, put the kids to bed, and get a conversation going.

A Call for Radical Honesty: The Essence of Communication

Once you've created the time and the setting for uninterrupted communication, I have only one piece of advice:

Tell Each Other Everything

Expose yourself completely to your spouse, and invite him or her to do the same. Wear your heart on your sleeve. Prudishness and secrecy have no place between a husband and wife. Remember the concept of river, kettle, and bird relationships? The only way to help your relationship go from river to kettle to bird is through extreme honesty. In the river relationship, when a husband seems preoccupied and his wife asks what's wrong, he replies, "Oh, nothing," because he believes his problems are all on his side of the river, nothing for her to worry about. In a kettle couple, the man answers, "You know, honey, I really just need some time to myself," and the woman nods knowingly and says, "I'll leave you alone, then." The kettle will always be in the way, impeding communication and connection.

Now for the bird couple. "What's wrong?" she asks. "This is hard for me to discuss," he begins, "but I'm not happy these days." And he shares his problems as they sit around the kitchen table over a cup of coffee.

In a bird relationship, both partners realize they need each other to keep them aloft. There's no such thing as a problem that's *his* or *hers*, because the two spouses are one flesh. Everything that happens is brought back into the relationship and used to make it stronger, to propel it forward. Neither partner thinks of himself or herself in terms of "I"; everything becomes "we."

I've long advocated that couples enhance their love lives by revealing even their petty attractions to strangers outside the relationship. To be sure, doing so can sometimes cause pain. But after a while such a deep level of trust is established between husband and wife that even this can bring greater passion into a marriage. One of the best ways to enhance marital passion is for husbands—and especially wives—to reveal their sexual fantasies to each other, especially during sex. (There's also no better way to nip a new crush in the bud than to mention it to your spouse.) Again, a very high level of trust and intimacy is required to do so without friction. But that's where our relationships should be headed.

A call for honesty doesn't have to make your partner feel small or weak or inferior. Honesty doesn't have to mean bluntness. It means truth with diplomacy. Radical honesty also means searching your heart to find the real reasons you love your spouse and then disclosing them. Don't interpret my suggestion as a call for constant criticism; instead, try to offer that kind of honesty in the most loving possible way. If you have something bad to say, ask yourself first if it's truly necessary, then make sure it's balanced with enough compliments that your spouse accepts it without getting defensive. And don't forget that timing is everything. There's nothing wrong with sharing a new sexual fantasy, but it can wait till all your dinner guests are safely gone.

4. Inquisitiveness

One of the main obstacles to the success of relationships today is boredom, which triggers inertia. Couples grow uninterested in each other, they no longer bother, and the relationship founders. Love is a journey that is meant to address the mystery of attraction. When a man and a woman are esoterically drawn to each other, they seek to learn as much about each other as possible.

Curiosity is the very engine of life. What most inspires us to act is the fact that we are endlessly inquisitive. This thirst for knowledge can be used to keep a relationship healthy and vibrant.

Imagine: A man sees a woman across a restaurant. She catches his eye. Sure, he's attracted to her, but he doesn't know her name, her interests, her background. What causes him to approach her is his desire to know all those things. So they start talking, and he invites her out on a date, which she accepts. They start dating. At first they share perfunctory conversation: their hobbies, their parents, the weather. Later, however, as time progresses, they begin to speak intimately. They start sharing secrets. And so long as they delve deeper and deeper into each other, so that their desire to know each other is never satiated, their relationship continues to flourish. But the moment they hit a brick wall, the moment he thinks he's got her all figured out, the relationship is dead.

Herein lies one of the great paradoxes of marriage: The comfort that we crave when we go into marriage is a factor that also has the power to destroy the marriage. If we allow ourselves to be too complacent, we stop bothering to make an effort, because it just doesn't seem worth it. To stay in love, not only do we have to make the effort, but we have to *want* to make the effort. We have to inspire action in our partner so that he or she feels we are still worth getting to know, and vice versa. The way to do this is to keep each other always guessing.

My friend Roberta is an astute wife. Her handsome and successful husband is on the road about half the year. A devoted husband, he calls nearly every night from his hotel to say hello to his wife. And while Roberta is often home when he calls, just as often she's out attending recitals or readings. The result is that her husband is always slightly on edge about where she is. His pursuit of what his wife is up to ensures that he isn't up to anything. He's too preoccupied thinking about Roberta.

Creating a Curious Environment

Inquisitiveness can exist only when two people don't give away everything about themselves; this is why modesty is essential in any relationship. Modesty is not about repression, but rather about creating curiosity and desire. Modesty is the thin veil we wear to shield ourselves from overexposure and boredom. It is designed to seduce in the best sense of the word, to invite your mate to lift that veil and enter your private domain.

Modesty is one of the great secrets of sustaining love in marriage. If someone dresses modestly, you might fantasize about what the body looks like underneath the clothes; if you always see the body, there's nothing left to fantasize about. If your body is always on exhibit, eventually your partner will tire of the display and move on to the next window.

The human body is incredibly magnetic. It has allure; we can't help looking at it. But if we look at it all the time, it loses its allure. Therefore, I advise wives who wish to preserve the love and excitement in their marriage never to parade around the bedroom naked. Make your husband earn a peek by paying attention.

As J. J. Wall once said, "My wife and I just celebrated our twelfth anniversary. I'm Catholic, so there's no real possibility of divorce. I'm Irish—so there *is* the possibility of murder." So if you and your spouse want to be in each other's heart rather than at each other's throat, exercise a bit of modesty and add mystery to your marriage.

Preserving Your Natural Mystery

The beauty of having a bird relationship is that both partners maintain the strengths of their individual identities. If we have no identity of our own, the bird won't fly; likewise, if we become entirely consumed by our partner's life, the bird will have two wings on the same side, neither of which will be functional when the bird wants to soar. Each partner, in other words, needs to indulge his or her natural mystery. This means two things:

1. *Get a life!* Though the relationship should be the most fundamentally important element of a married person's life, it cannot be the only important element. Your job, your relatives and friends, the books you read, your hobbies, and your athletic endeavors are also important. Investing in them is investing in your relationship.

2. *Expose yourself discriminately.* As we know, men are linear, and women are cyclical. Men are always moving toward or moving

away, and women make themselves either available or unavailable to those advances. In keeping with her natural mystery and to preserve the love in her relationship, a woman should open up to her man only insofar as he makes the effort to win her affections. She shouldn't go to bed with someone who hasn't tried to seduce her first, *and that includes her husband*. Just as you can't make love with a man who's across the room, you can't make love with a man whose heart is elsewhere.

A woman or man whose heart is always available, who never shows any reaction but acquiescence, will excite no interest in a spouse. If we become too easy, we rob our partners of the chance to prove their love for us. When we keep our partners curious about us, they stay active in their pursuit of us and in their desire to know us more and keep us happy.

Retaining Youthfulness

Just as we must keep our partners curious about our bodies, we should also work to keep them inquisitive about our minds. Become an inquisitive person: Ask questions, read, have opinions, think. Share your innate intelligence with your partner, and offer your own insights and wisdom into what is happening in his or her life.

One of the things we find so endearing about children is the wide-eyed innocence with which they view the world. They are always asking why and how; they are open to discovery and new ideas. As we grow older, though, we adults often stop asking questions, either because we feel we have most of the answers or because things just don't interest us as much anymore.

The key to staying young in the mind is to keep asking the questions. Never assume that you already know everything there is to learn in this big wide world. My advice is to resist the lifelong pressure to "grow up." Once in a while it's healthy to regress; allow your love to be the release from the adult pressures of life. Let it be carefree. Couples should tease each other and do silly things together. They should flirt with each other, because when they do they become kids again, in the best way.

When a popular magazine contacted me to ask what my millennial resolution was, I thought for a few minutes and said, "In the coming year I hope to make my wife laugh a lot more." People who are in love are carefree and happy, and if you're playful with your spouse, you'll find that these traits will follow. So find things to laugh at together with your spouse. Do something silly for the sole purpose of amusing your spouse. These good vibes will help establish you firmly for the next step in a RACIER relationship.

5. Eroticism

Sex in a marriage is like gas in a car; without it, nothing can move. Sex is a fundamental part of staying in love, because in the whole man-woman complex, sex is the final piece that brings them, figuratively and literally, together. It is the strongest form of communication between a man and a woman. Because sex can create tidal waves of positive feelings for both the man and the woman, it is an act that brings them together emotionally as well. The sexual act not only supports their differences but uses these differences to enhance their feelings for each other.

We all know how good sex can be; if we don't, we can at least imagine. Yet, as I mentioned at the start of this chapter, after many couples have been married for a while, sex seems to disappear from the menu. As the joke goes: Why are married women always fatter than single women? Because single women come home, check what's in the fridge, and then go to bed. Married women come home, check what's in the bed, and then go to the fridge. When sex is no longer exciting, it no longer seems necessary. If couples cannot grow closer together through sex, they will stop wanting to grow together at all.

Love equation: attraction + obstacles = excitement

This equation, which I discovered in Jack Morin's book *The Erotic Mind*, captures the paradox of pursuit: The more difficult the chase, the more meaningful the end result. To keep your sex life lusty, to make it more erotic, I recommend that you create barriers and obstacles. Erotica is based on the effort taken to overcome these obstacles; that is why you never read in an erotic story, "And

she was immediately available, and three minutes later it was over."
Eroticism draws part of its strength from the forbidden nature of the
fruit. Its unavailability becomes its attraction.

Any relationship needs erotic barriers to be healthy. If two people have sex all the time, for months on end without a break, at
some point they'll lose interest in sex and forget about it altogether.
On the other hand, the spouse who successfully overcomes erotic
obstacles confirms his spouse's desirability. This is recognized in the
Bible, which contains laws imposing a period of sexual separation
between a husband and wife for twelve days (the five days of men-
struation and seven days thereafter). During those twelve days, a
couple's libido is given a chance to renew itself. We are recharging
our sexual batteries.

I recommend that you follow this period of sexual separation.
During these twelve days, couples should distance themselves physically from each other as much as possible. Do not engage in
extended foreplay sessions. Sleep in separate beds, if possible. The
beauty of this period of sexual separation is that it allows couples to
become best friends as well as lovers. Let the stormy passions of
lovemaking give way to gentle conversation and conviviality. The
deep emotions that were garnered by sex can now move from the
bedroom to the other rooms in the house, teaching you how to be
close in ways other than the physical. We can stay in love only
when our bodies and our minds are nurtured; this is why erotic barriers are so important. Only in that way can our hearts remain
focused.

When you return to sexuality, have yourselves a mini-honeymoon;
you might even book a beautiful hotel room for your monthly
reunion. The more difficult the abstention, the more wonderful the
reward will be.

Sensuality: Remembering Our Bodies

We commonly associate our bodies with animal physicality, our
souls with celestial spirituality. Though we try to keep our body
healthy by eating properly and going to the gym, we do little to
keep our body holy, because we don't see the body as holy. We can't

believe that spirituality can come in the guise of a hunk of flesh that goes through such sloppy rituals as sex, and worse, on a regular basis. That is just too base. So we nurture our body physically, care for our soul spiritually, and seldom synthesize the two.

In Judaism, the body has never been treated as merely an adjunct of the soul, to be used and discarded. Judaism has always recognized the body's holiness, and this is why sensual stimulation is an integral part of the laws of familial relations. The physical contact of hugging, kissing, and lovemaking is seen by Judaism not as a capitulation to animal instincts, but rather as the holy medium of a committed relationship.

Lovemaking is a celebration of the senses, but the problem today is that our culture values the visual over all else. We go crazy trying to look our best. We diet, we lift weights, we jog, we get nose jobs, and we have our breasts stuffed with silicone, nipping and tucking ourselves into attractiveness. We seldom put the same kind of energy into making our personalities better or into stimulating our minds. Thus lovemaking has become a purely visual activity as well. Gone are the days when a woman's scent could drive her husband wild. The sense of touch no longer sends us to the moon. We're always focused on what the person who is touching us looks like and whether we find him or her sufficiently attractive to look at. If a man and a woman cannot find stimulation through the art of human touch, then something precious has been lost to them. The rabbis of the Talmud forbade physical contact between unmarried men and women. Some people have told me they find this ridiculously prudish, but in the ancient rabbis' time, touch was so powerful that it was held back until a man and a woman were ready to surrender themselves to its power.

We have forgotten, too, about the erotic quality of sound. Though phone sex is a multimillion-dollar industry, embarrassment and laziness have caused us to overlook the role of sound as an essential part of our lovemaking. Today we speak either with great vulgarity or not at all. And the beauty of taste has been lost. We associate taste only with erogenous zones, to the exclusion of all the other body parts. Once upon a time taste meant more than oral sex; it meant kissing the skin all over each other's bodies.

If you want to enhance your marriage, it's time to reacquaint yourself with the instinctive and intuitive nature of sex. Stop placing so much emphasis on sight, and open yourself up to the pleasures of smell, taste, touch, and sound as well. Make each the object of your erotic instincts. If one of you goes on a business trip, instead of watching porn movies all alone, watch an erotic home movie that you have made with each other. Rather than calling a phone-sex line, couples should have phone sex with each other.

In the bedroom, communication should not be about demanding that your partner make certain moves. It should be about expressing what feels good, and how those feelings make you *feel*. Communication should be a way of communing with the whole body so that sex becomes sensual.

A Call for Darkness

To wean ourselves from the visual, I believe we should return to an old practice: making love in the dark. Immersing ourselves in darkness, shutting out the sense of sight and the "noise" of light, allows the other senses to come to the fore and be fed. The ancient rabbis of the Talmud advocated that sex primarily occur in darkness, because they knew that light inhibits us; the cloak of darkness, on the other hand, enables us to free our inner spirit.

Darkness has gotten an unfair rap. For thousands of years, clerics of various religious denominations have been encouraging us all to run from the darkness to the light. But the Jewish mystics taught that the most powerful light is the light that comes out of the darkness, which represents the illumination of the spirit. When couples embrace each other in the dark, they end up creating their own light, the sparks of each other's bodies and the illumination of each other's souls.

Going without physical light in the bedroom can make room for spiritual light in many ways. Light reveals our flaws, making us feel exposed and vulnerable. And even the very experience of darkness is more intense and vivid, more exhilarating, than mundane everyday light. For the same reasons that sight is more important to most of us than sound, darkness is a more vivid experience than silence. Darkness is palpable. Immersed in darkness, we feel all our other senses that would normally be hidden by the light suddenly springing to life. In darkness, the sense of touch brings glorious sensations precisely because it is sudden and unexpected. The touch comes from nowhere. The element of surprise makes all the difference. Darkness is also the perfect place to entertain fantasy in a relationship. It invites the mind, our principal sexual organ, to engage. Lovemaking in the light is a two-dimensional experience that grabs only our external features. But sex in the dark is a three-dimensional experience that lifts the spirit above the body and sews two personalities together as one, indivisible flesh.

Every night, observe at least fifteen minutes of complete, erotic darkness together, even if you don't actually make love. (And that's *before* sleeping.) Each and every light in the bedroom should be extinguished. Revel in the sense of delight brought by touch, sound, even your twin rates of breathing. This is pure sensuality, pure eroticism, and it's guaranteed to heighten your sense of emotional intimacy with your spouse.

6. Respect

It is appropriate that respect is our final subject, because respect is the crowning glory of love. People get married because they want to love and be loved. They want to feel important to someone and to have the pleasure of making someone else feel important. In other words, they want some respect. They want to be heard when they speak. They want to be noticed when they undress. They want to be consulted when important decisions are made. And they want to feel chosen. If they've taken the time to look great, they want to *hear* that they look great. If they've nursed you through an illness, they want to be told that you appreciate what they've done, that you don't take them for granted.

We all understand the importance of respect. But most of us think of respect as an emotion, as something we feel on the inside. I would venture a different interpretation: In healthy relationships, respect is not just something you feel but something you show.

For husbands, that means, among others things:

❤ Never interrupting your wife midsentence.

❤ Never shouting at your wife, especially in front of other people.

- ♥ Always apologizing if you've hurt your wife, verbally or emotionally.

- ♥ Never making important decisions without consulting your wife.

- ♥ Never flirting outrageously with another woman, especially in your wife's presence—and even if she'll never know.

- ♥ Never staring intently at another woman, especially in your wife's presence.

- ♥ Helping with the dishes and other household chores.

- ♥ Not leaving things around the house for your wife to clean up.

- ♥ Granting your wife the space to pursue her personal interests.

- ♥ Always respecting, encouraging, and assisting your wife in her professional goals.

- ♥ Never making love to your wife before you've showered.

For wives, showing respect means, among other things:

- ♥ Never making your husband feel professionally unsuccessful.

- ♥ Never being critical in a way that's demeaning rather than constructive.

- ♥ Not comparing your husband with other men in your conversations.

- ♥ Not putting your husband down in front of the children.

- ♥ Not putting your husband down in front of your or his parents or friends.

- ♥ Granting your husband leeway to pursue his interests.

- ♥ Supporting your husband's professional ambitions.

- ♥ Not ordering your husband around.

- ♥ Not making important decisions without first consulting your husband.

- Not making fun of your husband in public or in private.

- Not using sex as a weapon in your marriage.

- Faking orgasms (just kidding).

One other thing. For both partners, I recommend calling a moratorium on marriage jokes. There are endless jokes about the trials and tribulations of marriage, most of them not terribly funny, all of them diminishing the value of the institution. Don't be tempted; it will only degrade your self-respect, and there are plenty of better ways to be funny.

Let Your Spouse Be

A bird relationship intrinsically involves mutual respect. When we respect our spouses, we allow them their identity and never try to change them or mold them into our idea of what we think a spouse should be. We do not impose ourselves on them. We let them be, and we appreciate that their unique qualities are responsible for half the value of the relationship.

Unfortunately, too many couples believe that respect means learning to tolerate or stomach each other's differences. But that kind of respect, where you simply put up with each other's differences, is not enough to help a marriage flourish. Couples succeed only when husband and wife each feel enriched by the other.

My friends Natalie and Jonathan have a strong marriage, largely because of their emphasis on respect. Natalie explains: "When Jonathan and I started dating, he was still living in this toxic environment at home with his mother. Jonathan was always the creative type. He preferred painting pictures and writing music to doing anything more practical. His mother wanted him to be a lawyer or a doctor, and when he enrolled in art school she made his life miserable. She would rail against him, 'Stop choosing a useless career. One day you're going to have a family to support, and you can't give your children bread if you're a struggling artist.' These diatribes didn't exactly help his self-esteem.

"When we met it was clear that we were opposites. I was the reliable type. I may have lacked spontaneity, but I was really good at mastering practical living. When Jonathan and I met, I loved his artistic temperament. He was so down on himself on the first date that he practically apologized for being an artist. But I encouraged him to go to art school. I said, 'You are so talented, it would be such a waste if you didn't develop those talents. This is who you are—you are an artist.' Now Jonathan has just had his third exhibition, and all his paintings sold, and he is also writing the music for an upcoming play. The reason Jonathan fell in love with me, I think, was that I let him be him. I encouraged his choices, and I didn't impose my ideas of what a husband should be. He told me I was the first person who truly respected him."

The truth is that respecting someone takes a lot of self-assurance. We have to feel good enough about ourselves to understand that our spouse does not have to be exactly like us. Unfortunately, many of us feel so insecure that this self-assurance is hard to come by. We come into marriage scarred by years of rejection in the dating scene, and all too often we're unable to trust the other person sufficiently to let him or her alone. Rather than feeling enhanced by our spouse's differences, we feel threatened, and very often these are the feelings we share, instead of healthier, more affirmative emotions.

The way to remedy this situation is to remember to be as respectable as possible in your own life. The more comfortable you feel in your own skin, with your own decisions, the easier you'll find it to respect your spouse. Live nobly and honestly. Carry yourself with confidence. Tackle your life with gusto. The less frustrated you are about yourself, the less frustrated you will be with your spouse. The rule in life is that miserable people treat other people miserably. If you don't respect yourself, you won't respect your spouse either.

To use the old adage, treat people as you would want them to treat you. Be polite and courteous, and whenever possible rely on yourself before you ask others for help.

Eizer Kenegdo: The Helpmate Who Is Against You

The Bible tells us that God told Adam that he would create a woman who would be *eizer kenegdo:* a helpmate who was his oppo-

site. Biblical commentators have long puzzled over this turn of
phrase. If you are put on earth to help someone, then how can you
be opposed to that person? How would having someone in opposition to him help Adam?

The answer is that often we help our spouses most when we
challenge them. The whole point of a relationship is that we find
love in our opposite. When there is too much sameness, we don't
grow. But that growing is predicated on opening up our hearts to
the possibility of being enriched through sharing and being challenged.

We asked a question at the beginning of this chapter: Why go
into a relationship or marriage? If a man needs love, he can get it
from his parents. If he needs companionship, he can get it from his
male friends or from his dog. If he needs sex he can pay for it, and if
the paternal instinct strikes him he can become a sperm donor and
make babies in a test tube. So why bother with introducing a whole
other person into this life to upset the equation?

The reason is that only a woman can give a man the gift of masculinity, and only a man can give a woman the gift of femininity.
The bird of love can soar only when the two partners are helpmates
who challenge each other, who flap in opposite directions while
being component parts of one organism, a single unit. We won't
stay in love if we are exactly the same; we will just get bored with
each other. We will stay in love only if we support each other's differences and use them as wings in our special union of souls.

The Twelve LoveSteps

*The Love Prophet's Recovery
Program for Dating Dependents
and Love Anorexics*

1. Admit That You Can't Fall in Love

'Fess up. You are lonely, and loneliness is causing serious pain in your life. It hurts, and it stinks. There, you said it, and lightning didn't strike you dead. Now take responsibility; you can't blame the opposite sex forever.

No matter how many times you date, you find fault. If Brad Pitt or Jennifer Aniston showed up as your blind date, you'd find a mole on Jennifer's ear or discover to your horror that Brad isn't a natural blond. Subliminally, you *want* to find flaws. It saves you from having to commit and possibly making a mistake. *Not* falling in love has the added benefit of keeping you in your comfort zone, where things many not be perfect, but at least you're in control.

If you valued love as a necessity rather than a luxury, you'd have realistic expectations, and you'd get over the idea that no one out there is worthy of you. What you need to do is admit that the problem is internal, not external. If you hadn't been eating for weeks, would you tell your family that you're hungry, it's just that the food's so lousy? No, you'd have to admit you were anorexic and take steps to do something about it. And just as you can't fool your doctor, well, you can't fool the Love Prophet, either.

Confront the truth: You're a love anorexic who's lost touch with the deep-seated human appetite for love. You date and date, but no one sticks, because your Teflon coating negates the love adhesive. The problem's with you, not with the people you're meeting. Confess that you've become committed to noncommitment, addicted to dating, and that this is no different from any other addiction. As in any program that effectively breaks you of a drug or alcohol dependency, recognizing the fact that the buck stops with you is the first healthy step toward rehabilitation.

2. Get Help

Lord knows you've tried to kick the dating habit on your own, but this has gotten way beyond your control. You can't do this alone. Confide—to a trusted friend, a family member, a professional counselor, a spiritual adviser, even your spouse!—that you've lost the ability to love freely, openly, and fully. Confess that you've unwittingly joined the ranks of the Love Mafia: You will love only someone who makes you an offer you can't refuse, whose virtues— attractiveness, wealth, celebrity—are out of this universe. Go sit with someone who is mature and wise, who you think would understand. Ask for help in finding your way back to that space in your heart where love still lurks, that pool of tenderness that will never dry up—even if you've lost track of where it's hidden.

Telling someone else you've got a problem makes it more real and will help lift some of the burden from your shoulders. Confiding in and unburdening yourself to a trusted friend or counselor also removes the emotional stoppages and allows the love to start flowing freely. The complicity of a third party will force you to be more accountable. If you fall off the wagon, your friend will understand and encourage you to get back on. Falling in love is all about inspiration and feeling uplifted. You need someone who can foster that inspiration. Expect to fall off several times. If this were easy, you'd already be in love.

Invite the person you've chosen to ask you the hard questions, and make sure you answer them honestly, ruthlessly. Take on questions like these:

❤ *What am I looking for?* Be extremely honest about this question. Do you even know what you want? Are you looking vaguely for some fantastic life partner, with no realistic sense of what that means? Search for a complementary mate, for your "helpmate who is your opposite," as the Bible says. And remember that love is not a luxury but a necessity.

♥ *How am I going about looking for it?* List five things you've done or places you've gone in search of your heart's desire. What was your experience with each? What worked and what failed? What do you wish were different *about yourself* on dates? For instance, perhaps you feel anxious and wish you could be more confident and natural. Set your mind to correcting one flaw at a time. On your next date, rather than laughing hysterically at something that isn't funny, be more authentic. Just smile politely and bring the conversation back to subjects you are familiar with.

♥ *What am I finding instead?* List the last five dating or relationship experiences you've had, whether they go back five weeks or five decades, and closely scrutinize the types of people you've been involved with. Do they fit a certain category? Similar income bracket? Artists versus professionals? Personality types? Buttoned-down or free spirit? Able or unable to commit? Too independent? Recently separated or divorced? What patterns do you see emerging? Are you sabotaging your relationships before they even begin? Are you dating people who you know deep down are the wrong ones, giving yourself a convenient excuse to get frustrated and break off the relationship? Have you subtly made peace with loneliness, to the point that you don't even admit it to yourself?

♥ *What have I been doing wrong?* It ain't gonna happen sitting around waiting for the phone to ring. Neither will it happen by scanning the wedding pages of the Sunday *Times*, drooling over the ones that got away. If it didn't work out with the married person once, it's likely not to happen the fifth time either.

♥ *What must I change to do it right?* This is the tough part. Deconstruct your patterns, then attempt to reconstruct a new you who goes about the noble search for true love in a realistic and optimistic manner. If you're the type of person who always falls in love at conventions with people who live hundreds of miles away—a passive commitment-phobe, in other words—take a break from the conventions, and try falling in love in your hometown. If you're the kind of guy who can't seem to get sex off his mind and engineers every date to end up in the woman's bed, make a personal commitment that you will not have sex for six months. Take up knitting instead.

3. Heal the Love Wounds

Make amends with former and present lovers you may have hurt in the past. The same thing applies to everyone you may have offended, insulted, or hurt in the past. Try to mend any wounds you have caused, unless doing so would harm an innocent party or make a situation worse.

Write letters, send E-mails, make calls and personal appearances. Take responsibility for the role you played in the demise of the relationship. In male-female relationships, this is especially important for the man who dumped a woman after she offered her body in sex, or the woman who rejected an utterly decent guy who worked in a dead-end job. Apologize for sins of omission as well; sometimes it's the things you don't say or don't do that hurt more than the things you do. Apologize for behavior that you now realize hurt both of you. In doing so, you will also mend self-inflicted wounds, guilt, misgivings, and bad feelings about yourself. Admitting that you caused others pain and asking their forgiveness is a tremendously effective self-correcting mechanism that can prep you for love in future relationships. Saying you're sorry, and accepting responsibility, also helps you regain the humility you need to fall in love.

Granted, this might be the most difficult task in this entire program. Saying "I'm sorry" may be just as hard as, if not harder than, saying "I love you." Perhaps it might be easier to start with friends and family or professional colleagues. Writing a practice script might help. Try drafting it and rehearsing it out loud, alone in your room, in front of a mirror. Here are some samples:

♥ I was arrogant to assume I was better than you because I drive a Mercedes SUV and you drive a Taurus.

💜 It was my own insecurity that kept me from showing you how much I appreciated that two-week all-expenses-paid trip to Hoboken, New Jersey.

💜 I'm sorry I made you feel inadequate when I laughed at the size of your manhood.

💜 I didn't realize that my sleeping with your best friend would upset you.

💜 You never told me marriage was important to you, and I never assumed that dating for fifteen years without asking you to be my wife was a big deal.

Helping to restore people's dignity will help you earn back yours. It will allow you to move into future relationships with a clean slate and a clear conscience.

4. Take Your Love Pulse

Just how loving are you? To love *specifically*, you first need to love generally. To love one person, you need to love all people (okay, maybe not that guy who posted pictures of you naked and drunk on the Internet, but almost everyone). This is the holistic approach to love. You can't fall in romantic love if you're not practicing overall love. Practice makes perfect, so start showing love today. Commit yourself to becoming a sensitive, caring, and feeling individual in every area of life. Carry out acts of loving-kindness every day. Your daily "to do" list should include entries like "Compliment someone" (this might come right after "Floss") and "Be nice to a person who can't help my career or improve my social status in any way." The greatest test of whether or not you're a loving person is how you treat those from whom you need nothing. Here are some small ways to start practicing:

💜 At a dinner party where each guest is more boring than the next, rather than rudely getting up and excusing yourself, sit through it, nodding and smiling, as you endure a passionate soliloquy on the maintenance of sod. Enjoy the company of these people, even if you need a Zoloft drip to do it. If you force yourself to be interested, you'll discover that every human being is a player in a fascinating tale. Everyone has a story from which we may learn.

♥ Show patience to some pain in the neck at work or misfit at a social occasion who normally exasperates you. Do so out of a sincere desire to be kind and get to know the person.

♥ Practice generosity of spirit, ranging from giving the parking attendant a decent daily tip to judging people favorably when you hear nasty gossip about them.

♥ Start giving 10 percent of your earnings to charity. If you find it hard, start with 3 percent, and every year increase by another two percentage points.

Now you're ready for the main event. Closely scrutinize the behaviors that keep you from loving. Do you look for the negative rather than the positive in people? List three things you've done or said in the last week to those near and dear to you (including parents, grandparents, siblings, offspring, closest friends) to show you love them. Say "I love you" for no reason, except that you mean it. Do you assume they know how you feel? Do your actions match your words, and vice versa? Give a gift that has no utilitarian value. Show caring in small ways. Make your own list of ways you can demonstrate more love to them all.

5. Call a Moratorium on Dating

While you're practicing your LoveSteps, gaining more self-knowledge and becoming more loving, don't run out and start dating again immediately. Before you jump back into the fray, try that short break from dating I discussed earlier in this book. More dating is just going to confuse you while you're trying to get hold of yourself. Honor the moratorium until you actually miss dating. Separate yourself from intimate emotional and physical contact with the opposite sex until you hunger for passion and intimacy again. The void caused in your social life will reawaken your appreciation for people, put it back into perspective with everything else in your life (money, career, possessions).

Not only will you have a foundation that will allow you to fall in love; you'll also come back fresh and unfettered, rediscovering the fundamental magic and attractiveness of the opposite sex. And you'll stand a far better chance of being swept off your feet than of feeling that you want to flee with your feet.

Once you return to dating, use the two-date minimum to ensure that you don't fall into the same old patterns. It'll make good practice in enjoying human company and tempering the impulse to judge, dismiss, and justify hurting people. When we hurt others without pausing to consider our actions, we're only encouraging a coldness in our hearts that's incompatible with love.

6. Increase Your Possibilities

If only 10 percent of the men or women you meet approach your minimum criteria for consideration as a lifelong mate (having a pulse is a fair bottom line), the problem is probably with your criteria, not the available gene pool. So work on expanding that percentage to 20 percent, at least. If you reject any woman who has 30 percent body fat, for example, make more room in your attraction meter for women who approach 40 percent. If you'd never date a guy who's bald, watch a few *Kojak* reruns until you realize how sexy it can be to see your own reflection in your date's head. Stop looking for the best. As the Love Prophet says, sometimes good enough is good enough—in refrigerators, jobs, restaurants, and love.

Focus on experiencing your own internal pangs of loneliness. Once you do so, you'll automatically increase the pool of potential partners you're attracted to by 50 percent. Let me be clear: This isn't about "settling." It's about emotional intelligence. The person who suits all your needs and makes you feel loved and cherished is "the best" for you, even if he or she isn't the best on paper. I'm suggesting that you be a little more selfish, not less. Focus on what's right for you, not what will impress your friends.

7. Commit First, Fall in Love Later

Sounds crazy, right? Just the opposite of what you've always thought. But isn't that the case in every other area of life? Doesn't commitment to your children bring out love, even when you're infuriated? Open your mind. Consider the possibility that true love is what comes from commitment, not the other way around. What if you lived your entire life alone because you were waiting to fall in love and then discovered that if you'd only committed to someone with whom at least the essentials were present—he or she was attractive, compatible, good-natured, and interested—you would have flourished together?

If you're in a good relationship but haven't felt able to commit, imagine making a life with this person. Don't dwell on your doubts; there will always be doubts. Think positively. Remember, without the press of commitment, the oils of love will never flow out. Love comes from the daily struggle of a life lived together in dedication and commitment.

8. Avoid Meaningless Sex

You know the feeling. What seemed like a grand idea in the heat of passion last night has left you with a severe love hangover the morning after. You feel more empty than full. Casual sex numbs the heart and dulls the body. If you violate this step, return to step 1 and start all over.

Because sex involves and absorbs our strongest impulses, it has the power to leave us in confusion, to create more problems than it solves. So you're dating a guy and having sex, and now you don't know if it's love, lust, commitment, or recreation you're dealing with. Worse, it seems that the more you have sex, the less you talk. Hormones have replaced healing; motion has replaced emotion; and the deep soul connection you seek has been preempted by the mere friction of two bodies. With casual sex, objectivity is replaced by a subjectivity born of false intimacy.

Great sex is about being natural. In sex with love, both participants can let go of control over their most active sex organ: their heart! They can enjoy the experience of being totally natural and totally naked. They can bask in the joy of allowing their bodies to be propelled by the motor of their affection, and they can burn brightly for a long, long time, as a result. If you feel you've lost sight of the difference between love and lust, consult a sex therapist, professional counselor, or wise and trustworthy friend.

If the joy of sex is gone for you, consider the joys of abstinence. Abstinence makes the heart (and other body parts) grow fonder. A little time off can remind us that sex is not an end, but an organic means of expressing deep intimacy. Some people actually wait until they're married before making love. What a concept, huh? But we here at the Love Prophet School of Love are realists. What's most important is to resist jumping into the sack until you're both ready to get *emotionally* undressed.

9. Let Go of People Who Are Wasting Your Time

Again, steer clear of commitment-phobes of either sex. There are plenty of ways to recognize them. If they're all about the line, all about the forward thrust, you can bet they'll have trouble with the follow-through. They push, but they don't pursue. They give you pressure without pleasure. They want to go out right away, tonight. Then they want to get sexually involved right away, tonight. They're charming and forceful and pseudo-sincere. But they don't call when they say they will, and if you're not available tonight, you may never hear from them again.

My friend Myron, who owns a beautiful beachfront house in Florida, was honest enough to tell me this: "When I'm interested in a woman only for sex, I'll call her up and sort of pressure her to come over to my house. I won't even make the effort to pick her up myself. But the same is not true when I'm really interested in a woman. Then I would never dream of not taking her places myself." If a guy is pushing you, and it feels like pressure rather than pleasure, you can bet he wants something *from* you rather than wanting *you*. And when he gets it, be prepared to say good-bye.

If you see a guy making that old about-face, watch out. Here are a few signs of these types; I'll bet they're familiar:

❤ They're adamant about reaching you by phone or E-mail but are abrupt once they call. If they get beeped, they take the other call and either hang up on you or leave you on hold endlessly. If their every other word to you on the phone is "Gotta go, I'll get back to you later," you may be waiting a very long time.

🖤 They commit at the last minute. A simple plan to go out for coffee or dinner appears to involve consulting the entire UN Security Council.

🖤 They cancel dates frequently (apparently the Council needs them).

🖤 In their defense, they *are* often committed to one thing: their jobs. They get in early, stay late, work through lunch, take work home at night, and work weekends. Their social engagements revolve around colleagues at work or work-related social events.

🖤 They don't invite you to meet their parents, brothers, sisters, or other friends. Heck, they don't even *have* any, at least as far as they've let on.

🖤 They hate going to weddings and seem to have no friends who are married. Even saying the word *marriage* or *commitment* requires coaching from a speech therapist.

Learn to spot these symptoms. And when you do, give a polite but firm good-bye and move on.

10. Recapture Your Mental Virginity

Wipe your mind clean of the ghosts of lovers past. That was then, this is now. If you're having problems with this step, repeat step 3. Avoid comparison dating. No two people are supposed to be alike. Each person is unique and should be appreciated for his or her own special qualities. While on a date, be completely present in the moment. If you find your mind wandering, focus on your date's voice or eyes. Look deeper into the person for his or her less obvious qualities.

I can't say this often enough: Avoid pornography. Men especially should not buy porn mags, visit porno websites, or even look too long at the brassiere ads in the Sunday *New York Times*. The media bombard us with images of people of both sexes in various seductive stages of undress; practice diverting your glance. Get angry, rather than turned on, at how easily you're being manipulated by some Madison Avenue ad man whose new BMW is entirely dependent on your infatuation.

Judge less—another toughie, since we're such a judgmental society. But for every negative judgment you have, replace it with a positive one. Find virtue in your dates. Be creative. Slowly retrain your mind to look for the good rather than the bad. As the cliché goes (clichés become popular only when they work, after all), learn to see the cup as half full, not half empty. In fact, see it as almost completely full.

Finally, if you've got too many opposite-sex platonic relationships going on, step back. Familiarity robs you of the excitement and attraction of the opposite sex.

11. Go Deeper

If we've become bored with dating, perhaps it's because we've all become boring. But enough about everyone else: Maybe *you've* become boring. If you think you're shallow—if you look at the price of a thing, so to speak, rather than its value—replace superficial activities with those that will add to your depth.

Start with a week of abstaining from trivial pursuits (except for the board game of the same name). Whatever your vice—reading *People*, watching *Seinfeld* reruns, cruising malls, gorging yourself on self-help books (present company excepted)—replace it with something that will broaden your mind and heart. Volunteer at the local soup kitchen. Read *Pride and Prejudice*. Watch the History Channel. Learn to play chess. Read the Bible and try to draw lessons about your own life from its stories. Seek out great romantic classics, from *Romeo and Juliet* to *The Philadelphia Story*. Share the knowledge you're gaining with someone you're dating, or invite that person to join you in your new activities. The idea is not just to become more knowledgeable but to grow personally and spiritually.

Rediscover curiosity. Tap into your insatiable desire to explore. Whenever you feel you're getting bored in a relationship because you already "know" your partner, remember that you don't. We all have unknown depths. It's your challenge to explore them in your partner. Arrogance in a relationship says, "I know you already." Conceit says, "I have nothing more to learn." But the humble heart that can fall in love says, "I have known you all these years, yet every day I discover something new."

To encourage the process, engage in a new activity together. Let your partner take you on a trip of discovery to a new place or to engage in a new interest. Read new books and articles to each other. Write each other humorous or romantic poems. Take a trip to a new shore. Leave functional conversation—about daily chores and responsibilities—behind. Use your time to explore each other's depth and intensity. Dating in natural environments can help stave off cynicism. The woman who looked average on Fifth Avenue might acquire a special glow against the backdrop of a colorful sunset.

12. Keep Taking Your Love Pulse, and Spread the Word

This is an ongoing remedial program. It took you a lifetime to develop your dating addiction; you won't be cured in a day. It could take two days or two years. You were maybe in a hurry?

Ask your helpful friend from step 2 to help you follow up on step 4, and take your love temperature on a regular basis to make sure you don't fall back into old, counterproductive habits. Get a reading once or twice a week from this friend, someone whose perspective you admire and whose feedback and advice you'll follow; it should be someone wise, loving, and courageous enough to be a little tough on you when necessary.

Each session should end with an assignment or project, as drawn from the LoveSteps or elsewhere in this book. And the next session should begin with a report on how it went. In your conversations, report honestly on how you're doing, on your own sense of your chances for falling in love. This isn't a whining session, nor is it a beat-yourself-up session. The purpose is simply to track your progress. If you're really obsessive, make a graph or keep a diary to chart your improving condition.

Spread the Word

Once you've had your heart opened, you'll be in a position to promote the rewards of love. Without being too obnoxious, you're encouraged to become a missionary of love (and I'm not talking about the position). Carry the message to singles you know who are still struggling with the dating scene. There's security in numbers. Help make the world a place where no one needs to be ashamed to admit that he or she is alone. Let no one you know spend another moment feeling ashamed that what she really wants is someone who can lean on her and on whom she can lean in return. The greatest human gift is to alleviate someone else's loneliness.

Become an amateur matchmaker. Fix available people up with each other. (Try not to give away your husband.) Offer an ear or a shoulder to couples obviously stuck in a love rut. Always offer a kind word to a husband about his wife, so that he is reminded of her beauty. Give your girlfriend a compliment about her husband, so that she never takes him for granted. It takes a village to raise a marriage. We all need to be reminded by each other of the importance of love and the priority it deserves. Be a beacon to strangers who are mysteriously drawn to your love-generated light. Become a Love Prophet too.

Even if you haven't found the love of your life, this step will help you. The good vibes you spread will eventually be reflected back to you.

And don't forget . . .
to sign the Declaration.

Once you've begun the LoveSteps program, there's no better way to express your commitment than to sign the Declaration of Dependence in chapter 8. Make blank copies for your friends; show it to potential mates; most important, post your signed copy in a place where it won't be far from your thoughts. Remember, need is good.

ML